중학내신
통합영문법1

저자 **오세용**

대학에서 영문학 전공 후 한양–Oregon Joint TESOL(3기)을 마치고 TOEFL 성적 우수 장학금을 받고
Oklahoma-city University에 입학하여 2009년 5월 TESOL(영어교수법) 석사학위를 취득했다.
귀국 후 서울 오세용어학원에서 학생들을 가르치며 오세용 영어연구소를 운영하고 있다.
학생들의 입장에서 어떻게 하면 영문법을 쉽게 정복하게 할 수 있을까 늘 고민하고 있다.

중학내신 통합영문법 1

저자 오세용 영어연구소
초판 1쇄 인쇄 2015년 11월 8일 **초판 1쇄 발행** 2015년 11월 15일

발행인 박효상 **총괄 이사** 이종선 **편집장** 김현 **기획 · 편집** 박혜민 **디자인책임** 손정수
디자인 the PAGE 박성미
마케팅 이태호, 이전희 **디지털콘텐츠** 이지호 **관리** 김태옥

종이 월드페이퍼 **인쇄 · 제본** 현문자현

출판등록 제10-1835호 **발행처** 사람in **주소** 121-839 서울시 마포구 양화로 11길 14-10 (서교동) 4F
전화 02) 338-3555(代) **팩스** 02) 338-3545 **E-mail** saramin@netsgo.com
Homepage www.saramin.com

책값은 뒤표지에 있습니다.
파본은 바꾸어 드립니다.

ⓒ 오세용 영어연구소 2015

ISBN
978-89-6049-567-8 54740
978-89-6049-566-1 (set)

사람이 중심이 되는 세상, 세상과 소통하는 책 사람in

중학내신
통합영문법

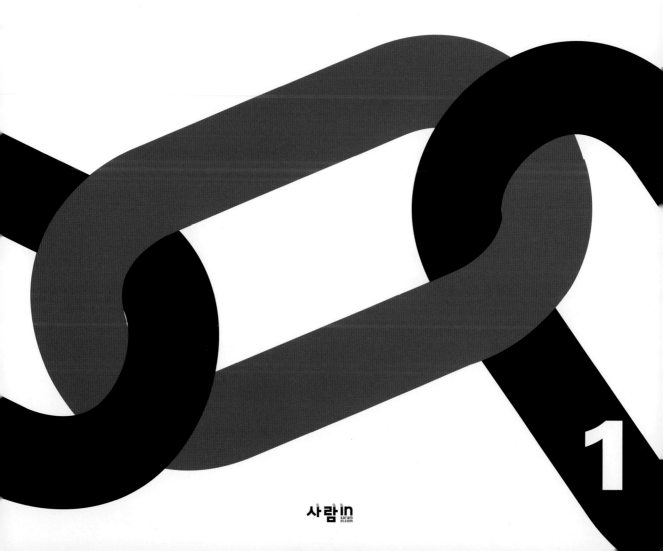

1

사람in
saram
in.com

통합 영문법의
특징과 시리즈 구성

통합(Integration) 영문법이란?

많은 학생들이 영문법을 공부하지만 정확하게 개념을 이해한 학생은 많지 않습니다. 그 이유는 따로따로 공부하다 보니 그것을 통합하여 유기적으로 시험에 활용할 수 있게 하는 장치와 기회가 없었기 때문입니다. 그런 학생들을 위해 묶어서 공부하는 통합(integration) 영문법을 고안해 냈는데, 이 통합 영문법에는 다음과 같은 장점이 있습니다.

1. 문법 개념을 분명하게 이해할 수 있다!
관련된 문법 파트를 비교해 함께 공부함으로써 각 문법 개념을 분명히 이해할 수 있게 됩니다. 개념 이해가 되면 응용 문제를 풀 때도 시너지 효과를 내게 되죠.

2. 영문법 실력 향상에 도움이 된다!
파트별로 나뉘어 있는 기존 영문법 책으로는 문법 전반을 이해하고 학습하기에 한계가 많은 게 사실입니다. 한 파트를 공부한 다음 다른 파트로 넘어가다 보면 그 전에 배웠던 건 까맣게 잊어버리고 말지요. 하지만 통합 영문법은 다릅니다. 관련된 사항을 묶어 공부하고 통합 유형을 다져 주는 문제를 풀고, 문법 전체를 평가하는 통합 실전 문제를 풀다 보면 자신도 모르는 사이에 영문법 전반에 대한 실력을 쌓을 수 있습니다.

통합 영문법의 supporter, 단계별 문제 수록

이 통합 영문법의 장점을 극대화하고 중요해지는 내신에 대비할 수 있게 새 교과 과정의 최신 기출 문제를 철저히 분석해 4단계에 걸쳐 다양한 문제를 수록했습니다.

단계 1 기본 실력 다지기 문제
통합으로 학습하여 문법의 기본 개념을 장착한 후 풀어 보는 문제입니다. 앞에 배웠던 내용을 바로 확인하기 때문에 복습 효과가 큽니다.

단계 2 통합 유형 문제(챕터 당 3회분)
관련 문법 단원들을 묶어 실제 시험처럼 풀면서 해당 문법에 대한 이해도를 높입니다. 기본 실력 다지기보다 많은 어휘력과 응용력이 요구되는 문제로 영문법 핵심 잡기에 최적화돼 있습니다.

단계 ③ 통합 실전 문제(10회 분)

5개 챕터를 학습한 후 영문법 전반에 관해 실전 문제를 풀면서 종합적인 인지능력을 기릅니다.

단계 ④ 최신 신경향 기출 서술형 100제

100% 최신 기출 서술형 문제로 점점 비율이 높아지는 서술형 문제에 완벽하게 대비하면서 동시에 영문법 전반에 대한 자신감도 갖게 됩니다.

『중학내신 통합영문법』 시리즈 구성

이 책의 구성

본 교재는 관련된 문법 부분을 묶어서 공부하는
통합 영문법의 큰 기치 아래 영문법을 5개 단원으로 묶었고,
각 단원은 다음과 같이 구성되어 있습니다.

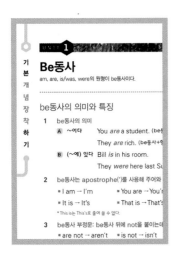

기본 개념 장착하기
관련된 영문법을 통합하여 묶어 설명했으며, 시험에 안 나오거나 활용도가 떨어지는 내용은 빼고 꼭 필요한 내용만 엄선했습니다.

기본 실력 다지기
앞에서 공부한 영문법 개념의 확인 차원으로 주관식으로 된 기본 실력 다지기를 꼭 풀어보세요. 막히는 부분이 있다면 기본 개념 장착하기로 다시 돌아가서 공부하세요.

통합 유형 1~3회 (회당 30문제)
묶어서 공부한 문법 내용을 응용한 문제입니다. 객관식 20문제와 서술형 10문제로 구성되어 있으며 이 문제를 풀다 보면 자신이 어느 부분에서 어려워하고 막히는지 알 수 있습니다. 막히는 부분이 있다면 반드시 해당 문법을 다시 공부해 정확하게 숙지해야 합니다.

이렇게 5개 단원에 걸친 영문법 학습이 끝났습니다.
하지만 이게 다가 아닙니다.
통합 영문법의 정수는 바로 통합 실전 문제와
최신 신경향 기출 서술형 문제입니다.

- 문법은 지겨운 게 아니라 영작과 독해에 도움이 되고 내신과 수능 고득점에 꼭 필요해요. 이왕에 하는 것, 즐거운 마음으로 재미있게 공부하세요.

- 각 단원의 기본 개념에 대한 이해를 분명히 하고 넘어 가셔야 해요.

- 문법을 이해만 해서는 안 됩니다. 필수 문법 사항에 대해서는 반복 암기도 필요해요.

- 반복해 출제되는 문제는 중요하다는 뜻입니다. 반드시 확실히 알아두세요.

- 개념 이해만으로는 충분하지 않아요. 통합 유형 문제를 통해 확인 학습을 꼭 하세요.

- 통합 실전 문제 풀이 후에는 꼭 오답노트를 정리하세요. 나중에는 오답노트를 보는 것만으로도 크게 도움이 됩니다.

- 실전 문제를 풀면서 막혔던 부분이나 부족하다고 여겨지는 문법 개념 부분은 다시 확인하세요

통합 실전 문제 1~10회
(회당 30문제)
통합 실전 문제는 영문법 전반을 아우르는 객관식 20문제와 서술형 10문제로
구성되어 있습니다. 배운 내용을 떠올리고 응용하면서
풀어야 하는, 통합 영문법의 진수라고 할 수 있습니다.

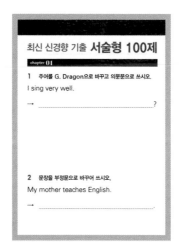

최신 신경향 기출 서술형 문제
(100문제)
내신에서 비중이 높아가는 서술형 문제에 철저히 대비할 수 있게
최신 기출 문제에서 뽑은 서술형 문제 100개를 실었습니다.
하나하나 풀면서 영문법 실력을 점검하고 틀린 부분은
확실하게 짚고 넘어가야 합니다.

목차

Chapter 1　Be동사 · 8품사 · 문장

Chapter 2　조동사 · 시제 · 수동태

Chapter 3　부정사 · 동명사 · 분사

이 책의 학습 진도표

A
type

50분씩 40시간 공부 공부할 때

Day	Day 1	Day 2	Day 3	Day 4	Day 5
진도	**Chapter 1** 기본 개념 장착하기	기본 실력 다지기	통합 유형 1-1	통합 유형 1- 2	통합 유형 1- 3
Day	Day 6	Day 7	Day 8	Day 9	Day 10
진도	**Chapter 2** 기본 개념 장착하기	기본 실력 다지기	통합 유형 2-1	통합 유형 2- 2	통합 유형 2- 3
Day	Day 11	Day 12	Day 13	Day 14	Day 15
진도	**Chapter 3** 기본 개념 장착하기	기본 실력 다지기	통합 유형 3-1	통합 유형 3- 2	통합 유형 3- 3
Day	Day 16	Day 17	Day 18	Day 19	Day 20
진도	**Chapter 4** 기본 개념 장착하기	기본 실력 다지기	통합 유형 4-1	통합 유형 4- 2	통합 유형 4- 3
Day	Day 21	Day 22	Day 23	Day 24	Day 25
진도	**Chapter 5** 기본 개념 장착하기	기본 실력 다지기	통합 유형 5-1	통합 유형 5- 2	통합 유형 5- 3
Day	Day 26	Day 27	Day 28	Day 29	Day 30
진도	통합 실전 1	통합 실전 2	통합 실전 3	통합 실전 4	통합 실전 5
Day	Day 31	Day 32	Day 33	Day 34	Day 35
진도	통합 실전 6	통합 실전 7	통합 실전 8	통합 실전 9	통합 실전 10
Day	Day 36	Day 37	Day 38	Day 39	Day 40
진도	최신 신경향 기출 서술형 1- 20	최신 신경향 기출 서술형 21- 40	최신 신경향 기출 서술형 41- 60	최신 신경향 기출 서술형 61- 80	최신 신경향 기출 서술형 81-100

급한 마음으로 한번에 너무 많이, 혹은 하루는 많이 하고 또 하루는 안 하는 그런 식의 학습은 도움이 되지 않습니다.
조금 시간이 걸리더라도 꾸준히 하는 게 가장 중요합니다.
다음에 제공하는 진도표에 따라 자기 컨디션에 맞게 공부해 보세요.

60분씩 30시간 공부할 때

Day	Day 1	Day 2	Day 3	Day 4	Day 5
진도	**Chapter 1** 기본 개념 장착하기 기본 실력 다지기	통합 유형 1-1	통합 유형 1-2	통합 유형 1-3	**Chapter 2** 기본 개념 장착하기 기본 실력 다지기
Day	Day 6	Day 7	Day 8	Day 9	Day 10
진도	통합 유형 2-1	통합 유형 2-2	통합 유형 2-3	**Chapter 3** 기본 개념 장착하기 기본 실력 다지기	통합 유형 3-1
Day	Day 11	Day 12	Day 13	Day 14	Day 15
진도	통합 유형 3-2	통합 유형 3-3	**Chapter 4** 기본 개념 장착하기 기본 실력 다지기	통합 유형 4-1	통합 유형 4-2
Day	Day 16	Day 17	Day 18	Day 19	Day 20
진도	통합 유형 4-3	**Chapter 5** 기본 개념 장착하기 기본 실력 다지기	통합 유형 5-1	통합 유형 5-2	통합 유형 5-3
Day	Day 21	Day 22	Day 23	Day 24	Day 25
진도	통합 실전 1 최신 신경향 기출 서술형 1-10	통합 실전 2 최신 신경향 기출 서술형 11-20	통합 실전 3 최신 신경향 기출 서술형 21-30	통합 실전 4 최신 신경향 기출 서술형 31-40	통합 실전 5 최신 신경향 기출 서술형 41-50
Day	Day 26	Day 27	Day 28	Day 29	Day 30
진도	통합 실전 6 최신 신경향 기출 서술형 51-60	통합 실전 7 최신 신경향 기출 서술형 61-70	통합 실전 8 최신 신경향 기출 서술형 71-80	통합 실전 9 최신 신경향 기출 서술형 81-90	통합 실전 10 최신 신경향 기출 서술형 91-100

초 · 중등어휘 동사의 불규칙 과거형-과거분사형

동사 (verb)	뜻 (meaning)	과거형	과거분사형
drink	마시다	drank	drunk
grow	자라다	grew	grown
throw	던지다	threw	thrown
write	쓰다	wrote	written
know	알다	knew	known
get	얻다, 받다	got	got(ten)
tell	말하다; 구별하다	told	told
fall	떨어지다	fell	fallen
keep	간직하다, 유지하다	kept	kept
become	~이 되다	became	become
fly	날다	flew	flown
break	깨다, 부수다	broke	broken
stand	서다	stood	stood
say	말하다	said	said
quit	그만두다, 끊다	quit	quit
sleep	잠자다	slept	slept
find	찾다	found	found
sit	앉다	sat	sat
take	잡다, 쥐다, 택하다	took	taken
catch	잡다	caught	caught
begin	시작하다	began	begun
read	읽다	read	read
put	놓다, 두다	put	put
run	달리다; 운영하다	ran	run

동사 (verb)	뜻 (meaning)	과거형	과거분사형
bring	가지고 오다	brought	brought
think	생각하다	thought	thought
come	오다	came	come
speak	말하다	spoke	spoken
fight	싸우다	fought	fought
drive	운전하다	drove	driven
see	보다	saw	seen
forget	잊다	forgot	forgotten
cut	자르다	cut	cut
teach	가르치다	taught	taught
give	주다	gave	given
go	가다	went	gone
meet	만나다	met	met
eat	먹다	ate	eaten
wear	입다	wore	worn
make	만들다	made	made
have	가지다	had	had
feel	느끼다	felt	felt
buy	구입하다, 사다	bought	bought
sing	노래하다	sang	sung
do	하다, 행하다	did	done
swim	수영하다	swam	swum
hear	듣다	heard	heard
ring	울리다	rang	rung

동사 (verb)	뜻 (meaning)	과거형	과거분사형
hit	치다, 때리다	hit	hit
pay	(돈을) 지불하다, 갚다	paid	paid
bite	물다, 깨물다	bit	bitten
set	놓다; 설정하다; 세우다	set	set
cast	던지다; 투표하다	cast	cast
let	~가 …하게 놔두다, 허락하다; ~하겠다	let	let
dig	(구멍 등을) 파다, (땅에서) 파내다[캐다]	dug	dug
lose	잃다; 잃어버리다; 지다	lost	lost
win	이기다, 승리하다; 얻다, 획득하다	won	won
build	짓다, 건설하다; 만들다	built	built
burn	(불에) 타다, 태우다; 화상을 입다	burnt / burned	burnt / burned
lie	눕다, 누워있다; 놓여있다	lay	lain
lie	거짓말하다	lied	lied
sell	팔다, 판매하다, 팔리다	sold	sold
leave	떠나다, 출발하다; 남기다	left	left
ride	타다; 말을 타다	rode	ridden
choose	선택하다, 고르다; 선출하다	chose	chosen
rise	오르다, 뜨다; 증가하다	rose	risen
understand	이해하다, 알다	understood	understood
bet	(내기, 경주 등에) 돈을 걸다; 틀림없다	bet	bet
shake	흔들리다, 흔들다, 떨다	shook	shaken
wake	깨다, 깨우다	woke	waken
bend	(몸을) 굽히다, 숙이다; 구부리다	bent	bent
send	보내다, 발송하다	sent	sent
fit	맞다, 적합하다	fit	fit
shine	빛나다, 반짝이다; 비추다	shone	shone
hurt	다치게 하다, 아프게 하다, 아프다	hurt	hurt
spend	(돈을) 쓰다, 소비하다; (시간을) 보내다	spent	spent
hide	숨기다, 숨다	hid	hidden
lead	이끌다, 안내하다; 《to》 ~에 이르다	lcd	led

동사 (verb)	뜻 (meaning)	과거형	과거분사형
lay	~을 놓다; (알을) 낳다	laid	laid
found	설립하다, 세우다	founded	founded
draw	(그림을) 그리다; (관심 등을) 끌다, 이끌어 내다	drew	drawn
mean	의미하다, 뜻하다	meant	meant
slide	미끄러지다, 미끄러뜨리다	slid	slid / slidden
steal	훔치다, 도둑질하다	stole	stolen
hold	잡다; 유지하다; 개최하다	held	held
freeze	얼다, 얼리다; 매우 춥다	froze	frozen
blow	(입으로, 바람이) 불다, 날리다, 날려 보내다	blew	blown
feed	먹이를 주다, 먹다	fed	fed
spread	확산되다, 퍼지다; 펼치다	spread	spread
beat	이기다, 능가하다; 두드리다	beat	beaten
stick	붙이다; 꼼짝 못하다	stuck	stuck
tear	찢다, 찢어지다	tore	torn
forgive	용서하다	forgave	forgiven
deal	《with》 다루다, 처리하다	dealt	dealt
swing	휘두르다; 흔들다	swung	swung
hang	걸다, 매달다; 걸리다, 매달리다	hung	hung
burst	터지다, 터뜨리다; 불쑥 오다	burst	burst
swear	맹세하다	swore	sworn
sew	바느질하다, 꿰매다	sewed	sewn
shut	닫다	shut	shut
sink	빠지다, 가라앉다	sank	sunk
shoot	(총 등을) 쏘다; 촬영하다; 슛을 하다	shot	shot
spill	흘리다; 쏟아져 나오다	spilt	spilt
sweep	쓸다	swept	swept
sow	씨를 뿌리다	sowed	sown / sowed
strike	치다, 때리다; 공격하다	struck	struck
overcome	극복하다, 이기다	overcame	overcome

chapter

01

Be동사

8품사

문장

기본개념장착하기

Be동사

am, are, is/was, were의 원형이 be동사이다.

----

be동사의 의미와 특징

1 be동사의 의미

　Ⓐ ～이다　　You *are* a student. (be동사+명사)

　　　　　　　They *are* rich. (be동사+형용사)

　Ⓑ (～에) 있다　Bill *is* in his room.

　　　　　　　They *were* here last Sunday.

2 be동사는 apostrophe(')를 사용해 주어와 줄여 쓸 수 있다.

　▪ I am → I'm　　　▪ You are →You're　　▪ He is → He's　　▪ She is → She's

　▪ It is → It's　　　▪ That is →That's

　＊ This is는 This's로 줄여 쓸 수 없다.

3 be동사 부정문: be동사 뒤에 not을 붙이는데 be동사와 축약해 쓸 수 있다.

　▪ are not → aren't　　▪ is not → isn't

　▪ was not → wasn't　▪ were not → weren't

　　▪ She *is not* my sister. = She *isn't* my sister.

4 be동사 의문문: 주어와 be동사의 자리를 바꾸고 물음표를 붙인다.

　You are a student. → *Are you* a student?

　Kate is in the playground. → *Is Kate* in the playground?

5 be동사 의문문에 대한 대답

　Ⓐ 긍정: Yes, 주어+be동사

　　A: Is this a map? **B:** *Yes, it is.*

　Ⓑ 부정: No, 주어+be동사+not

　　A: Are these your shoes? **B:** *No, they aren't.*

➕ P·L·U·S

There is+ 단수명사: ～이 있다　There are+ 복수명사: ～들이 있다

▪ *There is* a park near my house. (긍정문)

▪ *There are* good films on TV this evening. (긍정문)

▪ *Is there* a hotel near here? (의문문)

8품사

- -

1 명사: 사물이나 동식물, 사람, 장소 등의 각각의 이름

  A **셀 수 있는 명사**: 단수형과 복수형(명사+-s/명사+-es)으로 표시 가능

  a cat(고양이 한 마리), two dogs(개 두 마리), three bananas(바나나 세 개),

  four potatoes(감자 네 알), etc.

  B **셀 수 없는 명사**: love(사랑), friendship(우정), faith(믿음), etc.

2 대명사: 명사를 대신해 쓰이는 말 (인칭 · 지시 · 의문 · 부정 대명사 등)

	인칭대명사 주격	인칭대명사 목적격	인칭대명사 소유격
1인칭	I (나는)	me (나를)	my (나의)
2인칭	you (너는)	you (너를)	your (너의)
3인칭	he (그는) she (그녀는) it (그것은)	him (그를) her (그녀를) it (그것을)	his (그의) her (그녀의) its (그것의)
1인칭	we (우리는)	us (우리를)	our (우리의)
2인칭	you (너희들은)	you (당신들을)	your (당신들의)
3인칭	they (그들은, 그것들은)	them (그들을, 그것들을)	their (그들의, 그것들의)

	지시대명사 단수	지시대명사 복수
가까운 것을 지칭	this (이것, 이)	these (이것들, 이)
멀리 떨어진 것을 지칭	that (저것, 저)	those (저것들, 저)

3 동사: 사람이나 사물의 동작 또는 상태를 나타내는 말

  A **동작:** go(가다), come(오다), run(뛰다) ….

  B **상태:** like(좋아하다), love(사랑하다), know(알다) ….

4 형용사: 명사나 대명사의 성질, 모양, 상태 등을 묘사 또는 서술하는 말

  long(긴), short(짧은), big(큰), small(작은), young(어린), white(흰)

  A **명사 수식:** a *big* man, a *beautiful* girl (형용사+명사의 순서)

  B **명사 서술:** I am *tall*. You are *pretty*. (보어로서 명사의 상태 서술)

5 부사: 동사, 형용사, 다른 부사, 문장 전체를 수식하는 말

  A **본래부터 부사:** very(매우), there(거기에), too(너무), often(자주), well(잘) …

  B **형용사+-ly 형태의 부사:** slowly(느리게), happily(행복하게) …

  We work *hard*. (동사 수식)   That book is *very* big. (형용사 수식)

  You run *too* fast. (다른 부사 수식)   *Fortunately*, he saved her life. (문장 전체 수식)

6 전치사: 단독으로 쓰이지 않으며 전치사+명사/대명사의 형태로 구를 만듦

  Sung is going to France *for* a holiday.

There is a book *on* the desk.

Turn left *at* the traffic lights.

The girl is standing *under* a tree.

I'd like to have a house *with* a garden.

7 접속사: 단어와 단어, 구와 구, 절과 절을 연결해 주는 말

I am tall, *but* you are small. (절+절)

They like films, *so* they often go to the cinema. (절+절)

When I went out, it was raining. (절+절)

Please close the window *before* you go out. (절+절)

8 감탄사: 놀람, 기쁨, 슬픔, 분노 등의 감정을 나타내는 말

Oh, Alas(슬픔), Bravo, Hey

➕ P·L·U·S

관사 a/an과 the

- There is *a* pencil on the desk. (발음이 자음으로 시작하는 셀 수 있는 명사 앞)
- I have *an* apple in my pocket. (발음이 모음으로 시작하는 셀 수 있는 명사 앞)
- I have *the* pencil my father bought for me. (특정한 것을 지칭)

UNIT 3

문장

---

❶ 평서문과 일반동사

일반동사는 사물의 동작이나 상태를 나타내는 동사로 be동사와 조동사를 제외한 모든 동사를 뜻한다. 평서문은 〈주어+동사 ~〉 순으로 나열되며 마침표로 끝난다.

ex) like(좋아하다), speak(말하다), love(사랑하다), hate(미워하다) …

I *study* English hard. He *drives* a bus.

1 일반동사 현재형: 주어가 3인칭 단수(he, she, it ….)일 때는 동사 끝에 -s나 -es를 붙인다.

A -s, -sh, -ch, -o, -x로 끝나는 동사+-es

The earth *goes* round the sun.

B '자음+y'로 끝나는 동사는 y를 i로 고치고 -es

He always *studies* math.

C 예외 동사: have – has

She *has* a lot of pencils.

D 그 외 대부분 동사+-s

He *speaks* English very well. She *works* very hard.

2 일반동사 과거형: 주어의 인칭과 수에 관계없이 '동사+(e)d' 또는 불규칙 동사의 과거형

We *watched* the baseball game yesterday.

❷ 부정문

1 일반동사 현재형: 주어가 3인칭 단수일 땐 doesn't+동사원형, 그 외에는 don't+동사원형

She studies very hard. → She *doesn't study* very hard. (주어가 3인칭 단수)

I like tennis. → I *don't like* tennis. (3인칭 단수 외의 주어)

2 일반동사 과거형: 주어의 인칭, 수에 상관없이 did not[didn't]+동사원형

She *didn't study* hard for the English exam.

❸ 의문문

1 일반동사 현재 의문문: 주어가 3인칭 단수일 때는 Does, 그 외에는 Do+주어+동사원형 ~?

You like Music. → *Do* you *like* music? (주어가 2인칭)

He swims very well. → *Does* he *swim* very well? (주어가 3인칭 단수)

A: *Do* they *eat* bread? **B:** Yes, they do. / No, they don't. (주어가 3인칭 복수)

2 일반동사 과거 의문문: Did+주어+동사원형 ~?

A: *Did* you *turn* off the computer? **B:** Yes, I did. / No, I didn't.

3 의문사 의문문: '의문사+일반동사 의문문'의 형태로 yes나 no로 답하지 않는다.

A: *What* did you do yesterday afternoon? **B:** I played tennis with my friends.

4 선택의문문: 주어진 두 개 중에서 선택하는 의문문으로 yes나 no로 답하지 않는다.

A: Is this a wolf *or* a fox? **B:** It's a wolf.

5 부가의문문: 평서문 뒤에 짧게 덧붙인 의문문으로 '그렇지 않니?'의 뜻.

He is happy, *isn't he*? (be동사 평서문, be동사 부정형+대명사?)

Jun doesn't have a book, *does he*? (일반동사 부정문, do/does/did+대명사?)

You will go there, *won't you*? (조동사 긍정문, 조동사 부정형+대명사?)

You finished your homework, *didn't you*? (일반동사 긍정문, don't/doesn't/didn't+대명사?)

6 부정의문문: 의문문에 not이나 no가 들어간 의문문

A: *Doesn't* he like Su-mi?

B: Yes, he does. (아니, 좋아해.) / No, he doesn't. (응, 좋아하지 않아.)

❹ 명령문

1 긍정 명령문: you가 생략된 형태로 동사원형으로 시작한다.

Look at those flowers.

Give me that book.

2 부정 명령문: Don't/Never+동사원형

Don't phone me.

Don't hit me like that.

❺ 청유문

타인에게 어떤 행동을 하자고 권유하는 문장으로 기본 형태는 〈Let's+동사원형 ~〉이다.

Let's go see a movie together.

❻ 감탄문

1 What+a[an]+형용사+명사+주어+동사!

It is a very cold day. → *What a* cold day it is!

These are very expensive books. → *What* expensive books these are!

2 How+형용사[부사]+주어+동사!

They are very small. → *How small* they are!

This book is very interesting. → *How interesting* this book is!

의문문으로 고칠 때 빈칸에 알맞은 말을 쓰시오.

1 You have a radio.

→ _____ _____ have a radio?

2 He gets up at six.

→ _____ _____

_____ up at six?

3 Su-jin likes soccer.

→ _____ Su-jin _____

soccer?

4 Mike has a bicycle.

→ _____?

대화의 빈칸에 알맞은 단어를 쓰시오.

5 A: Do they like your friends?

B: Yes, _____ _____.

6 A: Does he read English books?

B: No, he _____.

7 A: Does Mrs. Baker walk to school?

B: No, she _____.

8 A: Doesn't he like tennis?

B: Yes, _____ _____.

부정문으로 고칠 때 빈칸에 알맞은 말을 쓰시오.

9 They use spoons.

→ They _____ use spoons.

10 Mr. Baker teaches English.

→ Mr. Baker _____ teach English.

11 Su-mi has a piano.

→ Su-mi _____ _____ a piano.

12 My father works in a bank.

→ My father _____ _____ in a bank.

괄호 안의 단어를 이용하여 복수형으로 바꾸어 쓰시오.

13 He has a bus. (two)

→ _____.

14 They have a box. (three)

→ _____.

15 A dog has a leg. (four)

→ _____.

16 There is an apple in the box. (seven)

→ _____.

17 A tree is in the garden. (ten)

→ _____.

각 문장에서 밑줄 친 부분의 품사를 쓰시오.

18 My brother <u>walks</u> to the library.

_____

19 My pencils are in <u>my</u> schoolbag.

_____

20 <u>She</u> has ten pencils. _____

21 This is my <u>book</u>. _____

22 <u>That</u> book is Tom's. _____

23 Jane is my <u>sister</u>. _____

24 You are <u>a</u> student. _____

25 <u>This</u> is Mr. Kim. _____

감탄문으로 고칠 때 빈칸에 알맞은 말을 쓰시오.

26 She is a very nice teacher.

→ _____ _____

_____ _____ she is!

27 They are very large balls.

→ _____ _____

_____ they are!

28 He is very strong.

→ _____ _____ he is!

29 She runs very fast.

→ _____ _____ she

_____!

밑줄 친 곳에 알맞은 부가의문을 쓰시오.

30 The girl has many books, _____

_____ ?

31 My sister went to the movies,

_____ _____ ?

32 You can speak English, _____

_____ ?

주어진 단어들을 이용하여 영어 문장을 쓰시오.

33 그녀는 매우 행복해 보인다.

(looks / she / very / happy)

→ _____ .

34 그 음악은 감미롭게 들린다.

(the / sounds / music / sweet)

→ _____ .

35 저녁 밥이 맛있는 냄새가 난다.

(good / smells / dinner / the)

→ _____ .

우리말에 맞도록 빈칸에 알맞은 말을 쓰시오.

36 조용히 하세요.

→ Please _____ quiet.

37 점심 먹자.

→ _____ eat lunch.

38 책상 위에 앉지 마세요.

→ _____ sit on the desk.

낱말을 바르게 배열하여 문장을 완성하시오.

39 a, beautiful, this, what, dress, is, !

→ _____

40 you, how, tall, are, !

→ _____

1 단어의 관계가 나머지와 <u>다른</u> 것은?

① easy - difficult
② light - heavy
③ learn - take
④ strong - weak
⑤ remember - forget

2 A:B = C:D의 관계가 <u>어색한</u> 것은?

① fast : faster = help : helper
② colder : coldest = easier : easiest
③ large : small = exciting : boring
④ length : long = height : high
⑤ shock : shocking = interest : interesting

3 밑줄 친 부분의 의미가 나머지와 <u>다른</u> 것은?

① His name <u>is</u> Mike.
② She <u>is</u> kind and pretty.
③ There <u>is</u> a desk in the classroom.
④ The boy <u>is</u> my friend.
⑤ Mr. Kim <u>is</u> our English teacher.

4 빈칸에 들어갈 순서로 알맞은 것은?

> - _____ Minwha go to church early?
> - _____ your friend studying well?
> - _____ his teacher like baseball?

① Does - Is - Is
② Does - Does - Does
③ Do - Is - Does
④ Does - Is - Does
⑤ Do - Does - Is

5 빈칸에 들어갈 순서로 알맞은 것은?

> - I _____ from Korea, but Pavarotti is from Italy.
> - My hair _____ very long.

① am not - are
② am - is
③ am - are
④ are - is
⑤ is - is

6 빈칸에 들어갈 알맞은 것은?

> _____ your friends like baseball?

① Am ② Are ③ Does ④ Do ⑤ Is

7 밑줄 친 부분을 바르게 줄여 쓴 것은?

① <u>You do not</u> work hard. →You're
② <u>This is</u> a teacher. →This's
③ Bomi <u>is not</u> late for school. → is'nt
④ <u>It is</u> 9 o'clock in the morning. → Its
⑤ She <u>does not</u> feel very happy. → doesn't

8 빈칸에 들어갈 알맞은 것은?

> _____ interesting books they are!

① How ② Which ③ When
④ What ⑤ That

9 빈칸에 들어갈 말이 같은 것끼리 짝지어진 것은?

> ⓐ _____ his friends exercise every day?
>
> ⓑ _____ they teach English to the students?
>
> ⓒ _____ your friend sing a song well?
>
> ⓓ _____ she go to school by car?
>
> ⓔ _____ his brother like the movie?

① ⓐ, ⓒ, ⓓ   ② ⓐ, ⓓ, ⓔ
③ ⓐ, ⓒ, ⓔ   ④ ⓑ, ⓓ, ⓔ
⑤ ⓒ, ⓓ, ⓔ

10 빈칸에 들어갈 말이 다른 것은?

① _____ you have a car?
② _____ your cats cute?
③ _____ you hungry?
④ _____ Tom and Mary smart?
⑤ _____ they his close friends?

11 어법상 빈칸에 들어갈 알맞은 것은?

> She _____ exercise, does she?

① isn't   ② likes   ③ is
④ don't like   ⑤ doesn't like

12 밑줄 친 like와 다른 의미로 쓰인 것은?

> I use different toppings for the waffles <u>like</u> honey, ice cream, and fruit.

① I want to be a great artist <u>like</u> her.
② It sounds <u>like</u> an interesting place.
③ I <u>like</u> the way you express yourself.
④ Some animals <u>like</u> lions eat other animals.
⑤ Students <u>like</u> you usually sing well.

13 어법상 옳지 <u>않은</u> 것은?

① Your home looks lovely.
② The doll feels smoothly.
③ The candy tastes sweet.
④ The food smells good.
⑤ The story sounds interesting.

14 어법상 옳은 것은?

① She will make a good wife.
② He made his brother exciting.
③ The event made all the people angrily.
④ A sad movie makes me sadly.
⑤ She made a new suit to me.

15 밑줄 친 부분 중 어색한 것은?

① Jack doesn't like baseball, <u>does he</u>?
② She will do her best, <u>won't she</u>?
③ They are fighting, <u>aren't they</u>?
④ You didn't clean the classroom, <u>do you</u>?
⑤ Tom gave you a ring, <u>didn't he</u>?

16 어법상 <u>틀린</u> 것을 <u>2개</u> 고르면?

① Please show your presents for me.

② He will send a gift to me.

③ I'll buy you some snacks.

④ Jessica teaches English to us this year.

⑤ You can give some help poor people.

17 어법상 옳은 문장을 <u>모두</u> 고른 것은?

ⓐ Tom and Jason are in the classroom now.

ⓑ Is Jenny's friends angry?

ⓒ I am afraid of wild wolves.

ⓓ My three sisters was in Canada last year.

ⓔ How were your weekend?

① ⓐ, ⓒ   ② ⓒ, ⓓ

③ ⓒ, ⓔ   ④ ⓐ, ⓒ, ⓓ

⑤ ⓐ, ⓒ, ⓔ

18 밑줄 친 ⓐ~ⓔ 중 옳지 <u>않은</u> 것은?

You may be worried about ⓐ <u>making</u> friends. Making friends is necessary for living in our society. Here ⓑ <u>are</u> some advice. I think you should join a club activity. Also, you ⓒ <u>should</u> be kind to ⓓ <u>others</u> and talk to them first. I hope ⓔ <u>that</u> my advice will be helpful to you.

① ⓐ   ② ⓑ   ③ ⓒ   ④ ⓓ   ⑤ ⓔ

19 글의 흐름에 맞게 ①~⑤를 고치고자 한다. 바르게 고친 것 <u>2개</u>는?

If you are tired, your stress levels will go up. A good night's sleep is ① <u>one of the best way</u> to ② <u>increase</u> your stress. Make sure you ③ <u>go to the bed</u> on time and try to ④ <u>take</u> at least eight hours of sleep at night. You have to ⑤ <u>break</u> this rule even when you are studying for a big test.

① one of the best way → one of the best ways

② increase → add

③ go to the bed → go to a bed

④ take → sleep

⑤ break → keep

20 대화의 밑줄 친 ①~⑤ 중 옳지 <u>않은</u> 것은?

A: ① <u>Is this axe yours?</u>

B: ② <u>I can buy my boys computers</u> and shoes with that axe, but it's not mine.

A: ③ <u>I'll show you another.</u> Then, is this axe yours?

B: ④ <u>I can buy my girls clothes</u> and a few cookies with that axe, but it's not mine.

A: You are a very good man! ⑤ <u>I'll give all three axes for you.</u>

通 합 유 형

서 술 형

1 주어진 문장을 괄호 안의 지시대로 바꾸어 쓰시오.

Mr. Kim likes to go hiking. (부정문으로)

→ _____

_____ .

2 문장을 의문문으로 바꾸고 짧게 대답하시오.

His parents are professors.

_____ ? (의문문)

→ No, _____ . (대답)

3 문법적으로 어색한 문장 4개를 찾아 바르게 고치시오

> ⓐ Are you happy?
> ⓑ Is she study English hard?
> ⓒ Are you like Gimbap?
> ⓓ Are you live in Busan?
> ⓔ Is Boa play the piano?

_____

_____

_____

_____

4 음악 감독이 하는 말을 주어진 단어를 포함, 5개의 단어를 이용하여 명령문으로 완성하시오.

Your voice is too low.

_____ _____ _____

_____ voice. (큰 소리로 부르세요.)

5-6 제시된 조건과 해석을 참고하여 주어진 단어를 사용해 문장을 완성하시오.

> 〈조건〉
> · 반드시 주어진 단어를 모두 사용하되, 각 단어는 한 번씩만 사용할 것.
> · 필요 시 단어의 형태 변화 가능.

5 많은 아이들이 운동장에 있다.

(children / lot / the playground / of / at / be / a)

→ _____

_____ .

6 그들은 더 이상 초등학생들이 아니다.

(be / elementary school students / not / they / longer / any)

→ _____

_____ .

028

7 어법상 틀린 문장 4개를 찾아 바르게 고치시오.

> Jason's friends held a birthday party for him. Jane bought a basketball him. Tommy gave a book him about American culture. Jane made a pencil case him. They played games together. All the people at the party has a wonderful time.

❶ _____ .

→ _____ .

❷ _____ .

→ _____ .

❸ _____ .

→ _____ .

❹ _____ .

→ _____ .

8-9 표는 세 학생의 등교 방법이다. 표를 참고해 괄호 안의 단어들을 사용하여 물음에 답하시오.

	걷기	자전거 타기	버스 타기
Jenny		O	O
Mina	O		O
Tom		O	

8 버스를 타고 가는 학생(들)은 누구인가?

→ _____

_____ . (go / by)

9 자전거를 타고 가지 않는 학생(들)은 누구인가?

→ _____

_____ . (by / go / not)

10 주어진 단어를 사용하여 그림을 보고 누가, 누구에게 무엇을 주었는지 문장을 완성하시오.

> sent / gave / for / to / bought

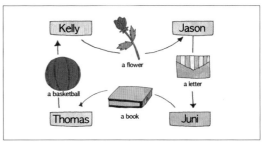

❶ Jason sent _____ .
   (4단어)

❷ Thomas bought _____

   _____ . (4단어)

❸ Juni gave _____ .
   (4단어)

1 단어의 관계가 나머지와 <u>다른</u> 것은?

① advise - advice
② health - healthful
③ serve - service
④ cook - cooker
⑤ speak - speech

2 A:B = C:D의 관계가 어색한 것은?

① sing : singer = teach : teacher
② famous : favorite = worried : nervous
③ delicious : tasty = remember : forget
④ sun : solar = use : useful
⑤ giraffe : animal = history : subject

3 밑줄 친 부분의 쓰임이 나머지와 <u>다른</u> 것은?

① <u>It's</u> Sunday.
② <u>What's</u> up?
③ <u>That's</u> too bad.
④ He is <u>John's</u> brother.
⑤ <u>There's</u> a pencil on the table.

4 빈칸에 들어갈 알맞은 것은?

| _____ don't go to school by bus. |

① Mr. Lee   ② Her mother
③ A child   ④ James's friends
⑤ Our teacher

5 밑줄 친 do의 쓰임이 나머지와 <u>다른</u> 것은?

① <u>Do</u> your best to succeed in getting a good grade.
② <u>Do</u> you play the violin?
③ What does she <u>do</u> in her free time?
④ My mother didn't <u>do</u> many things.
⑤ I <u>do</u> my homework after school.

6 ⓐ~ⓒ에 들어갈 단어를 바르게 나열한 것은?

| Jenny ⓐ (is / are) my best friend. We went to the same school, but we ⓑ (were / weren't) in the same class. Jenny has two sisters and they are so cute. ⓒ (Hers / Her) parents are doctors and they are such a happy family! |

	ⓐ	ⓑ	ⓒ
①	is	weren't	Her
②	is	were	Her
③	are	weren't	Hers
④	are	were	Hers
⑤	is	were	Hers

7 문장을 의문문으로 바르게 고친 것은?

| Jane and Tom go to England together. |

① Do they goes to England together?
② They does go to England together?
③ Do they go to England together?
④ Does they go to England together?
⑤ Does they goes to England together?

8 부정문으로 바꿀 때 알맞은 것은?

> Jinhui has an expensive car.
> → Jinhui _____ an expensive car.

① doesn't has   ② isn't has
③ have not   ④ don't have
⑤ doesn't have

9 답에 대한 질문으로 알맞은 것은?

> Yes, she does.

① Is Kelly sick?
② Did she look good yesterday?
③ Does your brother walk to school every day?
④ Does Kelly like to listen to music?
⑤ Did she come from America?

10 빈칸에 들어갈 말이 다른 하나는?
① They _____ good friends.
② Jun and I _____ not tall.
③ There _____ a dog in the garden.
④ In Atlanta, there _____ a lot of Korean people.
⑤ Jiyoung and Tommy _____ nice students.

11 빈칸에 들어갈 수 없는 것은?

> His mother made him _____.

① happily   ② angry
③ nice   ④ a doctor
⑤ sad

12 교실에서 학생들의 행동과 그에 대한 선생님의 충고로 적절치 않은 것은?

교실 내 학생들의 행동	충고
① 수업 중 휴대폰을 사용하는 경우	Don't use your cellphone.
② 학교에 지각한 경우	Don't be late for school.
③ 컴퓨터 게임에 빠져 있는 경우	Don't play computer games too much.
④ 수업에 집중하지 않는 경우	Listen to me carefully.
⑤ 떠들고 있는 경우	Speak in a loud voice.

13 부가의문문이 바르게 표현된 것은?
① Sujin and Nayoung are good friends, are they?
② Jiho can make pizza, can't Jiho?
③ Jinny is often late for class, isn't she?
④ You feel hungry, aren't you?
⑤ They don't want to travel to Italy, won't they?

14 어법상 옳은 것은?

① Jenny bought me a pair of shoes.

② Bomi gives her brother to a bag.

③ He showed a beautiful photo me.

④ I gave a difficult book for my sister.

⑤ I sent a Christmas card Jenny.

15 어법상 옳지 않은 문장을 모두 고르면?

① She felt so well.

② She can't see at all.

③ She looks kindly.

④ Her hands feel so warmly.

⑤ My new master is so nice to me.

16 어법상 옳지 않은 것을 2개 고르면?

① Be careful not to wake the baby.

② Goes to work by subway.

③ Study English on weekends.

④ Don't looks at the brown hamster.

⑤ Don't be angry at me.

17 어법에 맞는 문장은 모두 몇 개인가?

- If you can't guess the solution, think different.
- He can plays the violin.
- Are you good at swiming?
- Does he reads books every day?
- Can your mother make cookies?

① 1개　② 2개　③ 3개　④ 4개　⑤ 5개

18 어법상 옳은 문장을 모두 고른 것은?

> ⓐ My younger sisters gets up early.
>
> ⓑ James learns Korean every weekend.
>
> ⓒ My sister often stays at home.
>
> ⓓ My son always studys hard.
>
> ⓔ The girl doesn't plays tennis after school.
>
> ⓕ You can't use anything else.

① ⓑ, ⓒ, ⓕ　　　　② ⓐ, ⓒ, ⓓ

③ ⓑ, ⓒ, ⓓ, ⓔ　　④ ⓑ, ⓒ, ⓓ

⑤ ⓐ, ⓑ, ⓔ, ⓕ

19 밑줄 친 ①~⑤ 중 문맥상 자연스럽지 않은 것은?

> My father ① works every day. He doesn't get up ② lately. My mother ③ cooks well. She ④ doesn't like hamburger. My brother ⑤ plays computer games a lot, so he doesn't go to bed early.

20 밑줄 친 동사의 형태가 옳은 것은 모두 몇 개인가?

> Looking at this picture. This is my brother, Thomas. He wears glasses. He doesn't have long hair. He plays the piano well. He studys very hard. He do his homework every day. He goes to school by bus. It took about twenty minutes.

① 2개　② 3개　③ 4개　④ 5개　⑤ 6개

서 술 형

1 문장을 부정문과 의문문으로 고치시오.

> He watched his favorite TV show then.

❶ 부정문 _____

_____.

❷ 의문문 _____

_____?

2 밑줄 친 부분을 바르게 고치시오.

❶ <u>Are</u> nice to your parents.

→ _____ nice to your parents.

❷ <u>Do</u> touch! It's very hot.

→ _____ touch! It's very hot.

3 단어들을 <u>모두</u> 사용해 어법에 맞는 문장을 완성하시오.

> speaks / act / will you / didn't she / doesn't she / had

❶ Mrs. Lee _____ German,

_____?

❷ Don't _____ like a child,

_____?

❸ Jenny _____ good grades on the

exams, _____?

4 주어진 단어를 사용해 문장을 완성하시오.

❶ A: I'm making a Gimbap.

B: _____?

(will / you / to / who / it / give)

A: It is for my boyfriend.

❷ A: _____?

(will / on / card / you / what / write / the)

B: I'll write "Happy Birthday, Mom."

5 괄호 안의 말을 바르게 배열하시오.

I can't understand _____.

(you / why / it / need)

6-7 제시된 조건과 해석을 참고하여 주어진 단어를 사용해 문장을 완성하시오. (단어 형태 변형 및 추가 가능)

6 A: _____?

(what / told / do / to live / your family / like / you)

B: My family told me to live like I played basketball.

7 더 도와드릴 게 있나요?

(I / there / help / else / you / is / can / anything / with)

→ _____?

8 주어진 단어를 사용해 문장을 완성하시오.

> **A:** When is Nayoung's birthday?
> **B:** It's this Friday. Did you buy a gift for her?
> **A:** Not yet. ① <u>나는 나영이에게 책을 줄 거야</u>. (give / will)
> **B:** ② <u>나는 나영이에게 가방을 사 줄 거야</u>. (buy / will)
> **A:** Great. I hope she will like them.

① _____.

(7단어)

② _____.

(7단어)

9 다음을 영작하시오.

> 너 정말 친절하구나! (4단어)

_____!

10 주어진 단어를 사용해 영작하시오.

> 그것이 그들을 따뜻하게 해 줄 거야. (5단어)
> keep

_____.

1 단어의 관계가 나머지와 <u>다른</u> 것은?

① weather - windy

② job - writer

③ sport - badminton

④ color - red

⑤ capital city - the Netherlands

2 A:B = C:D의 관계가 옳은 것을 <u>2개</u> 고르면?

① open : close = start : begin

② physical : mental = valuable : invaluable

③ sister : brother = aunt : father

④ child : children = tooth : teeth

⑤ impressive : touching = hard : difficult

3 밑줄 친 apostrophe(')의 쓰임이 나머지와 <u>다른</u> 것은?

① I'm a salaried man.

② He's a soccer player.

③ What's that in your hand?

④ Why don't we join the reading club?

⑤ I sing and dance to music for our school's team.

4 빈칸에 공통으로 들어갈 단어는?

- I _____ to the nearest church.
- This computer doesn't _____.
- This machine doesn't _____ well.

① take　　② work　　③ run

④ have　　⑤ do

5 빈칸에 들어갈 순서로 알맞은 것은?

- The history book _____ interesting.
- His heart _____ so warm.

① sounds - feels　　② feels - looks

③ smells - sounds　　④ sounds - tastes

⑤ tastes - smells

6 빈칸에 들어갈 단어의 성격이 <u>다른</u> 것은?

① Tom _____ very nervous this morning.

② _____ she your English teacher?

③ _____ they looking for schools?

④ Jason and Jun _____ my best friends.

⑤ _____ they help you?

7 빈칸에 들어갈 알맞은 것은?

He looks _____ from his brother.

① happy　　② angry　　③ sad

④ close　　⑤ different

8 빈칸에 들어갈 알맞은 것은?

> **A:** Did Jinsu walk to school?
>
> **B:** _____. He went to school by bus.

① Yes, he was.   ② No, he doesn't.
③ Yes, he did.   ④ No, he wasn't.
⑤ No, he didn't.

9 문장을 부정문으로 바르게 고친 것은?

> I will clean the living room.

① I will don't clean the living room.
② I am not will clean the living room.
③ I not will clean the living room.
④ I don't will clean the living room.
⑤ I won't clean the living room.

10 빈칸에 들어갈 순서로 알맞은 것은?

> **A:** Hey, Jihae. How was your first day at school?
>
> **B:** Great! Everything _____ new.
>
> **A:** I know. There _____ different teachers for every subject.
>
> **B:** How _____ your classmates?
>
> **A:** I don't know many of them yet.

① is - is - am   ② are - am - am
③ is - are - are   ④ is - are - am
⑤ are - are - is

11 ⓐ~ⓒ에 들어갈 단어를 바르게 나열한 것은?

> Hi, everyone! I ⓐ (am / is) Tommy. I'd like to introduce my teachers. This is Ms. Kim. She teaches history. Mr. Oh ⓑ (is / were) my English teacher. He is from America. They all ⓒ (do / are) very kind to me. I like them very much.

	ⓐ	ⓑ	ⓒ
①	is	were	are
②	am	were	are
③	am	is	are
④	am	is	do
⑤	is	were	do

12 다음 괄호 속의 단어를 재배열하여 문장을 완성할 때 네 번째에 오는 단어는?

> Some friends have different interests and likes, but you can get along with them. Your differences (your / better / make / will / friendship).

① your   ② better
③ make   ④ friendship
⑤ will

13 문법적으로 옳은 것은?

① May I ask a favor for you?
② She showed her photo me.
③ He gave a book of me.
④ I told a surprising story to him.
⑤ She made a cake to me.

14 어법상 어색한 것은?

① Turn off the light.

② Be careful not to wake the baby.

③ Not eat too many sweets.

④ Wash your hands before meals.

⑤ Don't mix them up.

15 어법상 옳은 것을 모두 고르면?

① She does not good at speaking English.

② Jun don't like to play basketball.

③ They are pretty and is cute.

④ Everyone is different.

⑤ I like English, but I don't like English homework.

16 어법상 옳은 것을 2개 고르면?

① Most of the schools starts at 9 o'clock.

② She has one sister and two brothers.

③ He studys English very hard.

④ 30% of the students were for math homework.

⑤ My friends always watches TV.

17 어법상 옳지 않은 문장을 모두 고르면?

> ⓐ She doesn't have long hair.
>
> ⓑ Do Kate go to school by bus?
>
> ⓒ There is two middle schools in my village.
>
> ⓓ Tommy and Jane did their homework together.
>
> ⓔ Kate doesn't watches TV at night.

① ⓐ, ⓒ   ② ⓐ, ⓔ

③ ⓑ, ⓒ, ⓓ   ④ ⓑ, ⓒ, ⓔ

⑤ ⓑ, ⓒ, ⓓ, ⓔ

18 밑줄 친 동사의 형태가 옳지 않은 것은 모두 몇 개인가?

> Donghi <u>go</u> to Songpa Middle school. His class <u>start</u> at 9:00. His teacher <u>tells</u> his class some information about their school life. They <u>ate</u> lunch at 12:00. After school, he and his friends <u>like</u> playing soccer together.

① 1개   ② 2개   ③ 3개   ④ 4개   ⑤ 5개

19 어법상 옳지 않은 문장을 모두 고르면?

> ⓐ Where do we watch a movie this Saturday?
>
> ⓑ We help not doctors and nurses.
>
> ⓒ We don't have enough time.
>
> ⓓ Let's go not and watch it.
>
> ⓔ Tell me about your school life.
>
> ⓕ What is the weather like today?

① ⓑ, ⓓ   ② ⓐ, ⓑ, ⓓ

③ ⓑ, ⓓ, ⓔ   ④ ⓑ, ⓓ, ⓕ

⑤ ⓑ, ⓒ, ⓔ

20 ①~⑤ 중 어법상 옳지 않은 것을 2개 고르면?

> We ① <u>are</u> in the music club. We go to a children's hospital every Saturday. We ② <u>are teaching</u> music to sick children in the hospital. Jenny becomes a piano teacher for the children. Jun ③ <u>teaches</u> the guitar to sick children. Kelly ④ <u>isn't play</u> the instruments, but she ⑤ <u>is</u> a good voice. She sings along with the children.

서 술 형

1 같은 뜻이 되도록 괄호 안에 주어진 단어를 사용해 문장을 완성하시오.

The river isn't clean anymore.

= _____ .

(longer)

2 밑줄 친 부분을 복수형으로 바꾼 후 의문문을 완성하시오.

There is a big park in our city.

→ _____ there many _____

in our city?

3 각 문장을 3형식으로 바꾸시오.

① My mother makes our friends a cake.
② I sent my friend a cake.
③ I ask you an important favor.

❶ My _____ .

❷ I _____ .

❸ I _____ .

4 주어진 단어를 사용해 문장을 완성하시오.

개에게 초콜릿이나 아이스크림을 주지 마세요.

(give / ice cream / or / don't / to / chocolate / a dog)

→ _____ .

5 〈보기〉처럼 주어진 두 문장을 한 문장으로 연결하시오.

● 보기 ●

• When did she come to the party?
• I'd like to know it.
→ I'd like to know when she came to the party.

Can you tell me? + What does Judy want?

→ _____

6 ⓐ~ⓔ 중 어법상 옳지 않은 것을 3개 고르면?

Hi, everyone. Nice to meet you. My name is Tom. ⓐ I'm from Boston, America. I like soccer and music. ⓑ I also like K-pop very much and I have a big family. ⓒ There are ten of us: Dad, Mom, two brothers, five sisters, and me. ⓓ We have two dogs, either. ⓔ My dog's names are Happy and Sen. I'm really happy to meet you.

❶ _____ .

❷ _____ .

❸ _____ .

7-8 나영이가 지난 주말 동안 한 일과 하지 않은 일을 정리한 표를 보고 질문에 맞는 답을 쓰시오.

한 일	하지 않은 일
take a walk	study math
write a poem	learn English

7 What did she do?

→ She _____

_____ .

8 What didn't she do?

→ She _____

_____ .

9-10 ⓐ와 ⓑ에서 골라 자연스러운 문장이 되도록 완성하시오.

ⓐ	ⓑ
and	you won't get wet
or	you will be healthy
but	she won't hear you
for	you will break things inside

9 Take a walk every day, ⓐ ⓑ.

ⓐ _____

ⓑ _____ .

10 Carry this box carefully, ⓐ ⓑ.

ⓐ _____

ⓑ _____ .

chapter

02

조동사

시제

수동태

조동사

일반동사 앞에 놓여 동사에 없는 특수한 의미를 부여하는 보조동사

❶ 조동사의 정의와 특징

1 주어의 수·인칭에 따라 변하지 않는다.

You *can* swim well.

He *can* swim well. ⋯▸ *cans swim* (X)

2 조동사 뒤에 오는 동사는 항상 동사원형이다.

You *can swim* well.

He *can swim* well. ⋯▸ *can swims* (X)

3 의문문은 〈조동사+주어+동사원형 ~?〉, 부정문은 〈주어+조동사+not+동사원형 ~〉

Can she get home?

He *cannot* go there.

4 조동사는 두 개를 나란히 쓸 수 없다.

She will can swim well. (X)

She *will be able to* swim well. (O)

*will can은 쓸 수 없으므로 can의 의미를 지닌 be able to로 바꿔 써야 한다.

❷ 조동사의 종류

1 will+동사원형: ~할 것이다, ~하겠다

- **긍정문** I *will* play tennis.

- **부정문** I *will not (=won't)* play the tennis.

- **의문문 A:** *Will* you go with me?　　**B:** Yes, I *will*. / No, I *won't*.

> ➕ P·L·U·S
>
> 조동사 will은 'be going to+동사원형'과 바꿔 쓸 수 있다.
> - I *will* play tennis. = I'*m going to* play tennis.
> - He *won't* play tennis. = He *isn't going to* play tennis.

2 would

- Ⓐ **will의 과거형** He said that he *would* come back soon.

- Ⓑ **의문문에서 공손한 부탁** *Would* you lend me your pen?

- Ⓒ **~하고 싶다(희망)** I *would like to* go to Jeju Island.

3 may

- Ⓐ **허가: ~해도 된다**

- **긍정문** You *may* go there.

■ 부정문 You *may not* leave now.

■ 의문문 **A:** *May* I come in? **B:** Yes, you *may*. / No, you *may not*.

B 불확실한 추측: ∼일지도 모른다

■ 긍정문 It *may* rain tomorrow.

■ 부정문 He *may not* come back.

4 Can

A 능력: ∼할 수 있다 (=be able to)

■ 현재형 I *can* speak Japanese. = I *am able to* speak Japanese.

■ 미래형 I *will be able to* speak Japanese.

■ 과거형 I *could* speak Japanese. = I *was able to* speak Japanese.

■ 부정문 I *can't* speak Japanese. = I *am not able to* speak Japanese.

B 허가: ∼해도 좋다

You *can* use my phone.

C 강한 부정의 추측: ∼일 리가 없다

It *cannot* be true.   He *cannot* be an American.

5 Must

A 의무: ∼해야 한다 (=have to)

■ 현재형 You *must(=have to)* go there.

■ 미래형 You *will have to* go there. (will must X)

■ 과거형 You *had to* go there.

■ 부정형 You *must not* go there.

  * don't have to ∼: ∼할 필요가 없다 (=need not)
    You don't have to go there.

■ 의문문 *Must* I *(=Do* I *have to)* go there?

B 강한 추측: ∼임에 틀림없다

■ 긍정문 He *must be* sick today.

■ 부정문 He *cannot* be sick today.

6 Should: ∼해야 한다(=ought to: 도덕적 의무, 충고)

■ 긍정문 We *should* listen to our teacher.

      = We *ought to* listen to our teacher.

■ 부정문 You *shouldn't* drink too much coffee.

기본 개념 장착 하기

시제

❶ 현재시제

동사원형이 현재형으로 쓰이지만 주어가 3인칭 단수형일 때는 '동사+-(e)s'로 표현

1 현재의 반복되는 동작 · 상태 He *runs* very fast.

2 현재의 습관 I *study* for two hours every night.

3 진리 · 격언 Water *consists* of hydrogen and oxygen.

4 때나 조건의 부사절에서 미래 시제를 대신

Are you going anyplace if it *is* fine next Saturday?

❷ 미래시제

1 will+동사원형

- **긍정문** He *will* go to school.   He *will* be busy tomorrow.

- **부정문** I *will not (=wont')* go there again.

- **의문문** A: *Will* he come tomorrow?   B: Yes, he *will*. / No, he *won't*.

2 be going to+동사원형

- **평서문** I *am going to* play tennis tomorrow.

They*'re going to* visit me this summer.

- **부정문** We *are not going to* help her.

- **의문문** What *are you going to* do this afternoon?

❸ 과거시제

1 과거의 동작 · 상태 · 습관 His father *was* a poor farmer.

2 역사적인 사실 It is true that Dr. Schweitzer *died* in 1965.

3 규칙동사의 과거형

- 보통은 어미에 -ed를 붙인다. *ex.* play-played, walk-walked

- 어미가 -e로 끝나면 -d만 붙인다. *ex.* like-liked, love-loved

- '자음+y'로 끝나는 동사는 y를 i로 바꾸고 -ed를 붙인다. *ex.* study-studied

- '단모음+단자음'으로 끝나면 자음을 하나 더 쓰고 -ed를 붙인다. *ex.* stop-stopped

4 불규칙 동사의 과거형 They *came* back home at five.

❹ 진행 시제 (현재진행형, 과거진행형)

1 형태

be동사의 현재형+동사-ing **(현재진행형)**

be동사의 과거형+동사-ing **(과거진행형)**

2 용법

Ⓐ **현재진행형: 현재 말하는 시점에서 동작의 진행을 표현**

▪ **긍정문** I *am driving* a bus now.

▪ **부정문** I'*m not driving* a bus now.

▪ **의문문 A**: *Are* you *working* now?   **B**: Yes, I am. / No, I am not.

Ⓑ **과거진행형: 과거의 시점에서 동작의 진행을 표현**

▪ **긍정문** I *was driving* a bus at 4 o'clock.

▪ **부정문** I *was not (=wasn't) driving* a bus at 4 o'clock.

▪ **의문문 A**: *Were* you *working*?   **B**: Yes, I was. / No, I wasn't.

3 -ing형 만들기

Ⓐ **동사 끝이 -e로 끝나면 e를 빼고 -ing를 붙인다.**

동사원형	-ing형	동사원형	-ing형
live	living	move	moving
write	writing	love	loving

Ⓑ **동사 끝이 '단모음+단자음'으로 끝나면 자음 하나를 더 쓰고, -ing를 붙인다.**

동사원형	-ing형	동사원형	-ing형
stop	stopping	swim	swimming
plan	planning	sit	sitting

Ⓒ **동사 끝이 -ie로 끝나면, ie를 y로 고치고 -ing를 붙인다.**

동사원형	-ing형	동사원형	-ing형
die	dying	lie	lying

❺ 현재완료 have/has+과거분사(p.p.)

과거에 일어난 어떤 동작이나 상태가 현재까지 그 영향을 미치고 있음을 표현할 때 사용한다.

1 경험: ~한 적이 있다 ⋯ ever, never, before, once 등의 부사와 함께 쓰인다.

▪ **긍정문** I *have seen* the movie *before*.

▪ **부정문** I *have never seen* snow.

▪ **의문문** *Have* you *ever visited* Mexico?

2 계속: ~해 오고 있다 ⋯ since, for 등 기간을 나타내는 말이 함께 쓰인다.

I *have been* here *since* seven o'clock.

3 완료: 막 ~하였다 ⋯ just, already, yet, now 등의 부사와 함께 쓰인다.

- **긍정문** I *have already seen* that movie.
- **부정문** He *has not arrived* home *yet.*

4 결과: ~해 버렸다. 그 결과 지금~하다 ⋯ 동사 go, lose... 등이 주로 쓰인다.

He *has gone to* America. (=He went to America and he isn't here.)

* He has been to America. → have been to는 '~에 갔다 온 적이 있다'라는 경험의 뜻

UNIT 3

수동태

❶ 수동태 문장의 정의와 형태

주어가 누군가에 의해서 동작을 당하거나 상태에 처하게 됨을 의미한다. 〈주어+be동사+p.p.(과거분사)+by+행위자〉의 형태로 만든다. 행위자를 군이 밝힐 필요가 없을 때는 'by+행위자'를 쓰지 않는다.

He *was killed* in the war.   A new mayor *will be elected.*

❷ 능동태와 수동태의 차이

- **능동태:** S(주어)+V(동사)+O(목적어) ➡ 주어가 능동적으로 행위를 하는 것을 강조
- **수동태:** S(주어)+be동사+p.p.+by+행위자 ➡ 주어가 행위를 당하는 객체임을 강조

He *paints* those pictures. →Those pictures *are painted* by him.

Tom *broke* the dishes. →The dishes *were broken* by Tom.

❸ 수동태의 시제

수동태는 be동사 부분을 변화시켜 다양한 시제를 표현한다.

1 현재 Tom *opens* the door. →The door *is opened* by Tom.

2 과거 The hunter *caught* a bear. → A bear *was caught* by the hunter.

3 미래 Tom *will open* the door. →The door *will be opened* by Tom.

4 현재완료 Tom *has opened* the door. →The door *has been opened* by Tom.

5 현재진행 Kelly *is cooking* spaghetti. → Spaghetti *is being cooked* by Kelly.

❹ 능동태 → 수동태

1 3형식

He *made* a box. → A box *was made* by him.

(행위자에서 행위를 받는 객체로 초점 이동)

All the students *looked up to* him. → He *was looked up* to by all the students.

(look up to: '~을 존경하다'의 타동사 구)

2 4형식

He *gave* me a doll.

→ I *was given* a doll by him. (간접목적어가 주어로)

→ A doll *was given (to)* me by him. (직접목적어가 주어로)

3 5형식

We *elected* him chairman of our society.

→ He *was elected* chairman of our society by us. (목적어를 주어로)

4 조동사가 있는 경우: (조동사+be+p.p.의 형태)

You *must keep* the door open. → The door *must be kept* open by you.

5 by 이외의 전치사를 쓰는 경우

He *was surprised at* the news.

The bottle *is filled with* milk.

She *was satisfied with* the result.

He *is interested in* music.

1 동사의 과거형을 빈칸에 쓰시오.

❶ work - _____ ❷ live - _____

❸ wash - _____ ❹ come - _____

❺ go - _____ ❻ stand - _____

2 동사의 -ing형을 빈칸에 쓰시오.

❶ hear - _____ ❷ sit - _____

❸ come - _____ ❹ write - _____

❺ stop - _____ ❻ make - _____

❼ eat - _____ ❽ run - _____

괄호 안의 동사를 올바른 형태로 바꾸어 쓰시오.

3 It (is) fine tomorrow. _____

4 It may (is) true. _____

5 She is (goes) to write a letter to him.

_____

대화의 빈칸에 알맞은 말을 쓰시오.

6 A: Will you marry her?

B: No, _____ _____.

7 A: May I see it?

B: Yes, _____ _____.

8 A: Can he speak Chinese?

B: No, _____ _____.

문장을 우리말로 해석하시오.

9 You must do your best.

→ _____.

10 We don't have to go to school on Sundays.

→ _____.

11 She must be ill.

→ _____.

12 He may come back soon.

→ _____.

괄호 안에서 알맞은 것을 고르시오.

13 They (live / lives / lived) here last year.

14 He (play / plays / played) tennis every day.

15 (Were / Do / Did) you talk with your teacher yesterday?

16 What (do / are / did) you have for dinner yesterday?

두 문장의 뜻이 일치하도록 빈칸에 알맞은 말을 쓰시오.

17 I will play tennis with my mother.

= I _____ _____ to play tennis with my mother.

18 They will not go to the party this evening.

= They _____ _____ _____ to go to the party this evening.

문장을 괄호 안의 시제로 바꾸어 쓰시오.

19 I draw a picture. (현재진행형)

→ _____.

20 In-su studied English. (과거진행형)

→ _____.

수동태로 고쳐 쓰시오.

21 She sent for the doctor.

→ _____.

22 They called it a flower.

→ _____.

23 He will write his parents a letter.

→ _____.

현재완료의 용법을 쓰시오.

24 Have you done your homework yet?

_____

25 They have gone to Brazil. _____

26 It has been very hot since last week.

_____

27 My father has been to New York twice.

_____

틀린 곳을 바로 고쳐 쓰시오.

28 The vase was broken by I.

→ _____.

29 Her was loved by everybody.

→ _____.

30 His house built in the woods last year.

→ _____.

31 The movie made by Leigh Film Co.

→ _____.

32 The room was filled by smoke.

→ _____.

33 The mountain will be covered by snow in winter.

→ _____.

34 I have once climbed Mt. Seorak some years ago.

→ _____.

35 I will not go there, either, if it will rain tomorrow.

→ _____.

우리말에 맞도록 빈칸에 알맞은 말을 쓰시오.

36 그들은 첫 기차를 타야 했다.

→ They _____ _____ catch the first train.

37 그는 서두를 필요가 없다.

→ He _____ _____ _____ hurry up.

38 그녀는 바쁜 게 틀림없다.

→ She _____ be busy.

39 그는 의사가 될 것이다.

→ He _____ _____ _____ be a doctor.

40 메리는 그녀의 친구를 만나려고 한다.

→ Mary _____ _____ _____ meet her friend.

1 동사과거형 표에서 옳지 <u>않은</u> 것을 <u>모두</u> 고르면?

현재	과거	현재	과거
ⓐ sing	sang	ⓗ study	studied
ⓑ get	got	ⓘ meet	met
ⓒ drink	drank	ⓙ keep	kept
ⓓ find	founded	ⓚ sleep	slept
ⓔ set	sat	ⓛ tell	told
ⓕ catch	caught	ⓜ know	knew
ⓖ are	was	ⓝ read	read

① ⓓ, ⓘ, ⓝ   ② ⓓ, ⓔ, ⓖ   ③ ⓓ, ⓖ, ⓝ
④ ⓔ, ⓖ, ⓝ   ⑤ ⓓ, ⓖ, ⓝ

2 〈보기〉의 밑줄 친 last와 쓰임이 같은 것은?

● 보기 ●
The baseball game <u>lasted</u> by ten.

① The piano concert will <u>last</u> about two hours.
② You should catch the <u>last</u> chance.
③ I got up early <u>last</u> morning.
④ When did you see her <u>last</u>?
⑤ I am the <u>last</u> man to tell a lie.

3 문장을 현재진행형으로 맞게 고친 것은?

A dog comes over to the baby.

① A dog is comemings over to the baby.
② A dog is comeing over to the baby.
③ A dog are coming over to the baby.
④ A dog coming over to the baby.
⑤ A dog is coming over to the baby.

4 빈칸에 들어갈 알맞은 것은?

These pretty bags _____
by Jenny Kim.

① design   ② designing
③ designed   ④ were designing
⑤ were designed

5 밑줄 친 동사 ⓐ, ⓑ를 바르게 고친 것은?

Today was the first day of middle school. I was not only excited but also nervous. The first class was my homeroom teacher's. I ⓐ <u>know</u> anyone in my class, but I ⓑ <u>talk</u> to some of my classmates.

	ⓐ	ⓑ
①	knew	talk
②	knew	talked
③	don't know	talk
④	didn't know	talked
⑤	doesn't know	talked

6 두 문장이 같은 뜻이 되도록 빈칸에 들어갈 알맞은 것은?

You have to listen to your doctor.
= You _____ listen to your doctor.

① may   ② can
③ might   ④ must
⑤ will

7 빈칸에 들어갈 순서로 알맞은 것은?

> • I always _____ her while she was not here.
> • He'll pass the course by not _____ classes.

① miss - missing
② waited for - waiting for
③ missed - missing
④ waited for - waited for
⑤ missed - missed

8 빈칸에 들어갈 순서로 알맞은 것은?

> A: There are lots of clouds in the sky.
> B: It _____ rain tomorrow. If it rains tomorrow, we can't play a soccer game tomorrow.
> A: Right. We _____ study in the classroom tomorrow.

① can - will   ② should - will
③ should - should   ④ will - should
⑤ will - will

9 우리말을 바르게 영작한 것은?

> 그는 여기에서 10년 동안 살았다.

① He lived here ten years ago.
② He lived here since ten years.
③ He has lived here for ten years.
④ He has lived here since ten years.
⑤ He has been lived here for ten years.

10 ⓐ~ⓒ에 들어갈 단어를 바르게 나열한 것은?

> Only teenagers can hear the special sounds and adults can't ⓐ (hear / be heard) the sound at all. The device ⓑ (named / was named) the Mosquito because it sounds like the buzz of a mosquito. Some shop owners ⓒ (found / was found) the Mosquito very useful.

	ⓐ	ⓑ	ⓒ
①	hear	named	found
②	hear	was named	found
③	be heard	named	found
④	hear	named	was found
⑤	be heard	was named	was found

11 빈칸에 들어갈 순서로 알맞은 것은?

> My mom can make delicious cakes. She made cakes for me. I _____ her cakes since 13. Last week, I _____ myself to cookies. The cookies _____ me. They were great!

① ate - helped - excited
② ate - have helped - were excited
③ have eaten - have helped - were excited
④ have eaten - helped - excited
⑤ eaten - helped - exciting

12 빈칸에 들어갈 순서로 알맞은 것은?

> I have never made that promise before. You are ⓐ____. Am I ⓑ____? Of course, you are! You are a big ⓒ____!

	ⓐ	ⓑ	ⓒ
①	lieing	lying	liar
②	lieing	lying	a lier
③	lying	lying	liar
④	lying	lying	a lier
⑤	lying	lied	lier

13-14 어법상 옳은 것은?

13

① He cans cook Gimbap.

② The cat sounds angrily.

③ Nayoung can't going there.

④ The children look happily.

⑤ She cannot play the piano.

14

① Your room looks warmly with the orange color.

② When Jenny will do exercise, she listens to music.

③ When Jane feels cold, her face will turn red.

④ Tomorrow we had the soccer game with Italy.

⑤ I solved the science problem very difficulty.

15 문법적으로 옳은 것을 2개 고르면?

① I sent an email to my friend before I finished studying.

② Tom didn't stayed home yesterday afternoon.

③ They were not be in class yesterday.

④ Were you surprised when you got the birthday gift?

⑤ Jason has slept for eight hours last night.

16 동사의 형태가 옳지 않은 것을 모두 고르면?

① Jane has met him before.

② I have been here for three months.

③ He has left his hometown two days ago.

④ I've got your letter.

⑤ Have you cutten your wood?

17-18 어법상 옳은 문장을 모두 고르면?

17

> ⓐ A good eating habit will make you health.
> ⓑ Can you keep these apples fresh?
> ⓒ He is eating breakfast with his parents every day.
> ⓓ He can never get them fixed on time.
> ⓔ Watching TV before going to bed can keep you awake.
> ⓕ The scenes in the movie made us exciting.

① ⓐ, ⓓ, ⓔ   ② ⓐ, ⓒ, ⓔ

③ ⓑ, ⓓ, ⓕ   ④ ⓑ, ⓓ, ⓔ

⑤ ⓓ, ⓔ, ⓕ

18

> ⓐ He was playing soccer as I came.
> ⓑ Jane left before the concert ended.
> ⓒ My car has already been stolen when I reached my garage.
> ⓓ Tom had studied the English language since he was 8 years old.
> ⓔ When they arrived at the station, the bus has already left.

① ⓐ, ⓑ   ② ⓐ, ⓓ   ③ ⓑ, ⓔ
④ ⓒ, ⓓ   ⑤ ⓒ, ⓔ

19-20 어법상 옳지 <u>않은</u> 것은?

19

> One hot day, Thomas ① <u>was</u> very hungry. He ② <u>saw</u> some delicious water plants in the river. He ③ <u>dived</u> into the river, but he ④ <u>can't</u> catch them because the river ⑤ <u>became</u> very muddy.

20

> A: ① <u>What do you do last weekend?</u>
> B: I went to Busan with my mom.
> A: Great. ② <u>Did you finish the essay project</u> about the environment?
> B: Not yet. Can you do it with me?
> A: Sure. ③ <u>Do you have any ideas for the project</u>?
> B: ④ <u>Why don't we use</u> the story of Jane's sickness?
> A: How?
> B: She lives in a city. ⑤ <u>She becomes sick because of the dirty air.</u>
> A: That's a good idea!

📋 **서 술 형**

1 표를 보고 빈칸에 알맞은 말을 쓰시오.

	Thur.	Fri.	Sat.
Jenny	study math	read a book	do exercise
Tom	study math	read a book	do his homework

❶ Both _____ math on Thursday.

❷ Tom _____ a book on Friday.

❸ Jenny _____ exercise on Saturday.

❹ But, Tom _____ his homework on Saturday.

2 'know'의 알맞은 형태를 빈칸에 쓰시오.

> Let me introduce my friend, Junho. I met him three years ago. He is kind to everyone. He helps me with math. I _____ him for three years.
> (know를 사용할 것)

→ _____

3 문장을 주어진 단어로 시작하는 수동태 문장으로 쓰시오.

Tom wrote this novel.

→ This novel _____.

4 글에서 <u>잘못된</u> 한 문장을 골라 바르게 고쳐 쓰시오.

> Jane is on the bus now. But an hour ago, Jane and Tommy were at the school library. Jane reads a comic book. Tommy chose a novel. And then they borrowed some other books.

_____. → _____.

5 문장을 진행형으로 고쳐 쓰시오.

> She runs in the park.

❶ 현재진행형 _____ .

❷ 과거진행형 _____ .

6 두 문장을 한 문장으로 연결할 때 빈칸에 알맞은 말을 쓰시오.

> Jenny went to Canada, but now she is here in Korea.

→ Jenny _____ _____ to Canada.

7 대화 중 대답에서 <u>틀린</u> 부분을 찾아 고쳐 쓰시오.

> A: What did the passengers think?
> B: They thought that they will be going to land on the airport soon.

❶ _____ → _____

> A: Why did she check the plane twice after everyone was out?
> B: Because she wanted to make sure that no one is left behind.

❷ _____ → _____

8 주어진 단어를 사용해 영작하시오.

> 우리는 막 공원에 도착했다.
> (arrive / at the park)

→ _____ .

9 주어진 단어를 사용해 영작하시오. (단어 형태 변형 가능)

> 그는 책들을 집에 가져가면 안 된다.
> (should / the books / takes / he / not / home)

→ _____ .

10 아래 주어진 카드만을 이용하여 '과거에 일어난 일'을 나타내는 문장 세 개를 만드시오.

> 〈조건〉
> 1. 모든 카드를 사용하지 않아도 됨.
> 2. 카드는 한 번씩만 사용할 수 있음.

Thomas	I	You
did	not	was	were
do	take	read
the bus	thirsty	the book
yesterday	last week

❶ _____ .

❷ _____ .

❸ _____ .

1 불규칙 동사의 3단 변화가 잘못된 것은?

① beat - beat - beat

② see - saw - seen

③ choose - chose - chosen

④ fight - fought - fought

⑤ begin - began - begun

2 밑줄 친 단어의 뜻이 같은 것끼리 짝지어진 것은?

① He is <u>watering</u> the flowers.

  The <u>water</u> in this glass is hot.

② Peter <u>plays</u> the piano after dinner.

  She wrote many <u>plays</u>.

③ They <u>trick</u> the guests with special effects.

  He <u>tricked</u> almost everyone in that room.

④ We watched a movie which <u>lasted</u> 2 hours.

  He was the <u>last</u> one in line.

⑤ After we took some <u>rest</u>, we went out for dinner.

  He wanted to see the <u>rest</u> of my family.

3 현재진행형의 형태가 바르게 쓰인 것은?

① Jane and Anne <u>are ordering</u> food.

② Lora <u>is eatting</u> pasta.

③ Ned <u>is takeing</u> pictures of his friends.

④ Mike <u>is cuting</u> a hamburger.

⑤ The tiger <u>is walkking</u> to the forest.

4 〈보기〉의 밑줄 친 have finished의 쓰임과 같은 것은?

> ● 보기 ●
> They <u>have just finished</u> making a special present.

① I <u>have been</u> here for three months.

② How long <u>have</u> you <u>lived</u> in Seoul?

③ Jane <u>has known</u> him for six years.

④ Tom <u>has</u> already <u>arrived</u> at Seoul Station.

⑤ I <u>have learned</u> French since 2012.

5 〈보기〉의 밑줄 친 may와 쓰임이 <u>다른</u> 것은?

> ● 보기 ●
> <u>May</u> I go to Sujin's house, Mom?

① The new cellphone <u>may</u> be very cheap.

② <u>May</u> I use your book?

③ You <u>may</u> go there now.

④ <u>May</u> I order lunch food today?

⑤ You <u>may</u> stay my house as long as you want.

6 〈보기〉의 밑줄 친 will과 쓰임이 같은 것은?

> ● 보기 ●
> Where there is a <u>will</u>, there is a way.

① You need to have the <u>will</u> to live with.

② When <u>will</u> the conference be over?

③ It <u>will</u> be rainy tomorrow.

④ <u>Will</u> you clean the room?

⑤ I <u>will</u> always love you.

7 〈보기〉의 밑줄 친 make와 쓰임이 같은 것은?

> ──────────────● 보기 ●──
> It will <u>make</u> my family happy.

① My mom <u>makes</u> fresh air come in.
② I <u>made</u> Gimbap with my mother.
③ I will <u>make</u> my father a cake.
④ She will <u>make</u> a good reporter.
⑤ Chinese food <u>makes</u> you fat.

8 빈칸에 들어갈 말로 알맞지 <u>않은</u> 것은?

> My dad has taught me how to skate well
> _____.

① since 2014   ② since I was 5
③ for ten years   ④ for almost 10 years
⑤ ten years ago

9 대화의 빈칸에 들어갈 말로 알맞은 것은?

> **A:** What's the problem with you?
> **B:** I don't feel well today, and it is getting
>   worse.
> **A:** _____.

① You'd better not rest.
② You'd better go to the mental clinic.
③ You'd better skip going to hospital.
④ You'd better be late.
⑤ You'd better go to see a doctor.

10 문장을 수동태로 전환할 때 옳지 <u>않은</u> 것은?

① He gave me a piece of advice.
   → I was given to a piece of advice by
   him.
② She painted the door green.
   → The door was painted green by her.
③ You should clean your room.
   → Your room should be cleaned by you.
④ The man stole my book yesterday.
   → My book was stolen by the man
   yesterday.
⑤ You can use my laptop.
   → My laptop can be used by you.

11 ⓐ~ⓒ에 들어갈 단어를 바르게 나열한 것은?

> "If I ⓐ (have / don't have) the door key
> with me, thieves can't enter my house."
> "If I harm such poor people, I ⓑ (will be
> shamed / won't be shamed)."
> He didn't know that the fools ⓒ (would
> call / would be called) "foolish wisdom"
> in later times.

	ⓐ	ⓑ	ⓒ
①	have	won't be shamed	would call
②	don't have	will be shamed	would call
③	don't have	will be shamed	would be called
④	have	won't be shamed	would be called
⑤	have	will be shamed	would be called

12 밑줄 친 부분의 쓰임이 나머지와 <u>다른</u> 것은?

① I <u>have never tried</u> eating Thai food before.

② <u>Have</u> you ever <u>heard</u> of another Earth?

③ The players <u>have already finished</u> their match.

④ <u>Have</u> you ever <u>seen</u> the N Seoul Tower?

⑤ I <u>have never played</u> golf before.

16 어법상 옳은 것을 <u>2개</u> 고르면?

① When I reach the station, it'll rain.

② Someone will notice when it's too noisy.

③ James will visit the place when the sun rose.

④ Who will volunteer when the accident happen?

⑤ I didn't answer the phone when I hear the phone ring.

17 어법상 옳지 <u>않은</u> 것을 <u>모두</u> 고르면?

① He often rides a bike, jogs, and to exercise.

② For my health, I go swimming every day.

③ I did so because leftover food was polluted the environment.

④ I have met my girlfriend in 2014.

⑤ What did you do for your health?

13-15 어법상 옳은 것은?

13

① I was cooked spaghetti.

② The cat was slept on the sofa.

③ Dishes are washed by me.

④ You are cleaned the room.

⑤ Tom is taken a shower.

14

① Duri didn't lost his book.

② Hana ate apples tomorrow.

③ He doesn't watch TV last night.

④ The car hit a big tree a week ago.

⑤ When have you cooked this food?

18 어법상 옳은 것을 모두 고르면?

ⓐ I took off my shoes before I entered a room.

ⓑ You will get fat if you don't stop eating.

ⓒ If I will be late for the appointment, don't wait for me.

ⓓ When she gave some of her food for us, we were surprised by her kindness.

ⓔ I will wait here until you will come back.

ⓕ A new computer will be given to me by my mother.

① ⓐ, ⓑ, ⓓ　　　② ⓐ, ⓑ, ⓕ

③ ⓑ, ⓓ, ⓔ　　　④ ⓑ, ⓓ, ⓕ

⑤ ⓐ, ⓓ, ⓔ

15

① Have you heard about the movie?

② Don't shy.

③ He can plays the piano.

④ She won't be join our club.

⑤ I will visit my uncle last week.

19 밑줄 친 ①~⑤ 중 어법상 옳지 <u>않은</u> 것은?

Hi, everyone! My name ① <u>is</u> Suhyon Kim. I ② <u>come</u> from Korea. My lucky number is seven. ③ <u>My</u> favorite soccer player, Ji sung Park also has back number 7. I ④ <u>often play</u> soccer with my friends. I like to play with them. I hope ⑤ <u>you to come</u> to my house.

20 밑줄 친 ①~⑤ 중 형태가 옳지 <u>않은</u> 것을 <u>2개</u> 고르면?

After supper, we went to Gyoungpo Lake. The water was very clear. My father ① <u>caught</u> a big fish, but he ② <u>put</u> it back. He enjoyed fishing itself. My brother and I ③ <u>rode</u> a bike around the lake. We had a good time. At night, My brother and I heard a strange noise. We looked outside and ④ <u>see</u> a big shadow. We ⑤ <u>were frightening</u>. Then, it turned around. It was my dad.

서 술 형

1 문장을 지시대로 바꿔 쓰시오.

I write a new grammar book.

❶ 미래형 _____

_____ .

❷ 현재완료진행형 _____

_____ .

2 일과표를 보고 James가 주말에 하는 일에 대해 설명하는 말을 완성하시오.

James의 주말	
Saturday	play basketball with his friends
Sunday	help old people

❶ On Saturdays, James _____

_____ .

❷ On Sundays, James _____

_____ .

3 주어진 단어를 사용해 영작하시오.

너는 1주일 이내에 책들을 반납해야 한다. (7단어)
(return / should / within)

→ _____ .

4 두 문장을 and를 사용해 한 문장으로 바꿔 쓰시오.

> • James likes watching soccer games.
> • James enjoys playing basketball.

→ _____

   _____ .

5 같은 뜻이 되도록 빈칸에 알맞은 말을 쓰시오.

I came to Seoul ten years ago. And I still live here.

= I _____ _____ in Seoul

   _____ ten years.

6 주어진 단어를 사용해 문장을 완성하시오. (단어 형태 변형 가능)

> 이 편지는 며칠 전에 우리 선생님에 의해 쓰여졌다.
> (write / our teacher / a few)

→ This letter _____ .

7 문장을 수동태로 바르게 바꿔 쓰시오.

He bought Jenny a new bag.

→ A new bag _____ .
   (6단어 추가)

8 주어진 단어를 사용해 영작하시오. (단어 형태 변형 및 추가 가능)

> 그 그림들은 우리에게 그 돈이 어떻게 쓰이게 될지 보여준다.
> (pictures / use / the money / how)

→ _____ .

9 어법상 틀린 것을 바르게 고치시오. (3개)

> Last weekend, I was inviting to go on a trip with my friend Junho's family to Bulguksa in Gyeongju. I was very exciting although it was my first trip to the south of Korea. The trip was interesting and meaningful.

❶ _____ → _____

❷ _____ → _____

❸ _____ → _____

10 어법상 틀린 것을 바르게 고치시오. (4개)

> ⓐ Our teacher told us that Columbus had discovered the New Continent.
> ⓑ Water freezes at zero.
> ⓒ He haven't talked to me all day.
> ⓓ If it will rain tomorrow, our school will not go on a picnic.
> ⓔ The earth goes around the sun.
> ⓕ The World Cup is held every 4 years.
> ⓖ Have you ever catch a big fish?

❶ _____

   _____ .

❷ _____ .

❸ _____ .

❹ _____ ?

1 밑줄 친 run과 의미가 같은 것은?

Could you run the engine for a moment?

① We run 12-week courses with daily
   5-hour classes.
② He ran in the forest early in the morning.
③ When batteries run down, I can't use my
   phone.
④ The hospital runs a research center
   working on vaccine.
⑤ Please run the program again.

2 주어진 우리말에 맞게 문장을 완성할 때 네 번째에 오는
것은?

I'm _____.
(나는 너의 가족 사진을 보고 있어.)

① family   ② looking
③ your   ④ at
⑤ picture

3 빈칸에 들어갈 말로 어색한 것은?

My father is _____ next Sunday.

① going to America
② coming back home
③ visiting his hometown
④ leaving for New York
⑤ doing his project

4 〈보기〉의 밑줄 친 must와 의미가 같은 것은?

● 보기 ●
You must be curious about our plan.

① You must be tired after working.
② You must not say impolite things like
   that.
③ I must finish this report by tomorrow.
④ Cars must not be parked in front of the
   entrance.
⑤ I must go to school and study hard.

5 〈보기〉의 밑줄 친 부분과 쓰임이 같은 것은?

● 보기 ●
He has traveled to America for one month.

① Yong has been to Washington D.C.
   before.
② She has already finished her homework.
③ Jane has learned Korean since 2014.
④ She has never spoken to other men.
⑤ James has lost his bicycle.

6 빈칸에 들어갈 알맞은 것은?

Tommy cleaned the house for her mom.
→ The house _____ by Tommy
   for her mom.

① cleans   ② is cleaned
③ are cleaned   ④ was cleaned
⑤ were cleaned

7 글에서 that의 성격이 다른 하나는?

> He said ⓐ that I could not check out ⓑ that big green book from the library. So, I planned to show it to Jim in the corner. I didn't know ⓒ that my iguana would cause trouble in the library. My dad said ⓓ that it was my fault because I brought the iguana to the library. But I don't think ⓔ that a silent animal makes trouble in the library.

① ⓐ　②ⓑ　③ ⓒ　④ ⓓ　⑤ ⓔ

8 밑줄 친 be를 알맞은 형태로 고친 것은?

> Suyoung be a member of the club, Kids' Hope, since last January.

① was　② has been
③ were　④ been
⑤ have been

9 짝지어진 문장의 의미가 같지 않은 것은?

① Jackson lost his pen, and he doesn't have it.
→ Jackson has lost his pen.
② I started the work yesterday, and it is over now.
→ I have just finished the work.
③ Yesterday, she saw a lion for the first time in her life.
→ She has seen a lion once.
④ Nayoung went to Europe last year, and she is there now.
→ Nayoung has gone to Europe.
⑤ She came here seven years ago, and she still lives here.
→ She has lived here for seven years.

10 주어진 두 문장을 한 문장으로 바르게 연결한 것은?

> • He didn't have to go to school yesterday.
> • It was a holiday.

① He didn't have to go to school because it was a holiday yesterday.
② Because he didn't have to go to school, it was a holiday yesterday.
③ It's a holiday yesterday because he didn't have to go to school.
④ He didn't have to go to school, so it was a holiday yesterday.
⑤ So he didn't have to go to school, it was a holiday yesterday.

11 빈칸에 들어갈 순서로 알맞은 것은?

> Yesterday Junho ⓐ_____ up at 8 o'clock. He missed the bus, and he was late for class. He also ⓑ_____ his English book. During lunch break, he broke a window. On his way back home, he wasn't careful, so he ⓒ_____ down. It was a terrible day for Junho.

	ⓐ	ⓑ	ⓒ
①	wake	brought	fell
②	waked	brought	fell
③	waked	didn't bring	fell
④	woke	didn't bring	fell
⑤	woke	didn't bring	felled

12 빈칸에 들어갈 가장 알맞은 표현은?

> **A:** I'm so hungry now.
> **B:** _____.
> You may get a stomachache.

① You'd better eat too much.
② You'd not better eat too much.
③ You don't better eat too much.
④ You'd better not eat too much.
⑤ You'd better don't eat too much.

13-14 어법상 옳은 문장은?

13

① It was so windy yesterday. The wind makes the picture fall on the floor.
② When Ted was dancing, his mom called his name.
③ Get a good grade is a good habit.
④ You will can donate your talent.
⑤ When I will finish my homework, I will go out.

14

① He puts his bag on the desk yesterday.
② I had them with a cup of warm tea, and I begun to feel better.
③ Did you ate a lot of snacks?
④ I didn't do very well on the test, so I became sad.
⑤ They studied hard for the test last night.

15 어색한 문장을 모두 고르시오.

① If it's snowy outside, let's go out and play.
② Exercise if you want to be healthy.
③ Jenny went shopping yesterday.
④ If you will go with us, we'll be very happy.
⑤ When have you done the work?

16 옳은 문장을 2개 고르시오.

① She broked the plants.
② We should donates some money.
③ She did her art project last Monday.
④ She must get up early tomorrow.
⑤ I felted sorry that I didn't carefully listen to her.

17 어법상 옳은 것을 모두 고르면?

> ⓐ It may rains tomorrow.
> ⓑ May I try this shirt on?
> ⓒ Because the snow, she may be late for the party.
> ⓓ When I go to Jeju-do, I will have lots of seafood.
> ⓔ I saw a doctor, but I am still not feeling well.

① ⓐ, ⓑ, ⓓ   ② ⓑ, ⓒ, ⓔ
③ ⓑ, ⓓ, ⓔ   ④ ⓑ, ⓓ
⑤ ⓑ, ⓔ

18 어법상 틀린 문장은 모두 몇 개인가?

ⓐ Hyanggyo was a school for boys long time ago.
ⓑ What are you want to read?
ⓒ He wants to visits to Paris.
ⓓ He goes swimming every Saturday.
ⓔ Will he comes to the party tonight?
ⓕ They can't stayed out in the rain very long.

① 2개   ② 3개   ③ 4개   ④ 5개   ⑤ 6개

19 어법상 옳은 것을 모두 고르면?

Yesterday I did many things. I got up at 7. I had breakfast at 8. Then, I went to school at 9. After school, I ⓐ taken a piano lesson. After that, I ⓑ went shopping alone. I ⓒ was bought a birthday cake for my sister. It looked quite delicious and fresh. But I felt ⓓ disappointed because my sister told me that it tasted too ⓔ sweetly.

① ⓐ, ⓑ   ② ⓐ, ⓓ   ③ ⓑ, ⓒ
④ ⓑ, ⓓ   ⑤ ⓑ, ⓔ

20 밑줄 친 ⓐ~ⓔ 중 어법상 어색한 것 2개를 고르시오.

Today was Jihun's birthday, but no one ⓐ remembers. There was no present and no birthday cake. He got home and opened the door. "Surprise!" People ⓑ jumped from everywhere in the house. He ⓒ saw balloons, gifts, and a cake. His mother, father, and even his friends were there. He just ⓓ stood there. His eyes ⓔ filled with tears, but on his face, there was a big smile.

① ⓐ   ② ⓑ   ③ ⓒ   ④ ⓓ   ⑤ ⓔ

서술형

1 그림을 보고 영어로 답하시오.

Q: What are you doing?

A: _____ .

2 두 문장을 and를 사용해 한 문장으로 바꿔 쓰시오.

• Suji takes a dancing lesson on Friday.
• Suji goes to sing songs to the concert hall on Friday.

→ _____

_____ .

3 문장을 수동태로 바르게 바꿔 쓰시오.

Our students moved the boxes to the school.

→ _____ .

4 주어진 단어를 사용해 영작하시오.

나의 부모님은 결혼하신지 15년이 되었다.
(my parents / be / married)

→ _____ .

5 두 문장을 한 문장으로 나타낼 때, 괄호 안에 알맞은 말을 순서대로 쓰시오.

> • I started to writing books on English reading three years ago.
> • I still do.

→ I _____ _____ books on

English reading _____

_____ _____ .

6 표를 보고 빈칸에 들어갈 말을 알맞게 쓰시오.

	Me	Jenny	James
좋아하는 것	music	English	music
좋아하지 않는 것	science	math	science

Jenny ❶ _____ English, but

❷ _____ math. James and I

❸ _____ music, but we

❹ _____ science.

7 주어진 단어를 사용해 영작하시오.

> 한국사는 모든 학생들에게 가르쳐져야 한다.
> (should / every / teach)

→ Korean history _____

_____ .

8 용준의 용돈 기입장을 보고 문장을 완성하시오. (과거시제를 활용할 것)

날짜	내용	들어온 돈	나간 돈	남은 돈
10/8	allowance	50,000		50,000
10/9	games		10,000	40,000
10/10	books		20,000	20,000
10/13	savings		10,000	10,000

He _____ 10,000 won _____

games and only _____ 10,000 won

in the bank.

9 어법상 틀린 것을 바르게 고치시오.

❶ I have written an English book since three years.

_____ → _____

❷ You'd better attend not the presentation.

_____ → _____

❸ If it will snow tomorrow, I won't play badminton.

_____ → _____

10 주어진 단어를 사용해 영작하시오. (단어 형태 변형 및 추가 가능)

> 내가 세계 여행을 시작한지 거의 두 달이 되었다.
> (have / almost / month / since / start / my trip / around the world)

→ It _____

_____ .

Break Time!

Much learning does not teach understanding. (Heraclitus)

많은 공부와 지식이 곧 지혜로 연결되는 것은 아니다. (헤라클레이토스)

Education is the best provision for old age. (Aristotle)

교육은 노후를 위한 최상의 양식이다. (아리스토텔레스)

College isn't the place to go for ideas. (Helen Keller)

대학은 아이디어를 얻으러 가는 곳이 아니다. (헬렌 켈러)

Seek not every quality in one individual. (Confucius)

한 사람에게서 모든 덕을 구하지 말라. (공자)

Well done is better than well said. (Benjamin Franklin)

실천이 말보다 낫다. (벤자민 프랭클린)

Actions lie louder than words. (Carolyn Wells)

행동은 말보다 더 새빨간 거짓말을 한다. (캐롤린 웰스)

Strong reasons make strong actions. (William Shakespeare)

강력한 이유는 강력한 행동을 낳는다. (윌리엄 셰익스피어)

A happy childhood has spoiled many a promising life. (Robertson Davies)

행복한 어린 시절 때문에 많은 사람들이 촉망받는 인생을 망쳤다. (로버트슨 데이비스)

The foundation of every state is the education of its youth. (Diogenes Laertius)

어느 국가든 그 기초는 젊은이들의 교육이다. (디오게네스 라에르티오스)

Education is a state-controlled manufactory of echoes. (Norman Douglas)

교육이란 똑같은 생각을 찍어내는 국영 공장이다. (노먼 더글러스)

chapter

03

부정사

동명사

분사

부정사

'to+동사원형'이나 동사원형인 '원형부정사'의 형태로 문장에서 여러 역할을 담당한다.

❶ 문장 내 부정사의 다양한 역할

1 명사적 용법

Ⓐ 주어(~하는 것은)

To study English is fairly interesting.

It is a lot of fun *to play* the guitar.

*실제 구어체에서는 부정사 주어를 문장 뒤로 빼고 원래 자리에 it을 쓴다.

Ⓑ 보어(~하는 것은)

Your mistake was *to write* that letter.

My dream is *to become* a professor.

Ⓒ 목적어(~하는 것을)

We decided *to take* a picture.

I want *to work* with computers.

2 형용사적 용법

명사 뒤에 놓여 앞의 명사 수식(~하는, ~할)

He left me a dog *to take care of*.

I have a large family *to support*.

Can you give me something cold *to drink*?

*something, anything, everything은 꾸며 주는 형용사도 뒤에 온다.

3 부사적 용법

Ⓐ 감정의 원인(~해서) She was very glad *to hear* about her husband's winning.

Ⓑ 목적(~하기 위해서) I went to the station *to see* him off.

Ⓒ 결과(~해서 …하다) She has grown up *to become* a judge.

4 기타: 부정사의 의미상 주어와 부정형

Ⓐ for+명사/대명사 목적격: 일반적인 부정사의 의미상 주어

It is easy *for him* to solve the problem.

It is very important *for teachers* to understand young students.

Ⓑ of+목적격: 부정사 앞에 성격을 나타내는 형용사가 올 때

It was kind *of you* to help the friend in need.

It was foolish *of her* to make such a big mistake.

성격을 나타내는 형용사의 예

■ foolish(어리석은) ■ kind(친절한) ■ considerate(사려 깊은) ■ stubborn(완고한) ■ polite(예의 바른)
■ cold-hearted(냉정한) ■ conservative(보수적인)

C **부정사의 부정형: 부정사 앞에 not이나 never를 쓴다.**

I hurried to the station *not to miss* the train.

The man told me *never to touch* anything.

❷ 부정사 필수 패턴

1 사역동사+목적어+동사원형: make, let, have

I *made* many students *laugh*.   I *will let* you *study* English well.

2 지각동사+목적어+동사원형/동사원형-ing: see, watch, feel, hear

I *saw* him *run/running* to the park.   We *heard* the bell *ring*.

3 ask, allow, want, tell, order, get+목적어+to 동사원형

I *want* you *to receive* my gift.   The doctor *told* me *to stay* in bed.

UNIT **2**

동명사

동사원형+-ing의 형태로 동사의 기능을 하면서 문장에서 명사 역할을 한다.

❶ 동명사의 명사적 역할

1 주어

Reading history book is very interesting.

Studying all day is not efficient.

2 목적어

I really enjoy *playing* various musical instruments. (타동사 enjoy의 목적어)

Jean is good at *speaking* English fluently. (전치사 at의 목적어)

동명사만을 목적어로 취하는 타동사

■ enjoy(즐기다) ■ keep(유지하다, 계속하다) ■ mind(꺼려하다) ■ avoid(피하다) ■ finish(끝내다)
■ give up(포기하다) ■ consider(고려하다) ■ stop(~을 그만두다) ■ appreciate(감사해하다)....

3 보어

My hobby is *singing* classical songs.

My hope is *traveling* around the world.

② 동명사의 활용

1 동명사의 의미상 주어: 대명사의 소유격이 원칙이나 구어체에서는 목적격도 가능

He is proud of *being* rich. (being rich의 주체가 주어인 he. 이때는 따로 표기하지 않음)

I don't like *his making* an excuse. (making an excuse의 주체가 I가 아닌 his)

2 동명사의 부정형: 동명사 앞에 not이나 never를 쓴다.

She is ashamed of *not taking* care of the homeless.

3 뒤에 동명사가 오느냐 부정사가 오느냐에 따라 뜻이 달라지는 동사

	+동명사	+to부정사
try	한번 ~해 보다	~하려고 애쓰다
forget	~했던 걸 잊어버리다	~할 것을 잊다
remember	~했던 걸 기억하다	~할 것을 기억하다
regret	~했던 걸 후회하다	~해야 해서 유감이다
stop	~을 그만두다	~하기 위해 멈추다

I *tried making* it.   I *tried to make* it.

I *remember seeing* him before.   I *remember to see* him tomorrow.

I *stopped drinking*.   I *stopped to drink*.

③ 동명사의 관용적 표현

- be busy -ing: ~하느라 바쁘다   My mother *is busy cooking* breakfast.
- be good at -ing: ~을 잘하다   She *is good at baking* chocolate cookies.
- What[How] about -ing? (=What do you say to -ing?): ~하는 게 어때?

  What[How] about getting him a sweater?
- cannot help -ing (=cannot but+동사원형): ~하지 않을 수 없다

  She *couldn't help loving* him.

  =She *couldn't but love* him.
- go -ing: ~하러 가다   I'll *go shopping*.
- keep[go] on -ing: 계속 ~하다   They *went on talking* to one another.
- on[upon] -ing (=as soon as S+V): ~하자마자

  On[Upon] seeing me, she exclaimed.

  =*As soon as she saw* me, she exclaimed.
- feel like -ing: ~하고 싶다   Do you *feel like taking* a walk?
- be worth -ing: ~할 가치가 있다   They *are worth repairing*.

기본 개념 장착 하기

분사

동사와 형용사의 성질을 동시에 지니고 있는 것으로 현재분사와 과거분사가 있다.

분사의 종류와 역할

1 현재분사(동사원형+-ing): 능동, 진행의 의미(행하는, 행하고 있는)

A 명사 수식

I like the *dancing* girl.

That *sleeping* baby is cute.

B 상태 설명

He is *reading* a book now. (현재진행형)

She sat *reading* a novel. (~하면서)

2 과거분사(동사의 과거분사형): 수동, 완료의 의미(되어진, 다 된)

A 명사 수식

There are *fallen* leaves on the ground.

I want a book *written* in English.

*현재분사나 과거분사가 단독으로 오지 않고 뒤에 수식어구가 붙으면 명사 뒤에 놓여 수식한다.

B 상태 설명

The temple was *built* by him last year. (be+p.p.: 수동태)

I have just *finished* my work. (have+p.p.: 현재완료)

문장을 해석하시오.

1 I don't want to be late for school.

→ _____.

2 He told me to go to bed early.

→ _____.

3 I saw him go to church on Sunday.

→ _____.

4 I made him clean the room.

→ _____.

5 It is difficult for him to write a letter in English.

→ _____.

6 It is kind of you to say so.

→ _____.

7 Do you mind my waiting for you for a minute?

→ _____?

8 He really doesn't like her being late for school.

→ _____.

9 The policeman had a drunken man walk straight.

→ _____.

10 The girls stopped talking when they saw him.

→ _____.

밑줄 친 부분이 주어, 목적어, 보어 중 어느 것으로 쓰였는지 구별하시오.

11 They promised to do exercises every morning. _____

12 To read newspapers is useful to you.

_____

13 My hope is to get good grades.

_____

14 It is not good to tell a lie. _____

밑줄 친 부정사의 용법을 쓰시오.

15 He went to the station to meet her.

_____

16 To take a walk in the morning is very good. _____

17 Everyone needs a house to live in.

_____

18 Jerry and I like to play table tennis.

_____

19 He has a lot of work to do. _____

20 She grew up to be a good doctor.

_____

21 My wish is to live in peace.

_____

22 I was surprised to hear the news.

_____

23 He must be clever to answer such a question. _____

24 It is interesting to learn Chinese.

25 The baseball game was very (excited / exciting).

26 I am (interested / interesting) in dinosaurs.

27 I saw the beautiful moon through the (broken / breaking) window.

28 I smelled something (burnt / burning) in the kitchen.

29 Have you finished (to send / sending / sent) e-mails?

30 He can't but (to fall / fall / falling) asleep.

37 My father is proud that I teach Korean history.

= My father is proud of _____ _____ Korean history.

38 _____ _____ the news, he was shocked.

= As soon as he heard the news, he was shocked.

39 Let's go on a picnic.

= How _____ _____ on a picnic?

밑줄 친 부분이 현재분사인지 동명사인지 구별하시오.

31 Start practicing them today.

_____

32 Can you smell something burning?

_____

33 He is listening to the music.

_____

34 I hope it will stop raining. _____

35 One of my bad habits is biting my nails.

_____

주어진 단어를 사용해 영작하시오.

40 그들은 그 광경을 보고 웃지 않을 수 없었다. (help / laugh)

They _____ _____

_____ _____ at the sight.

41 너는 소파에 앉아 있는 그 신사를 아니? (sit / on)

Do you know _____ _____

_____ _____ the sofa?

42 열심히 책을 읽는 것은 중요하다. (read / hard)

It is important _____

_____ _____.

43 친구들과 어울리도록 노력해라. (try / get / along)

_____.

서로 같은 뜻이 되도록 빈칸을 채우시오.

36 She can dance very well.

= She is very good at _____.

44 나는 공부하러 학교에 간다. (school / to)

_____.

문장에서 틀린 부분을 고쳐 다시 쓰시오.

45 I heard him to sing a song.

    → _____.

46 I want him going to school now.

    → _____.

47 They had him to do it.

    → _____.

48 Did you decide being a singer?

    → _____?

49 He is ashamed of being not tall.

    → _____.

50 I don't feel like to study now.

    → _____.

51 What do you say to have some break?

    → _____?

52 Riding a horse is not as easy as to ride a bicycle.

    → _____.

53 My mother had that coat clean.

    → _____.

54 I bought a camera making in Korea.

    → _____.

1 동명사의 형태가 바르지 <u>않은</u> 것은?

① <u>Putting</u> something on the TV is dangerous.

② <u>Getting</u> up early in the morning is a good habit.

③ <u>Planting</u> trees is a good way to save the Earth.

④ <u>Lieing</u> on the bed late is bad for your back.

⑤ By <u>helping</u> the poor, we can be proud of ourselves.

2 빈칸에 알맞지 <u>않은</u> 것은?

> He _____ me to go to the room.

① wanted   ② expected   ③ advised
④ asked   ⑤ made

3 빈칸에 들어갈 주어진 단어의 형태가 나머지와 <u>다른</u> 것은?

① He considers _____ the detective novel. (read)

② She wants _____ the club. (join)

③ His hobby is _____ the piano at his free time. (play)

④ I enjoy _____ movies. (watch)

⑤ Please stop _____. It is unhealthy. (smoke)

4 빈칸에 들어갈 수 <u>없는</u> 표현을 2개 고르면?

> He _____ going on a picnic.

① enjoys   ② wants
③ avoids   ④ looks forward to
⑤ plans

5 빈칸에 공통으로 들어갈 단어를 <u>2개</u> 고르면?

> - She _____ to close the window.
> - She _____ to wash her face.
> - She _____ to go abroad.

① hoped   ② practiced
③ minded   ④ enjoyed
⑤ tried

6-7 빈칸에 들어갈 말로 알맞지 <u>않은</u> 것은?

6

> He looked forward to _____.

① the future   ② summer vacation
③ his next trip   ④ watching TV
⑤ visit Busan

7

> They _____ to practice it.

① continued   ② started
③ finished   ④ hoped
⑤ loved

8-10 밑줄 친 부분의 쓰임이 나머지와 <u>다른</u> 것은?

8

① <u>To tell</u> the truth is important.

② He wanted <u>to be</u> a chef.

③ My hobby is <u>to watch</u> a baseball game.

④ I like <u>to show</u> my pictures.

⑤ She had no chance <u>to succeed</u>.

9

① She brought some fruit <u>to make</u> a salad.

② They got up early <u>to join</u> the meeting.

③ He left for France <u>to study</u> pop music.

④ I went to the bookstore <u>to buy</u> some books.

⑤ He had some pictures <u>to show</u> her.

10

① She needed a chair <u>to sit</u> on.

② He wants some water <u>to drink</u>.

③ Would you give me something <u>to eat</u>?

④ He had a lot of things <u>to help</u> us.

⑤ I am going to meet him <u>to play</u> soccer.

11 〈보기〉의 밑줄 친 부분과 쓰임이 <u>다른</u> 것은?

> ● 보기 ●
> Is <u>taking</u> a shower every day good for our health?

① What he wants is <u>fixing</u> his bike.

② They enjoyed <u>watching</u> sports games.

③ She went out without <u>carrying</u> an umbrella.

④ Never touch <u>sleeping</u> dogs.

⑤ <u>Living</u> in foreign countries is an amazing experience.

12 밑줄 친 부분의 쓰임이 나머지와 <u>다른</u> 것은?

① He began <u>reading</u> her report.

② She enjoyed <u>playing</u> with her friends.

③ They are <u>talking</u> on the phone.

④ I gave up <u>playing</u> the instrument.

⑤ Do you mind <u>opening</u> the window?

13-14 어법상 옳은 문장은?

13

① He allowed her going to the party.

② She said that he will go to Seoul.

③ He told his daughter to not go shopping.

④ My mom wanted me to study hard.

⑤ The doctor advised me to not go to bed late.

14

① Play the piano is a good way to change one's mood.

② He didn't know how old are you.

③ It is impossible to catch the bus on time.

④ It is not interesting plays soccer with him.

⑤ Watching movies are her hobby.

15 밑줄 친 부분 중 어법상 옳은 것은?

① It is worth <u>watching</u> carefully.

② Think seriously before <u>buy</u>.

③ I made the list before <u>shop</u>.

④ <u>Keep</u> a rule is important.

⑤ He was too nervous to <u>saying</u> a word.

16 어법상 옳은 것은?

① He let me to go to the party.

② They helped her to clean the room.

③ Make the car fix.

④ She had her son to wash the dishes.

⑤ The man made his computer working again.

17 ⓐ~ⓒ의 형태를 어법에 맞게 바꾼 것을 고르시오.

Why isn't she ⓐ carry an umbrella? It may ⓑ rain soon. We need ⓒ prepare for our future.

	ⓐ	ⓑ	ⓒ
①	to carry	rain	preparing
②	carrying	rain	to prepare
③	carry	raining	to prepare
④	carry	to rain	prepare
⑤	carrying	rain	preparing

18 밑줄 친 부분이 어법상 옳지 <u>않은</u> 것은?

"You have ⓐ to go there." He heard someone's voice from a ⓑ waiting room. He didn't know what he ⓒ say. So he continued ⓓ talking and ⓔ playing with his friends.

① ⓐ   ② ⓑ   ③ ⓒ   ④ ⓓ   ⑤ ⓔ

19 (A), (B)와 같은 용법끼리 바르게 짝지어진 것은?

(A) To pass the exam, you don't need
(B) to look for another information.

ⓐ What would you like to eat?

ⓑ She got up early to catch the bus.

ⓒ They wanted to watch that movie.

ⓓ She went shopping to buy new shoes.

ⓔ They bought a new car to go there.

	(A)	(B)
①	ⓐ, ⓒ	ⓑ, ⓓ, ⓔ
②	ⓐ, ⓒ, ⓔ	ⓑ, ⓓ
③	ⓑ, ⓓ, ⓔ	ⓐ, ⓒ
④	ⓑ, ⓓ	ⓐ, ⓒ, ⓔ
⑤	ⓔ	ⓐ, ⓑ, ⓒ, ⓓ

20 밑줄 친 부분이 문법적으로 옳지 <u>않은</u> 것은?

My hobby is ⓐ taking pictures in my free time. Especially, I enjoy ⓑ doing it with my friends. We talk much about ourselves. And we take pictures of cars ⓒ to move on the street. After we finish ⓓ taking pictures, we go to the restaurant. We always like ⓔ eating delicious food.

① ⓐ   ② ⓑ   ③ ⓒ   ④ ⓓ   ⑤ ⓔ

📖 **서 술 형**

1 주어진 단어를 사용해 영작하시오.

> 시원한 마실 것을 좀 주세요.
> (something / drink / cool / to)

→ Please give me _____.

2 주어진 단어를 사용해 ①~③에 알맞은 단어를 쓰시오.
(단어 형태 변형 가능)

> I saw an ❶ _____ game tonight. It
> made me ❷ _____ . There are many
> ❸ _____ things to watch in the
> world.

❶ _____ (excite)

❷ _____ (excite)

❸ _____ (interest)

3 같은 뜻이 되도록 to부정사를 사용해 빈칸에 알맞은 말을 쓰시오.

He went to the party because he wanted
to meet her.

= He went to the party _____.

4 괄호 안의 단어를 바르게 배열하여 문장을 완성하시오.

> The man (him / give / to / asked) her
> this letter.

The man _____ her
this letter.

5 우리말에 맞게 주어진 단어를 사용해 문장을 완성하시오.

❶ 가난한 사람들을 돕는 것은 우리를 행복하게 만든다.

→ _____ the poor makes us

_____ . (help / happy)

❷ 집에 갈 시간이다.

→ It's time _____.
(go)

6 사역동사 have를 사용해 문장을 완성하시오.

그녀는 어제 컴퓨터를 수리되게 시켰다.

→ She _____ her computer

_____ yesterday.

7 우리말에 맞게 문장을 완성하시오.

그는 너무 어려서 그 영화를 볼 수 없다.

→ He is _____ _____

_____ watch the movie.

8 주어진 단어를 사용해 영작하시오.

> 우리는 축구 경기를 보는 것을 즐긴다.
> (enjoy / soccer games)

→ _____ .

9 주어진 단어를 사용해 영작하시오.

> for you / it / to / computer games / very /
> play / is / dangerous

→ _____

for a long time.

10 ⓐ~ⓔ 중 옳지 <u>않은</u> 문장을 고쳐 다시 쓰시오.

> ⓐ First, our parents wants us to prepare
> everything before going to school.
> ⓑ Next, they tells us to keep a rule of
> our home. ⓒ Our father also advises us
> to not come home late. ⓓ It's because
> our parents are worried about. ⓔ Finally,
> they want us to study harder.

❶ _____

_____ .

❷ _____ .

❸ _____ .

❹ _____ .

1 동명사 형태가 옳지 <u>않은</u> 것은?

① lie - lying
② swim - swimming
③ play - playing
④ help - helping
⑤ eat - eatting

2-3 빈칸에 들어갈 순서로 알맞은 것은?

2

> • Do you want _____ abroad?
> • By _____ your best, you can achieve your goal.

① to go - doing
② going - doing
③ to go - to do
④ go - do
⑤ to go - do

3

> • I think that movie will be _____.
>   So I don't want to watch it.
> • She was so _____ that she helped him.

① bored - impressing
② boring - impressed
③ bored - impressed
④ exciting - impressing
⑤ excited - impressed

4 빈칸에 들어갈 주어진 단어의 형태가 <u>다른</u> 것은?

① He was taking a walk and _____ to music. (listen)
② It is time _____ to bed. (go)
③ She enjoys watching TV and _____ a book. (read)
④ They heard him _____ in his room. (cry)
⑤ After finishing washing the dishes and _____ a shower, she went to bed early. (take)

5-6 빈칸에 알맞은 것은?

5

> She has a pen _____.

① to write with   ② to write on
③ to with write   ④ with to write
⑤ write with

6

> **A:** Now, we need to know each other.
> **B:** Let me _____ myself first. I was born in Seoul. My hobby is playing computer games.

① will introduce   ② to introduce
③ introducing   ④ introduced
⑤ introduce

7 밑줄 친 부분의 쓰임이 나머지와 다른 것은?

① I had a friend to play with.
② They decided to buy some food.
③ She needed a bed to lie on.
④ I have a lot of work to do.
⑤ He has much money to buy a house.

8 〈보기〉의 밑줄 친 to say와 쓰임이 같은 것은?

———● 보기 ●———
I went to his house to say good-bye.

① They practiced a lot to win the game.
② You don't need to go there.
③ She had to make some food to eat.
④ I forget to lock the door.
⑤ Nice to meet you.

9 〈보기〉의 밑줄 친 부분과 같은 용법으로 쓰인 것은?

———● 보기 ●———
I want to sing a song composed by him.

① He was sad to see that scene.
② My parents expected to go on a picnic.
③ She was glad to meet them.
④ He practiced very hard to win the medal.
⑤ She must be kind to say so.

10 밑줄 친 부분의 쓰임이 나머지와 다른 것은?

① I like taking a bath.
② Look at the man standing over there.
③ Eating breakfast is good for your health.
④ How do you feel about watching movies?
⑤ The woman finished reading her report.

11 〈보기〉의 밑줄 친 동명사의 용법과 다른 것은?

———● 보기 ●———
Do you enjoy playing computer games?

① Giving some gifts is good.
② He finished washing the dishes.
③ They enjoyed playing the violin.
④ I love taking a picture.
⑤ He was too fat but he couldn't stop eating.

12 빈칸에 들어갈 순서로 알맞은 것은?

• The game was very _____.
• They were _____ in music.
• I was _____ at the news.

① boring - interested - surprising
② boring - interested - surprised
③ boring - interesting - surprised
④ bored - interesting - surprised
⑤ bored - interesting - surprising

13 밑줄 친 동사의 형태가 옳은 것은?

① He let me watching the movie.
② The hot weather made her annoying.
③ He helped me do my homework.
④ His goal is to begin save money for the car.
⑤ She made her car wash in the morning.

14 어법상 옳지 <u>않은</u> 것은?

① He had his car washed.

② She let her hair cut by a hair dresser.

③ He made his chair repaired by his son.

④ She let him watch TV.

⑤ I helped my brother to making a kite.

15 어법상 옳은 것은?

① He wants see his daughter.

② He imagined to go to the beach.

③ He expects gaining more points.

④ He told me to clean my room.

⑤ He feels like to go to the hospital.

16 문법적으로 옳지 <u>않은</u> 것을 모두 고르면?

① I avoided to eat fast food.

② He finished washing the dishes.

③ I don't mind to open the door.

④ He began crying.

⑤ They expected me to go to the party.

17 어법상 쓰임이 <u>어색한</u> 것은?

① He went fishing with his father.

② He has started to do his work.

③ She took the subway not to be late for school.

④ She had him cleaned the window.

⑤ The teacher made his students stand up.

18 밑줄 친 ⓐ~ⓔ 중 옳지 <u>않은</u> 것은?

> ⓐ He helped her finish <u>doing</u> the dishes.
> ⓑ She has a lot of work <u>to do</u> this week.
> ⓒ She liked to spend her time <u>to playing</u> the piano.
> ⓓ I allowed her <u>to go</u> to the concert after she practiced playing the piano.
> ⓔ The man had me wash the dishes. It made me <u>feeling</u> sad.

① ⓐ, ⓒ   ② ⓑ, ⓒ   ③ ⓒ, ⓔ

④ ⓓ, ⓔ   ⑤ ⓑ, ⓔ

19 밑줄 친 단어 중 옳지 <u>않게</u> 고쳐진 것은?

> As soon as I ① <u>get</u> there, I will look for my items. I do not like ② <u>leave</u> them in the room. I enjoy ③ <u>play</u> with my brothers. I will make them ④ <u>stop</u> playing video games and ⑤ <u>go</u> to the park with me.

① get   ② leaving   ③ playing

④ stop   ⑤ going

20 밑줄 친 ⓐ~ⓔ의 동사 형태가 옳지 <u>않은</u> 것은?

> What do you ⓐ <u>do</u> in your free time?
> ⓑ <u>To watch</u> a movie is a way of filling time. Many people want ⓒ <u>to have</u> their own things. So they go shopping ⓓ <u>to buy</u> many kinds of things. If you like to spend time cooking, you may buy a cooker. If you like to take a picture, you might enjoy ⓔ <u>to go</u> to the countryside.

① ⓐ   ② ⓑ   ③ ⓒ   ④ ⓓ   ⑤ ⓔ

서술형

1 우리말에 맞게 문장을 완성하시오.

> 매일 아침 식사를 하는 것은 중요하다.

→ It _____ _____

_____ _____

_____ every day.

2 주어진 단어를 사용해 영작하시오.

> 그는 그녀가 동아리에 가입하기를 원했다.
> (want / he / join / a club / her)

→ _____.

3 단어를 재배열하여 문장을 완성하시오.

> he / to / them / let / go / the birthday
> party

→ _____.

4 주어진 단어를 사용해 영작하시오.

> 가 볼 만한 멋진 곳을 알고 있니?
> (a / visit / wonderful / place / to)

→ Do you know _____?

5 문장에서 틀린 부분을 2개 찾아 문장 전체를 다시 쓰시오.

> He knew the danced girl with strange
> something.

→ _____.

6 주어진 단어를 사용해 문장을 완성하시오.

> him / breakfast / eat / had

→ She _____ _____

_____ _____.

7 우리말에 맞게 문장을 완성하시오.

He has to write a letter. So he needs a

_____.

(그는 (편지를) 쓸 펜을 필요로 한다.)

8 주어진 문장을 〈보기〉와 같이 바꿔 쓰시오.

> ● 보기 ●
> She is too tired to say a word.
> → She is so tired that she can't say a
>   word.

The box was too heavy for her to lift.

→ _____.

9 주어진 단어를 사용해 문장을 완성하시오.

She heard someone call her name.

She saw _____ _____

_____ to her. (a / come / man)

The man was her science teacher.

10 표를 보고 빈칸에 들어갈 알맞은 표현을 쓰시오.

	좋아하는 것	싫어하는 것
I	축구 하기	영화 보기
Mia	피아노 연주	야구 경기 보기

• I like playing soccer but I _____

_____.

• Mia likes playing the piano but she

_____ baseball games.

1 밑줄 친 동명사 중 to부정사로 바꿀 수 없는 것은?

① He finished <u>taking</u> a shower.
② His goal is <u>entering</u> Seoul National Univ.
③ <u>Talking</u> too much is not good.
④ She likes <u>playing</u> the cello.
⑤ She continued <u>watching</u> the TV drama.

2 밑줄 친 단어 중 옳지 <u>않게</u> 고쳐진 것은?

She is ① <u>enjoy</u> watching movies with her friends. Her friends are ② <u>laugh</u> and ③ <u>cry</u>. Her boyfriend is ④ <u>sit</u> by her. They are ⑤ <u>have</u> a wonderful time.

① enjoying   ② laughing
③ crying   ④ siting
⑤ having

3-6 빈칸에 들어갈 순서로 알맞은 것은?

3

• She won the race. It really was amazing. She was so _____.
• I saw the movie last night. It was about the slave. I was _____.

① talent - touch
② talenting - touching
③ talented - touching
④ talenting - touched
⑤ talented - touched

4

• There was an _____ game in the gym.
• He was _____ by the music.

① interesting - exciting
② interested - excite
③ interesting - excite
④ interested - excited
⑤ interesting - excited

5

• Going fishing with my father _____ my favorite thing to do.
• He tried to stop _____, but he failed to do that.

① are - to smoke
② are - to smoking
③ is - smoked
④ is - smoking
⑤ is - has smoked

6

• We can save energy _____ on the light which is not used.
• He didn't finish _____ his homework.

① not by to turn - to do
② not by turning - doing
③ not by turn - to do
④ by not turning - doing
⑤ by not turning - to do

7 밑줄 친 부분이 다른 용법으로 쓰인 것은?

① It is surprising.
② She is playing the piano.
③ Where are you going now?
④ What do you like doing in your free time?
⑤ The dog is running.

8 〈보기〉의 밑줄 친 부분과 쓰임이 같은 것은?

> ● 보기 ●
> Sometimes he felt that he had too many things to do.

① He wants to take a picture.
② I went out with my friend to catch the train.
③ He wanted a friend to play with.
④ He wants to meet her at the park.
⑤ She must study English to enter the school.

9 〈보기〉의 밑줄 친 부분과 쓰임이 같은 것은?

> ● 보기 ●
> He went to his house to tell his parents the truth.

① Nice to meet you.
② She must be kind to say so.
③ He wanted to eat something.
④ We need something interesting to play with.
⑤ He went to America to meet his uncle.

10 밑줄 친 to부정사 중 쓰임이 다른 것은?

① He was surprised to hear the story.
② They went to Europe to meet their uncle.
③ She went to the library to borrow some books.
④ He woke up to know the truth.
⑤ He bought some pencils to write with.

11 ⓐ~ⓒ에 들어갈 단어를 바르게 나열한 것은?

> ⓐ (Meeting / Meet) her made me happy! By ⓑ (meeting / meet) her, I can know about her. Here is a girl ⓒ (make / making) people feel good.

	ⓐ	ⓑ	ⓒ
①	Meet	meet	making
②	Meeting	meet	make
③	Meeting	meeting	making
④	Meeting	meeting	make
⑤	Meet	meeting	making

12 밑줄 친 ①~⑤ 중 쓰임이 다른 것은?

> Some people like ① taking their pictures. ② Doing something can be very interesting. For others, ③ collecting some items can be a hobby. So they always try ④ looking for a new thing. Also they want to meet someone ⑤ trying to collect it.

13 어법상 옳지 <u>않은</u> 것은?

① He enjoyed watching TV.

② She imagined having her own house.

③ I finished doing my homework.

④ I'll never give up to play the piano.

⑤ Do you mind my telling the story about that?

14-15 어법상 옳은 것은?

14

① He was so tired that he couldn't get up early.

② She runs so fast that I hardly could catch up with.

③ The book was good so that he wants to read.

④ He was so nervously that he couldn't focus on it.

⑤ They always exercise so regular that they can be healthy.

15

① He always <u>makes me to clean</u> the room.

② The man <u>had her to wash</u> the dishes.

③ I <u>asked him help</u> my brother with the work.

④ His parents <u>allowed him to go</u> to the concert.

⑤ They <u>let her to play</u> the violin in the room.

16-17 어법상 옳은 문장을 <u>2개</u> 고르면?

16

① I watched an exciting sport game.

② She feels boring these days.

③ The play was not bored at all.

④ He was surprising at the news.

⑤ Many people are interested in politics.

17

① He enjoyed to travel around the world.

② I wanted to bring my bag.

③ He helped her doing the dishes.

④ Have you finished to make dinner?

⑤ He practices playing soccer after school.

18 쓰임이 같은 것을 <u>모두</u> 고르면?

> ⓐ I was glad <u>to see</u> you.
>
> ⓑ He was sad <u>to hear</u> the news.
>
> ⓒ He had so many books <u>to read</u>.
>
> ⓓ I felt happy <u>to meet</u> my friends.
>
> ⓔ He has a house <u>to live in</u>.

① ⓐ, ⓒ   ② ⓑ, ⓒ

③ ⓑ, ⓔ   ④ ⓒ, ⓔ

⑤ ⓓ, ⓔ

19 밑줄 친 ①~⑤ 중 어법상 옳은 것은?

> He liked ① <u>to watching</u> sports games. Last year he went to the soccer stadium and ② <u>will watch</u> the soccer game. It was really ③ <u>excited</u>. So, he felt happy ④ <u>to see</u> that great game. He planned ⑤ <u>going to see</u> other games.

20 어법상 옳은 문장을 모두 고르면?

ⓐ He told me not to go there.
ⓑ She told him to go to bed early.
ⓒ They closed the window in order to watch not the street.
ⓓ He asked her not talking too loudly.
ⓔ My mom wanted me not to join the club.

① ⓐ, ⓒ ② ⓑ, ⓓ
③ ⓒ, ⓔ ④ ⓐ, ⓑ, ⓔ
⑤ ⓑ, ⓓ, ⓔ

4 주어진 단어를 활용하여 그림과 어울리는 문장을 완성하시오.

him / his uncle / told / to / games / play / computer / not

→ _____ .

📝 서 술 형

1 문장을 바르게 고쳐 쓰시오.

He finished read and drink some water.

→ _____ .

2 주어진 단어를 사용해 영작하시오.

그는 함께 놀 많은 친구들이 있었다.
(to / he / play with)

→ _____ .

3 어법상 옳지 않은 단어를 찾아 고쳐 쓰시오.

He is going to have a party this weekend. He is going to invite his friends. They will be glad to be invited by him. He also wants to meet his girl friend, Sujin. He is looking forward to have a party.

_____ → _____

5 주어진 단어를 사용해 영작하시오.

그들의 취미는 강에서 수영하는 것이다.
(in / hobby / swimming / is / the / their / river)

→ _____ .

6 주어진 단어를 사용해 영작하시오.

서울은 방문할 만한 최고의 장소이다.
(is / to / Seoul / visit / the best place)

→ _____ .

7 우리말에 맞게 문장을 완성하시오.

> 그녀는 너무 아파서 학교에 갈 수 없었다.

→ She was _____ _____

_____ _____ to school.

8 대화를 읽고 〈보기〉와 같이 문장을 완성하시오.

> **Sujin:** Clean your room.
> **Tom:** Make pizza for me.

─● 보기 ●─
> Sujin wanted Tom to clean his room.

→ Tom told Sujin to _____

_____ _____ him.

9 〈보기〉의 예문처럼 문장을 완성하시오.

─● 보기 ●─
> draw pictures
> I saw women drawing pictures.

swim in the river

→ I watched boys _____.

10 주어진 단어를 사용해 영작하시오.

> 당신은 건강해지기 위해 규칙적으로 운동을 해야
> 한다.
> (exercise / be / healthy / regularly /
> must / to)

→ You _____.

Break Time!

A friend is a second self. **(Aristotle)**
친구는 제 2의 자신이다. (아리스토텔레스)

Have no friends not equal to yourself. **(Confucius)**
자기보다 못한 자를 벗으로 삼지 말라. (無友不如己者 / 무우불여기자) (공자)

My friends, there are no friends. **(Gabriel Coco Chanel)**
내 친구들이여, 세상에 친구란 없다네. (가브리엘 (코코) 샤넬)

All people want is someone to listen. **(Hugh Elliott)**
사람들이 원하는 모든 것은 자신의 얘기를 들어줄 사람이다. (휴 엘리어트)

Isn't it great when friends visit from afar? **(Confucius)**
벗이 먼 곳에서 찾아오면 또한 즐겁지 아니한가 (有朋自遠方來 不亦樂乎 / 유붕자원방래 불역락호) (공자)

Friends have all things in common. **(Plato)**
친구는 모든 것을 나눈다. (플라톤)

United we stand, divided we fall. **(Aesop)**
뭉치면 서고, 갈라지면 넘어진다. (이솝)

We are advertised by our loving friends. **(William Shakespeare)**
우리는 사랑하는 친구들에 의해서만 알려진다. (윌리엄 셰익스피어)

What is a friend? A single soul dwelling in two bodies. **(Aristotle)**
친구란 무엇인가? 두 개의 몸에 깃든 하나의 영혼이다. (아리스토텔레스)

To like and dislike the same things, that is indeed true friendship. **(Sallust)**
같은 것을 놓고 좋아하고 싫어하는 것. 그것이 바로 진정한 우정이다. (살루스트)

chapter

04

대명사
접속사
관계대명사

대명사

앞서 언급한 명사를 대신하여 쓰이는 명사를 말한다.

---

❶ 인칭대명사의 변화 총정리

	주격		소유격		목적격		소유대명사		재귀대명사	
1인칭	I	we	my	our	me	us	mine	ours	myself	ourselves
2인칭	you	you	your	your	you	you	yours	yours	yourself	yourselves
3인칭	he she it	they	his her its	their	him her it	them	his hers	theirs	himself herself itself	themselves

❷ 지시대명사

1   This(이것, 이): 가까운 것을 가리키며 복수형은 these(이것들, 이)

This is my room and *that* is my brother's. (이것: 대명사로 단독으로 쓰임)

This room is mine. (이: 지시형용사로 뒤에 단수 명사를 꾸며 줌)

These are my books. (이것들: 대명사로 단독으로 쓰임)

2   That (저것, 저): 먼 것을 가리키며 복수형은 those (저것들, 저)

That is my dad's car. (저것: 대명사로 단독으로 쓰임)

Who are *those* people? (저: 지시형용사로 뒤에 복수 명사를 꾸며 줌)

Those are his pencils. (저것들: 대명사로 단독으로 쓰임)

❸ 부정대명사: it, one, some, other

1   it: 특정한 것을 가리킴 one: 정해지지 않은 막연한 대상을 가리킴

A: Do you have a pencil? **B:** Yes, I have *one*. (연필이라고 생긴 것 아무거나)

A: Do you have the pen? **B:** No, I have lost *it*. (화자가 언급한 그 펜)

My watch is old. I have to buy a new *one*.

2   one ~ the other (둘 중에서) 하나는, 다른 하나는

She has two sons; *one* is a doctor and *the other* is a teacher.

3   one ~ another (여러 개 중에서) 하나는, 다른 것은

I don't like this *one*. Show me *another*.

4   some ~ others (여러 개 중에서) 몇 개는, 다른 몇 개는

Some like baseball and *others* like football.

5   some ~ the others (정확한 수가 제시된 상황에서) 일부는, 나머지 전부는

Our class has thirty students. *Some* are girls and *the others* are boys.

④ 비인칭주어 It의 용법

1 시간

A: What time is *it* now? B: *It*'s eleven o'clock.

2 요일

A: What day is *it* today? B: *It*'s Tuesday.

3 날짜

A: What's the date? B: *It*'s June 23rd.

4 날씨

A: How is the weather? B: *It*'s very cold.

5 거리

A: How far is *it* from here to the station? B: *It*'s two kilometers.

6 명암

It's dark outside.

⑤ 의문사

when 언제	where 어디	who 누가, 누구를
what 무엇을, 무엇이	how 어떻게, 얼마나	why 왜

의문사의 특징

- 의문문에 쓰이며 특수한 경우를 제외하고 문장 처음에 온다.
- 의문사가 있는 의문문은 문장의 마지막 강세에서 올려 말했다가 끝을 내린다.
- Yes나 No가 아닌 구체적인 사실로 대답한다.

A: *When* did Joe and Carol first meet? B: Last weekend.

A: *What's* your favorite color? B: Green.

A: *How* old are you? B: 15 years old.

A: *Where* are you going? B: To the library.

A: *Whose* pens are these? B: Tom's.

A: *Who* is your favorite singer? B: BoA.

A: *Why* were you late for school? B: I got up late this morning.

➕ P·L·U·S

이 외에도 which(어느 것), whose(누구의), whom(누구를) 등의 의문사가 있다. whose는 혼자 쓰이지 못하고 뒤에 명사가 와서 함께 쓰이며 whom의 경우 현대 영어에서는 거의 쓰이지 않고 who로 쓴다.

기
본
개
념
장
착
하
기

접속사
두 개 이상의 단어, 구, 절을 연결해 주는 단어를 총칭한다.

----

❶ 등위접속사
단어, 구, 절을 대등한 관계로 연결하는 접속사

She met a poet *and* an actor yesterday. (시인 한 명과 배우 한 명)

He is a poet *and* actor. (시인이자 배우)

I have bread *and* butter for lunch. (bread and butter: 버터 바른 빵)

Tom is in his room *or* in the garden. (전치사구를 연결)

Spring has come, *but* it is still cold. (문장과 문장을 연결)

She must be ill, *for* she looks pale. (문장과 문장을 연결)

*for가 등위접속사로 쓰이면 이유를 나타내는 문장 앞에 놓인다.

They did their best, *so* they won the game. (문장과 문장을 연결)

❷ 종속접속사

1 명사절: 접속사가 이끄는 절이 문장에서 주어, 보어, 목적어로 쓰임

It is certain *that* he is alive. (주어)

*that ~ 이하가 주어로 쓰이지만 앞에 가주어 it을 놓고 문장 뒤에 놓였다.

The problem is *that* we have no money. (보어)

The question is *whether* he will get well. (보어)

I don't know *if* he is honest. (목적어)

*if가 명사절을 이끄는 접속사로 쓰이면 '~인지 아닌지'의 뜻.

I know *that* he is here. (목적어)

I don't know *where* I should go. (목적어)

2 부사절: 접속사가 이끄는 절이 문장에서 때, 이유 등을 나타내는 종속절을 이끎

When she was a girl, she was very beautiful. (when: ~일 때)

It has been ten years *since* he came here. (since: ~ 이후로)

As he often tells a lie, I can't trust him. (as: ~이므로)

They could not stay outside *because* it was too cold. (because: ~이기 때문에)

It was *so* hot *that* I couldn't sleep. (so ~ that ···: 너무~해서 ···하다)

If you feel seasick, take one of these pills. (if: ~라면)

Though it was raining, I had to go out. (though: 비록 ~지만)

3 상관 접속사: 항상 세트로 같이 쓰여야 하는 접속사

Both he *and* I are high school students. (both A and B: A와 B 둘 다)

Either she *or* I have to go there. (either A or B: A나 B 어느 쪽이든)

Neither you *nor* he is wrong. (neither A nor B: A도 B도 아니다)

That is *not* a fox *but* a deer. (not A but B: A가 아니라 B다)

She plays *not only* the guitar *but also* the violin. (not only A but also B: A뿐 아니라 B도)

UNIT 3

관계대명사

❶ 관계대명사의 역할

1 역할: '접속사+대명사'의 역할과 선행사를 수식하는 형용사절 역할을 동시에 수행

- This is the man. + He teaches us English.
- → This is the man *who* teaches us English.

2 관계대명사의 종류와 격

선행사	주격	소유격	목적격
사람	who	whose	who(m)
사물, 동물	which	of which, whose	which
동물, 사람, 사물	that	X	that
X	what	X	what

❷ 관계대명사

1 who

A 주격일 때 who

- This is the man. + He helped me yesterday.
- → This is the man *who* helped me yesterday.

B 소유격일 때 whose

- This is the boy. + His father is a doctor.
- → This is the boy *whose* father is a doctor.

C 목적격 whom

- Tom is playing on the ground. + I helped him yesterday.
- → Tom *whom* I helped yesterday is playing on the ground.
- → Tom (*that*) I helped yesterday is playing on the ground.

*목적격일 때는 whom보다 that을 쓰거나 관계대명사를 생략하는 경우가 대부분이다.

2 which

A 주격의 which

- This is the pen. + It is blue.
- → This is the pen *which* is blue.

B 소유격의 whose

- Look at the house. + The top of it is covered with snow.

→ Look at the house *whose* top is covered with snow.

C 목적격의 which

- This is the house. + I live in it.

→ This is the house *which* I live in. (전치사 in의 목적어로 쓰임)

3 that: who와 which 대신 쓸 수 있음

- This is the bank. + He works at the bank.

→ This is the bank *which* he works at.

→ This is the bank at *which* he works.

→ This is the bank *that* he works at.

*관계대명사 who, which 앞에서는 전치사가 올 수 있지만 that 앞에는 전치사가 올 수 없다.

4 what: 선행사 없이 단독으로 쓰이며 the thing which로 풀어 쓸 수 있음

- *What* I want is your love. (=*The thing which* I want)

- I can't believe *what* he said. (=*the thing which* he said)

it과 there 중 하나를 쓰시오.

1 _____ rains a lot in summer.

2 _____ was a strong wind a few days ago.

3 _____ 's a dark cloud in the sky.

_____ 's going to rain.

4 _____ 's light in this room. Can you turn off the light?

대화에 알맞은 의문사를 쓰시오.

5 A: _____ is this?

B: It is a ball-point pen.

6 A: _____ does Ms. Kim live?

B: She lives in Seoul.

7 A: _____ is your father?

B: He is 45 years old.

8 A: _____ do you like Susan?

B: Because she is beautiful.

9 A: _____ books are these?

B: They are mine.

10 A: _____ is it today?

B: It's Friday.

밑줄 친 부분이 의문대명사인지 관계대명사인지 구별하시오.

11 I don't know <u>who</u> will go there.

_____

12 I don't know the man <u>who</u> will go there.

_____

13 <u>What</u> do you want to have?

_____

14 This is <u>what</u> I want to have.

_____

15 I know the children <u>whose</u> father is a doctor.

_____

문장을 해석하시오.

16 The cat which Betty loves so much is very small and cute.

→ _____.

17 Is this the American whom you met in the park yesterday?

→ _____?

18 This is the most useful book that I have ever read.

→ _____.

19 The man whose car was stolen has gone to the police.

→ _____.

옳은 것을 고르시오.

20 He has a son (who / whose / whom) name is Tom.

21 She is the lady (who / whom / which) teaches us music.

22 That is the boy with (who / whom / that) I played tennis yesterday.

23 Is this the girl (which / whom / whose) you met in the park?

24 Both the buses (or / and / but) the trains are running late.

25 I know a girl. She can speak English well.

= _____ .

26 That is the boy. His name is Jack.

= _____ .

27 Once there was a king in China. All the people loved him.

= _____

_____ .

28 Look at the house. Its roof is red.

= _____ .

29 This is the key. I have been looking for it.

= _____ .

30 The book is easy. I bought it last week.

= _____ .

31 I want those computers. Please give

_____ to _____ .

32 She wants the car. Please give

_____ to _____ .

33 She wants the keys. Please give

_____ to _____ .

34 We want love. Please give _____

to _____ .

35 They want the money. Please give

_____ to _____ .

36 She got out of the bath and dried

_____ with a towel.

37 When I am alone, I often talk to

_____ .

38 He fell off the building but he didn't hurt

_____ .

39 Be careful! The plate is very hot. Don't

burn _____ .

40 I'm not angry with you. I'm angry with

_____ .

41 I have two cats; _____ is black,

and _____ is white.

42 I have three brothers; _____ lives

in Seoul and _____ live in

Busan.

43 Here are four flowers; _____

is a rose, _____ is a lily, and

_____ are tulips.

44 I don't like this cap. Show me

_____ .

45 There are many students in our school.

_____ students come to school

by bus, _____ come to school on

foot.

1 단어의 관계가 나머지와 <u>다른</u> 것은?

① he - him
② you - you
③ it - it
④ we - our
⑤ they - them

2 대명사로 바꾸었을 때 잘못 연결된 것은?

① Mrs. Son - she
② the paper - it
③ the dogs - they
④ the boys - he
⑤ Jinsu and I - we

3 빈칸에 들어갈 순서로 알맞은 것은?

> **M1:** Hi, Sehun.
> **M2:** Oh, hello, Mr. Kim. Mom, _____ is my music teacher, Mr. Ramon Kim.
> **W:** Hello, Mr. Kim. Nice to meet you.
> **M1:** Nice to meet you, too. Sehun is a very good student in music class.
> **W:** That's great. Music is _____ favorite subject.

① This - he
② This - his
③ These - him
④ Those - he
⑤ He - him

4 밑줄 친 it의 쓰임이 나머지와 <u>다른</u> 것은?

① Is <u>it</u> too dark?
② <u>It</u> was very cold yesterday.
③ <u>It</u> is five o'clock now.
④ Is <u>it</u> your favorite song?
⑤ How far is <u>it</u> from here to your church?

5 빈칸에 들어갈 순서로 알맞은 것은?

> I live with my parents and Jeje. Jeje is _____ dog. He is very cute. _____ favorite food is fish.

① I - His
② my - His
③ you - Him
④ your - Our
⑤ my - your

6 빈칸에 들어갈 말과 일치하는 것은? (단, 관계대명사 that 제외)

> Susan _____ likes the park takes a walk in the park on weekends.

① He made a chair _____ looked comfortable.
② She bought the car _____ was not cheap.
③ She read a book _____ was really boring.
④ He met a boy _____ I saw yesterday.
⑤ They saw the movie star _____ volunteered at the nursing home.

7 두 문장의 뜻이 같도록 빈칸에 들어갈 말이 바르게 연결된 것은?

> She was sad _____ her dog was very sick.
> = Her dog was very sick, _____ she was sad.

① so - so
② and - but
③ because - so
④ but - because
⑤ or - though

8 〈보기〉의 밑줄 친 When과 쓰임이 같은 것은?

> ● 보기 ●
> When you go abroad, you sometimes get lost.

① When do you get up?
② I will tell you when to start.
③ He was seven when his mother died.
④ When did you go to bed yesterday?
⑤ They don't know when they will see together.

9 〈보기〉의 밑줄 친 that과 쓰임이 같은 것은?

> ● 보기 ●
> So this motto means that we have to do our best.

① I know who that boy is.
② He can't solve that kind of problem.
③ She didn't have dinner that much.
④ Do you think that is his car?
⑤ I hope that he will pass the test.

10 빈칸에 들어갈 순서로 알맞은 것은?

> ● I looked at the tree _____ had many red leaves.
> ● He is the man _____ is as brave as a soldier.

① whose - which
② that - whom
③ which - whose
④ who - which
⑤ which - that

11 빈칸에 공통으로 들어갈 말은?

> ● I'm sorry to hear _____.
> ● He says _____ he will go abroad next year.

① what
② when
③ this
④ that
⑤ those

12 빈칸에 들어갈 순서로 알맞은 것은?

> Jane and her family were in the house _____ it happened. Jane said, "Suddenly it got dark, and trees started to fall from the sky. My brother, Jim, started shouting. We didn't know _____ to do, so we just stayed down."

① what - where
② when - that
③ how - why
④ when - when
⑤ when - what

13 밑줄 친 의문사가 어법상 옳지 <u>않은</u> 것은?

① <u>Who</u> is the woman in the picture?

② <u>Why</u> do you like the computer?

③ <u>What</u> does Jinny go to bed early?

④ <u>Where</u> is the post office?

⑤ <u>When</u> do I have to do it?

14-16 밑줄 친 부분이 어법상 옳지 <u>않은</u> 것은?

14

① I said to <u>myself</u>.

② His parents are proud of <u>him</u>.

③ Jack took a picture of <u>himself</u>.

④ They can't do their homework for <u>themselves</u>.

⑤ She saw <u>himself</u> at the market.

15

① This is not <u>my</u> pen.

② That is <u>he's</u> book.

③ I will meet <u>her</u> at four.

④ <u>They</u> were wearing glasses.

⑤ His parents love <u>him</u>.

16

① He had a box <u>that</u> she made.

② She is the wisest girl <u>that</u> can solve the problem.

③ There was a girl <u>whose</u> was kind.

④ The man <u>whom</u> they liked is my friend.

⑤ That is the movie <u>which</u> he wants to see.

17 어법상 옳지 <u>않은</u> 것은?

① The tulip is a red flower.

② His uncle lived in a small house.

③ He didn't want cold something to drink.

④ Anything new didn't happen yesterday.

⑤ I have something special for you.

18 어법상 옳은 문장을 <u>2개</u> 고르면?

① She was a doctor who helped poor people in India.

② He is a pianist who have trouble doing his performance.

③ He is a firefighter that save people's lives.

④ She bought me the toy which have blue ribbons.

⑤ He is the boy that met her in the park.

19-20 밑줄 친 ①~⑤ 중 어법상 옳지 <u>않은</u> 것은?

19

James and Shilla are brother and sister. ① <u>They</u> are from Sydney. ② <u>There</u> family name is Marley. ③ <u>Their</u> friends, Gilbert and Susan, live near their house. Gilbert is ten and ④ <u>his</u> sister is twelve. ⑤ <u>Their</u> school is on King Street.

20

① <u>My</u> name is Mina. I have a dog. ② <u>His</u> name is Dodo. He is big and has long legs. ③ <u>My</u> friend, Tom, has a rabbit. ④ <u>Hers</u> name is Bobo. ⑤ <u>She</u> is small and brown.

📑 서 술 형

1 각 문장의 밑줄 친 주어를 she로 바꾸어 다시 쓰시오.

> - <u>They</u> go to the park.
> - Are <u>they</u> late? No, <u>they</u> aren't.
> - Do <u>they</u> help the unhappy? Yes, <u>they</u> do.

① _____.

② _____.

③ _____.

2 주어진 단어를 사용해 영작하시오.

> 그녀는 오전 8시에 아침을 먹는다. 하지만 그는 아침을 먹지 않는다.
> (eat breakfast / but / at 8 a.m.)

→ _____.

3 if절을 이용해서 다음 문장을 완성하시오.

_____ _____ _____ tomorrow, I will not go on a trip. (만일 내일 비가 내리면, 나는 여행을 가지 않을 것이다.)

4 빈칸에 적절한 단어를 쓰시오.

They enjoyed _____ at the party yesterday. (그들은 어제 그 파티에서 즐거운 시간을 보냈다.)

5 그림의 순서를 보고 접속사 before 또는 after를 사용하여 준호의 일과에 대한 문장을 완성하시오. (주어, 동사를 갖춘 완전한 문장으로 쓸 것)

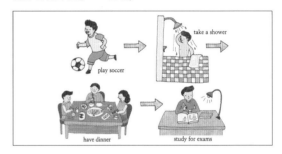

① Junho plays soccer _____

_____.

② _____,

he studies for exams.

6 두 문장을 한 문장으로 연결해서 쓰시오.

> - The tea is very hot.
> - He can't drink it.

→ The tea is _____ _____

_____ he can't drink it.

7-8 두 문장을 관계대명사를 사용하여 한 문장으로 쓰시오.

7

> I know the girl. + She is singing in the room.

→ _____ .

8

> - One good tip to the problem is to use the manual.
> - It is written in English.

→ _____

_____ .

(that은 사용하지 말 것)

9-10 주어진 단어를 사용해 영작하시오.

9

> 나는 그녀가 나를 위해 만들었던 쿠키를 먹었다.
> (ate / made / she / that / some cookies / for me / I)

→ _____ .

10

> 그는 그들이 존경하는 축구 선수이다.
> (that / the soccer player / they / is / respect / he)

→ _____ .

1 빈칸에 들어갈 순서로 알맞은 것은?

> • I will do _____ homework.
> • They are washing _____ hands.

① I - their
② my - ours
③ my - their
④ we - it
⑤ me - hers

2 〈보기〉의 밑줄 친 It과 쓰임이 같은 것은?

> ● 보기 ●
> <u>It</u> is important to study English.

① <u>It</u> is Saturday today.
② <u>It</u> is our gift.
③ <u>It</u> takes two hours by plane.
④ <u>It</u> is not my own fault.
⑤ <u>It</u> is inconvenient to live without a car.

3 빈칸에 들어갈 순서로 알맞은 것은?

> **A:** _____ is he doing?
> **B:** He is practicing.
> **A:** _____ does he visit his grandma?
> **B:** He visits her on weekends.

① Where - When
② What - Where
③ Why - Why
④ What - When
⑤ Who - Which

4 빈칸에 들어갈 말로 알맞은 것은?

> He eats all kinds of snacks, _____ he doesn't like ramen.

① but
② either
③ why
④ or
⑤ so

5 밑줄 친 while의 쓰임이 다른 것은?

① <u>While</u> he was taking a shower, somebody broke into the room.
② <u>While</u> they walked along the street, they got to meet him.
③ He likes the lake, <u>while</u> his wife prefers the seaside.
④ Make hay <u>while</u> the sun shines.
⑤ I watched the movie <u>while</u> I was having dinner.

6 두 문장을 한 문장으로 고칠 때 빈칸에 들어갈 순서로 알맞은 것은?

> She knew the house. He lived in the house.
> = She knew the house _____ he lived in.
> = She knew the house which he lived in.
> = She knew the house he lived in.
> = She knew the house _____ he lived.

① that - in which
② where - in which
③ where - in where
④ that - what
⑤ that - in that

7 빈칸에 공통으로 들어갈 단어로 가장 알맞은 것은?

> Do you like to listen to music _____ you study? _____ you listen to the radio, sometimes it may bother you.

① what
② when
③ why
④ which
⑤ how

8 빈칸에 들어갈 말이 <u>다른</u> 것은?

① He felt hungry _____ he came home.
② _____ she was young, she lived in Seoul.
③ _____ you called me, I was not in my office.
④ I didn't buy a book _____ it was very expensive.
⑤ He and I like to play soccer _____ we are free.

9-10 빈칸에 들어갈 순서로 알맞은 것은?

9

> "Oh, no! I'm late, Mom. Where's my uniform? Where's my bag?" Then her mom says, "Jisu, you don't need _____. It's 7:30 in the evening!" Jisu's mom looks around _____ room and takes out a list.

① it - our
② its - his
③ them - my
④ them - her
⑤ their - him

10

> A little girl held the truck driver's arm and said something. _____, the driver did not listen. The girl did so again. This time, the truck driver listened and smiled. _____ the truck moved.

① However - At last
② And - Also
③ Therefore - At last
④ So - Finally
⑤ However - Or

11 ⓐ~ⓒ에 들어갈 단어를 바르게 나열한 것은?

> What is your favorite day? Is it your birthday or Christmas ⓐ (while / because) you get presents from your parents? Easter may not be people's favorite holiday, ⓑ (and / but) for Christians, it is definitely the most important. ⓒ (Like / Unlike) most holidays, Easter is celebrated on a different date every year.

	ⓐ	ⓑ	ⓒ
①	because	but	Unlike
②	because	and	Like
③	because	but	Like
④	while	but	Unlike
⑤	while	and	Like

12 그림에 대한 설명에 맞게 @~@에 들어갈 단어가 바르게 나열된 것은?

There are seven boys and six girls in the classroom. One of the @ (boy / boys) is reading an art book. ⓑ (Each / Some) of the girls ⓒ (is / are) wearing a school uniform. ⓓ (One / Some) of the girls are standing by the window.

	@	ⓑ	ⓒ	ⓓ
①	boy	Each	are	One
②	boys	Each	is	One
③	boy	Some	are	Some
④	boys	Each	is	Some
⑤	boys	Some	are	Some

13 밑줄 친 부분이 적절하지 않은 것은?

① He likes her hair style.
② She is my uncle, Joe.
③ His bag is very big.
④ My sisters are students.
⑤ His homeroom teacher is very nice.

14 밑줄 친 that을 생략할 수 없는 것은?

① He believes that the boy is wise.
② She knows that Tom will move to London.
③ He thinks that she will come back soon.
④ She believes that everything will be fine.
⑤ They said that was delicious.

15-16 어법상 옳은 문장은?

15

① Matt and I studies in the same school.
② Suho and Tom plays soccer.
③ She watch TV every weekend.
④ The babies cry a lot when they are hungry.
⑤ She have dinner with her family at 6 o'clock.

16

① Books whose authors are famous sell well.
② The movie which she saw it yesterday was boring.
③ He met an old woman she asked him the way to the subway station.
④ He likes those whom help the poor.
⑤ She is the singer that voice can heal our hearts.

17 어법상 옳은 문장 2개를 고르면?

① They knew the man I played tennis with yesterday.
② He knew everything that was important.
③ She wants to visit the city which they have never been.
④ His brother and he that like to play the piano.
⑤ The doctor is from England which speaks Korean well.

18 ⓐ~ⓕ 중 it의 쓰임이 〈보기〉의 문장과 같은 것을 <u>모두</u> 고르면?

> → 보기 →
>
> <u>It</u> is cloudy and rainy in London.

> ⓐ <u>It</u> rains a lot in my country. Last year, I couldn't go to school for weeks because we had floods again. Father said, "The floods are becoming worse. The ice in the Himalayas is melting more these days, so ⓑ <u>it</u> rains more often."
> ⓒ <u>It</u> was the first day of school today, and something was coming to me. ⓓ <u>It</u> was a school boat. ⓔ <u>It</u> was going to come from Monday to Friday and stay at the village for two hours. My little brother and I were ready for school very early in the morning. We went outside and waited with other children. When ⓕ <u>it</u> finally came, we all got excited.

① ⓐ, ⓔ
② ⓓ, ⓔ
③ ⓐ, ⓑ, ⓒ
④ ⓓ, ⓔ, ⓕ
⑤ ⓐ, ⓑ, ⓒ, ⓕ

19 밑줄 친 ①~⑤ 중 쓰임이 <u>어색한</u> 것은?

> ① <u>My</u> name is Suzan. ② <u>I am not pretty</u>. My best friend is Thompson. ③ <u>He is not quiet</u>. He is funny. ④ <u>He and I are not tall</u>, but ⑤ <u>they are good at sports</u>.

20 어법상 옳은 것을 고르시오.

> Jenny is my classmate. She often goes to a nursing home ① <u>that</u> is very far from her house. She helps old people there. It is not an easy job. But she never says ② <u>what</u> it is difficult.
> She admires Lee Sunshin. He was an admiral ③ <u>what</u> saved our country from naval battles. He was brave and smart. He had only a small number of soldiers and ships, ④ <u>or</u> he won every battle. He loved his people and his country, ⑤ <u>but</u> they also loved him.

📰 **서 술 형**

1-2 A와 B의 내용이 자연스럽게 이어지도록 주어진 접속사를 사용하여 연결하시오.

A	B
he is in the museum	he does not take a picture
he got up late	he missed the train

1 when 사용

→ _____ .

2 because 사용

→ _____ .

3 주어진 단어를 사용해 영작하시오. (단어 형태 변형 가능)

> 직접 채소를 기르는 것이 건강한 삶에 좋다.
> (you / grow / healthy)

→ _____ vegetables _____

　　is good for a _____ life.

4 우리말에 맞게 문장을 완성하시오.

> 나는 하얀색 집을 찾고 있다.

→ I'm looking for a house _____
　　color is white.

5 주어진 단어를 사용해 영작하시오.

> 주의 깊게 듣고 그녀가 말했던 대로 정확하게 해라.
> (as / do / carefully / said)

→ _____ _____ _____

　　_____ exactly as _____

　　_____ .

6 두 문장을 관계대명사를 사용해 한 문장으로 쓰시오.

> - He liked the food.
> - It was made by his mom.

→ _____ .

7 두 문장을 관계대명사를 사용해 연결할 때 표현 가능한 문장을 <u>모두</u> 쓰시오. (3가지)

> - I have a computer.
> - I can search the information with the computer.

❶ _____ .

❷ _____ .

❸ _____ .

8 주어진 단어를 사용해 문장을 완성하시오.

> the place / I / which / last / year / was / wanted / London / to visit

→ _____ .

9 주어진 단어를 사용해 영작하시오.

> 그는 그녀에게 그가 가진 모든 책들을 주었다.
> (he / all the books / he / her / that / had / gave)

→ _____ .

10 밑줄 친 부분을 영어로 쓰시오.

> He used different techniques so as to create new picture images _____.
> 그는 <u>아무도 이전에는 본 적이 없는</u> 새로운 영상 이미지들을 만들어 내기 위해 색다른 기술들을 사용했다. (that, ever 사용)

→ _____ .

(7단어)

1 대명사와 재귀대명사의 연결이 바르지 <u>않은</u> 것은?

① I - myself   ② they - themselves

③ he - himself   ④ she - herself

⑤ it - itselves

2 빈칸에 들어갈 말이 〈보기〉와 <u>다른</u> 것은?

> ● 보기 ●
>
> She lives with her father, mother,
> _____ her brother Jack in London.

① Open the door, _____ you'll feel fresh.

② John _____ his friends are playing music together.

③ Do your best, _____ you'll pass the test.

④ Put on your coat, _____ you'll feel cold.

⑤ The bookstore is between the flower shop _____ the post office.

3 빈칸에 들어갈 순서로 알맞은 것은?

> ● She hasn't decided _____ to stay during her trip.
> ● Do you know _____ to make pizza?

① why - what

② where - what

③ where - how

④ who - how

⑤ when - why

4 밑줄 친 who의 쓰임이 다른 것은?

① Can you guess <u>who</u> will be the next boss?

② I'm not sure about <u>who</u> can solve it.

③ <u>Who</u> do you think can climb the mountain?

④ I want to know the person <u>who</u> invented that.

⑤ <u>Who</u> will come on time?

5-6 빈칸에 들어갈 순서로 알맞은 것은?

5

> ● She liked to paint people _____ were working or dancing.
> ● It is a movement _____ was looked at in a party.

① what - who

② where - that

③ whom - which

④ that - which

⑤ who - why

6

> **A:** Oh, this is not _____. Is this _____?
> **B:** Yes. It is my favorite book.

① me - your

② me - you

③ my - your

④ mine - you

⑤ mine - yours

7 빈칸에 들어갈 말로 알맞은 것은?

> People often make mistakes. _____, they have trouble doing their works.

① But

② Still

③ Additionally

④ As a result

⑤ At most

8 빈칸에 들어갈 표현으로 알맞은 것은?

> Welcome to my Cooking Class. Today, we'll make a cake. Tomorrow is Mother's Day, _____.

① and I will make spaghetti for you

② so you can make a cake for your mom

③ and you will take a picture

④ so I can go shopping with my friends

⑤ but I like making spaghetti

9 〈보기〉의 밑줄 친 If와 의미가 다른 것은?

> ──● 보기 ●──
> If she doesn't hurry, she will miss the bus.

① She doesn't know if he did his homework.

② If she asks him, she will know the truth.

③ He will make cookies if she wants to eat them.

④ It will take an hour if she takes the subway.

⑤ If it is rainy tomorrow, she will not go on a picnic.

10 재귀대명사의 용법이 나머지와 다른 것은?

① He made dinner himself.

② She is talking to herself now.

③ They really enjoyed themselves.

④ She is proud of herself.

⑤ I went to the mountain by myself.

11 빈칸에 들어갈 순서로 알맞은 것은?

> I watched the 2002 World Cup on TV last summer. _____ Korea lost the game against Germany, I wasn't sad. At first, I thought Korea lost its chance for the round of 16. _____, Korea made history in the game with Portugal! The Korean team made it to the second round! I almost cried with joy.

① If - So

② Though - However

③ If - But

④ Though - Until

⑤ However - If

12 ⓐ~ⓒ에 들어갈 단어를 바르게 나열한 것은?

> Boys and girls live all around the world. They look ⓐ (differently / different) and they wear different clothes. ⓑ (So / But) they are the same in many ways. They love to play, and they want to have friends. ⓒ (However / Most of all), they have dreams.

	ⓐ	ⓑ	ⓒ
①	different	But	However
②	different	But	Most of all
③	differently	But	Most of all
④	differently	So	However
⑤	differently	So	Most of all

13 어법상 옳은 것은?

① She didn't have a friend to talk.

② He built the house their family would live in.

③ Unless you don't exercise regularly, you will not be strong.

④ If he will take a subway, he will not get lost.

⑤ I feel tired, so I need a chair to sit.

14 밑줄 친 의문사가 어울리지 <u>않는</u> 것은?

① <u>Why</u> do you like that game?

② <u>What</u> does he go to bed in the evening?

③ <u>When</u> do you get up?

④ <u>Who</u> is the girl in this picture?

⑤ <u>Where</u> is the flower shop?

15-17 문장의 쓰임이 자연스러운 것은?

15

① He and she is not happily.

② I and Paul doesn't do our work.

③ She watch TV every weekend.

④ My mother and father don't late for the meeting.

⑤ John, my friend, is the fastest runner in our class.

16

① Hurry up, or you will catch the first train.

② I have a bag she talked about it.

③ Sujin looked at herself in the mirror.

④ I have a bad headache, so I don't need to take some medicine.

⑤ The man looks happily.

17

① People in the party is smiling.

② Are this man a teacher?

③ She lives in a big towers.

④ The students are singing on the stage.

⑤ My best friend and I am in the same age.

18 ⓐ~ⓒ에 들어갈 단어를 바르게 나열한 것은?

His success was special ⓐ (because / because of) he couldn't move the lower half of his body. He climbed the rock, holding the rope tightly and pulling ⓑ (his / himself) up. When reporters asked him ⓒ (how / what) he made it, he said, "Just 5 centimeters at a time."

	ⓐ	ⓑ	ⓒ
①	because	his	how
②	because	himself	how
③	because	himself	what
④	because of	himself	how
⑤	because of	his	what

19-20 글을 읽고 물음에 답하시오.

We can do many things with a cellphone. ⓐ_____, cellphones are a problem for many people. They are sometimes very noisy. We can hear the ringtone of cellphones here and there. ⓑ_____ people do not turn off their cellphones in class. ⓒ_____ talk on their phones during a movie. Some students play games or send their friends text messages in class. One ⓓ_____ three Korean students sends over 50 text messages a day.

19 ⓐ에 들어갈 말로 적절한 것은?

① After　　② Like
③ However　④ Therefore
⑤ In other words

20 ⓑ~ⓓ에 들어갈 말을 바르게 나열한 것은?

① One - The others - in
② Some - Others - out of
③ One - Another - as
④ Some - Others - of
⑤ Some - Another - from

📋 서 술 형

1 우리말 뜻에 맞게 문장을 완성하시오.

> 그가 그것을 살 것인지

→ She wanted to see _____

_____ would _____

_____.

2 그림을 보고 If(조건절)를 사용하여 〈보기〉와 같이 만드시오.

〈보기〉 If he walks to school, it will take 30 minutes.

❶ _____.

❷ _____.

❸ _____.

3 우리말에 맞게 문장을 완성하시오.

I enjoy movies _____ make me cry. (나는 나를 울게 만드는 영화를 좋아한다.)

4 관계대명사를 사용해 한 문장으로 완성하시오.

> That building is my house.
> Its roof is round.
> 지붕이 둥근 저 건물이 나의 집이다.

→ _____.

5 ⓐ와 ⓑ에서 한 문장씩 골라 의미가 통하게 연결하여 문장을 완성하시오.

ⓐ
• Get up early,
• Study harder than you used to,
• Open the window,

ⓑ
• and you will have better scores.
• and you can see the wonderful lake.
• and you will catch the school bus.

❶ _____

_____.

❷ _____

_____.

❸ _____

_____.

6 so ~ that ...구문을 사용하여 문장을 완성하시오.

그 상자는 너무 무거워서 그가 옮길 수 없었다.

→ The box _____.

(heavy, move 사용, 7단어)

7 우리말에 맞게 문장을 완성하시오.

이것은 나의 가족들을 보여주는 사진이다.

→ This is the _____ _____
shows my family members.

8 주어진 단어를 사용해 밑줄 친 부분을 영작하시오.

학교에서 나는 곰처럼 생긴 조각상을 보았다.
At the school, (a / a / I / saw / bear /
like / statue / which / looked).

→ _____.

9 우리말에 맞게 문장을 완성하시오

The paintings _____ _____
_____ _____ wonderful.
(그가 그린 그림들은 멋있었다.)

10 ⓐ와 ⓑ에서 한 문장씩 골라 〈보기〉와 같은 문장으로 완성하시오. (3개의 문장 만들기, 한 번 사용한 관계대명사는 반복 불가)

ⓐ
- The dog is mine.
- The bird is white.
- He knows the girl.
- The book is thick.

ⓑ
- The dog has short ears.
- She carries the book.
- I like it best.
- They play with the girl.
- The boy picked the leaves.
- The bird's tail is long.

━━● 보기 ●━━
He likes the boy who is wearing a green cap.

❶ _____.

❷ _____.

❸ _____.

chapter

05

전치사

명사와 관사

형용사

부사

비교급, 최상급

전치사

❶ 전치사의 역할과 목적어

전치사는 명사나 동명사 앞에 놓여 형용사구와 부사구를 만든다. 한 단어로 된 전치사 외에 두 단어 이상으로 된 전치사도 있다.

1 전치사의 목적어로 올 수 있는 어구

I love to work *with the man*. (명사)

It's *for you*. (대명사 목적격)

He is proud *of being* rich. (동명사)

2 형용사구, 부사구의 역할

The girl *with roses* is my daughter. (형용사구: 명사 the girl 수식)

I saw him *in the distance*. (부사구)

❷ 전치사의 의미

1 시간 · 기간

He was born *at* 7 *on* April 8, *in* 1977. (~에)

Father will come home *in* a week. (~ 후에)

She returned home *after* a few hours. (~ 후에)

You must be back at the office *by* nine. (~까지: 완료)

Last Sunday I was in bed *till* noon. (~까지: 계속)

He has lived in London *for* three years. (~ 동안: 숫자+시간)

Did you go anyplace *during* the summer vacation? (~ 동안: 특정한 시간)

2 장소 · 방향

He stopped *at* a bus stop *in* Seoul. (~에)

There is a picture *on* the wall. (~에)

The moon rose *above* the hill. (~ 위로)

There is a bridge *over* the river. (~ 위에)

John sat *beside* the tree. (~ 옆에)

Please take a seat *between* the two men. (~ 사이에)

There was a beautiful rose *among* the flowers. ((셋 이상) 사이에)

She stood *before* him. (~ 앞에)

A car parked *in front of* the building is mine. (~ 앞에)

She stood *behind* a tree. (~ 뒤에)

She closed the door *after* her. (~를 뒤따라)

3 수단 · 도구

I usually go to work *by* bus. (~로)

He cut the wood *with* an axe. (~을 가지고)

4 원인 · 이유

He died *of* hunger.

He died *from* overwork.

5 재료

The bridge is built *of* stone. (~로 (된)–물리적 변화)

Butter is made *from* milk. (~로 (된)–화학적 변화)

6 ~에 관하여

Bob was sorry *about* the mistakes.

He gave us a lecture *on* Asia.

UNIT **2**

명사와 관사

❶ 명사의 복수형과 소유격

셀 수 있는 명사를 복수형으로 만들 수 있다.

1 명사의 복수형 만들기

Ⓐ 대개 단어 끝에 -s를 붙인다.

cat → cat*s* (고양이들)　　　　bag → bag*s* (가방들)

Ⓑ 단어 끝이 -s, -x, -sh, -ch, -o인 경우에는 -es를 붙인다.

bus → bus*es* (버스들)　　　　tomato → tomato*es* (토마토들)

Ⓒ 단어 끝이 '자음+y'일 때는 y를 i로 고치고 -es를 붙인다. '모음+y'일 때는 -s만 붙인다.

lady → lad*ies* (숙녀들)　　　city → cit*ies* (도시들)　　　family → famil*ies* (가족들)

boy → boy*s* (소년들)　　　　toy → toy*s* (장난감들)

➕ P·L·U·S

복수형 어미 -s, -es 발음하기

- 단어가 [f], [t], [k], [p] 같은 무성음으로 끝나고 -s가 붙으면 [s]로 발음한다.
  cake[keik]→ cake*s*[keiks]
- 단어가 [s], [z], [ʧ], [ʃ]로 끝나고 -s, -es가 붙으면 [iz]로 발음한다.
  horse[hɔːrs] → horse*s*[hɔːrsiz]
- 이 외에는 [z]로 발음한다.
  apple [æpl] → apple*s*[æplz]

2 명사의 소유격

Ⓐ **사람과 동물: 단어+'s**

my friend*'s* house   a cat*'s* tail   a girl*'s* school

your parent*s'* car

*-s로 끝나는 복수명사는 '만 붙인다.

Ⓑ **사물: of+명사**

the legs *of* the desk   the door *of* the car

② 물질명사

일정한 형태가 없는 물질을 나타내는 명사로 복수형을 만들거나 a, an을 붙일 수 없다.

물질명사의 수량을 나타내는 표현

a cup of tea   two cups of tea

a glass of water   two glasses of water

a piece of paper   **단수 →**   two pieces of paper   **복수**

a loaf of bread   two loaves of bread

a bar of soap   two bars of soap

③ 명사와 관사

1 부정관사 a/an: 셀 수 있는 명사 앞에

I had *a* sandwich and *an* apple for lunch.

*자음으로 시작하는 명사 앞에는 a, 모음으로 시작하는 명사 앞에는 an을 붙인다.

2 정관사 the: 특정한 것, 화자와 청자가 모두 아는 명사 앞에

I cleaned my car yesterday. *The* car (=my car) is an expensive car.

I bought a book. *The* book is very interesting.

A man and a woman were sitting. *The* man was American but I thought *the* woman was British.

UNIT **3**

형용사

① 형용사의 역할과 위치

1 명사를 수식하거나 성질이나 상태를 설명한다.

I heard the *wonderful* story.

기본 개념 장착하기

We saw an *interesting* movie.

This flower is *beautiful*. (flower의 성질 설명)

He is very *quiet*. (he의 상태 설명)

2 형용사의 위치

    A 꾸며 주는 명사 앞에 위치

a *beautiful* lady

    B something, nothing, anything, everything+형용사

I want to eat *something cold*.

Do you want to eat *anything hot*?

    C 수식어구가 붙은 형용사는 명사 뒤에 위치

Korea is a *famous* country.

Korea is a country *famous for the Seoul Olympics*.

❷ 부정 수량 형용사

1 많은

    A many(수) = a lot of(=lots of)

There are *many* students in the class.　How *many* books do you have?

    B much(양) = a lot of(=lots of)

There is *much* water in the pool.　　How much *money* do you have?

2 약간의, 거의 없는

    A a few(수) / few(수)

I have *a few* friends.　　　　I have *few* friends.

    B a little(양) / little(양)

I have *a little* money.　　　I have *little* money.

3 얼마간의, 약간의

    A some (긍정문, 권유, 제안의 의문문에서 사용)

Bring me *some* water, please.　　We bought *some* flowers.

Will you have *some* coffee?　　Can I have *some* sugar, please?

    B any (부정문, 의문문, 조건문에서 사용)

Do you have *any* brothers?　　He never does *any* work.

부사

부사의 형태와 역할

1 부사의 형태

Ⓐ **본래 부사:** then, already, too

Ⓑ **형용사+-ly:** careful*ly*, ful*ly*, happi*ly*, easi*ly*....

Ⓒ **형용사와 형태가 동일:** late, hard, fast, early....

Ⓓ **형용사+-ly가 다른 뜻으로 쓰이는 것**

late 늦게	lately 최근에	high 높게	highly 매우
near 가까이	nearly 거의	hard 열심히	hardly 거의~않은

2 부사의 역할

▪ **동사, 형용사, 부사, 문장 수식**

All his family rise *early*. (동사 수식)

This book is *too* expensive. (형용사 수식)

The horse runs *very* fast. (부사 수식)

Happily, he did not die. (문장 수식)

> ➕ **P·L·U·S**
>
> **주의해야 할 부사의 쓰임**
> ▪ already(긍정문), yet(의문문, 부정문)
> They have ***already*** gone home.
> Have they gone home ***yet***? He has not come ***yet***.
> ▪ so(긍정문), neither(부정문)
> A: She likes bananas. B: ***So*** do I.
> A: She doesn't like bananas. B: Neither ***do*** I.
> ▪ ago(과거시제), before(완료시제)
> I saw the movie two years ***ago***. I have seen the movie ***before***.

3 부사의 어순 및 위치

Ⓐ **어순: 작은 단위+큰 단위, 장소+방법+시간**

I stayed *at a hotel on the hill in the town*. (작은 단위 → 큰 단위)

They went to *Yeongjoo by train last week*. (장소+방법+시간)

Ⓑ **빈도부사의 위치: 일반동사 앞, be동사와 조동사 뒤에 온다.**

He *usually* goes to bed at ten. (일반동사 앞)

He is *seldom* late for work. (be동사 뒤)

UNIT **5**

비교급, 최상급

❶ 형용사의 비교급, 최상급 만드는 방법

1 규칙 변화

Ⓐ 형용사 원급에 -er, -est를 쓰고 비교급, 최상급을 만든다.

small – smaller – smallest

Ⓑ -e로 끝난 단어에는 -r, -st를 붙인다.

wise – wiser – wisest, large – larger – largest

Ⓒ '자음+y'로 끝나면 y를 i로 고쳐 -er, -est를 붙인다.

easy – easier – easiest, happy – happier – happiest

Ⓓ '모음+자음'으로 끝나면 자음 하나를 더 쓰고 -er, -est를 붙인다.

big – bigger – biggest, hot – hotter - hottest

Ⓔ 3음절 이상의 형용사와 2음절 형용사 일부 앞에 more, most를 붙인다.

beautiful – *more* beautiful – *most* beautiful

Ⓕ 2음절 형용사가 -ous, -ful, -ing, -less, -ive 등으로 끝나면 more, most를 붙인다.

famous – *more* famous – *most* famous, useful – *more* useful – *most* useful

2 불규칙 변화

원급	비교급	최상급
good/well	better	best
bad/ill	worse	worst
many/much	more	most
old	older elder	oldest (나이) eldest (항렬)
little	less	least

❷ 원급 – 동등비교, 비교급 – 우열비교

1 동등비교

Ⓐ as+원급+as+비교 대상: ~만큼 …하게

She is *as* beautiful *as* my mother.

He can run *as* fast *as* I.

Ⓑ not so(=as)+원급+as+비교 대상: ~만큼 …하지 않은

She is *not so* beautiful *as* my mother.

He can*not* run *as* fast *as* I.

2 우열비교

비교급+than+비교 대상: ~보다 …한(하게)

A giraffe is *taller than* a horse.

He loved me *more than* you.

This car is *less expensive than* that car.

❸ 최상급

셋 이상의 것 중에서 '가장 ~한'의 뜻을 가진다.

최상급 표현

Ⓐ the+최상급+of+복수명사: ~ 중에서 가장 …하다

He is *the oldest of* the three boys.

Ⓑ the+최상급+in+장소, 집단: ~에서 가장 …하다

She is *the most beautiful* girl *in* her family.

➕ P·L·U·S

형용사의 최상급에는 the를 붙이지만, 부사의 최상급에는 the를 붙이지 않는다.

- I get up **earliest** in the family.
- Carl Louis ran **fastest** in the world.

1 단어의 복수형을 쓰시오.

❶ family - _____ ❷ bus - _____

❸ radio - _____ ❹ box - _____

❺ dish - _____ ❻ ox - _____

❼ city - _____ ❽ piano - _____

빈칸에 a, an, the 중 알맞은 것을 쓰시오. (필요 없으면 x 표시)

2 That is _____ egg.

3 She can play _____ piano well.

4 Look at _____ cat on the chair.

5 He plays _____ tennis every day.

6 I like _____ honest girl.

빈칸에 a few, a little 중 알맞은 것을 쓰시오.

7 I'm going to study here for _____ days.

8 There is _____ water in the well.

9 _____ students play baseball after school.

10 A: Can you speak English?

B: Yes, but just _____.

빈칸에 some, any 중 알맞은 것을 쓰시오.

11 Is there _____ surviving family member?

12 He doesn't have _____ brothers.

13 Will you have _____ cookies?

14 Min-su has _____ friends in New York.

괄호 안에서 알맞은 것을 고르시오.

15 There is (many / few / much) oil in the bucket.

16 Tom has (many / any / much) friends in Seoul.

17 There is (many / little / few) water in this lake.

18 He came (a few / a little) minutes later.

두 문장의 뜻이 같도록 빈칸에 알맞은 말을 쓰시오.

19 She doesn't have any money.

= She has _____ money.

20 Jane has a lot of pretty dolls.

= Jane has _____ pretty dolls.

21 We have a lot of snow in January.

= We have _____ snow in January.

22 There are many trees in the garden.

= The garden _____ many trees.

괄호 안에서 알맞은 것을 고르시오.

23 Bill is (so / as) tall as Tom.

24 Washington is not (too / as) large as New York.

25 He is not so old (than / as) she.

26 Do they play tennis (well / better / best) than we?

27 Which is (useful / more useful), a donkey or a horse?

28 This is the (more / most) beautiful (in / of) all.

29 The Han River is one of the longest (river / rivers) (of / in) Korea.

30 Seoul is (larger / large) than any other city in Korea.

31 Jane is (beautiful / more beautiful / as beautiful) as her sister.

32 We had (many / more / much / most) rain this year than last year.

33 He was as (poor / poorer / more poorer) as a church mouse.

34 He had (little / less / most) money than she.

35 He became (bad / worse / badder) after he took the medicine.

36 That building is (very / much) higher than this building.

우리말에 맞게 주어진 단어를 사용해 영작하시오.

37 건강은 돈보다 중요하다.
(money / important / health / more / is / than)

→ _____.

38 그는 나보다 키가 크다. (tall)

→ _____.

39 그것은 내가 본 것 중에서 최악의 영화다. (ever)

→ _____.

40 그녀는 자기 반에서 가장 키가 큰 소녀이다.
(in her class)

→ _____.

통 합 5-1 유 형

1 주어진 단어의 관계가 <u>다르게</u> 짝지어진 것은?

① use - useful　　② peace - peaceful

③ beauty - beautiful　④ think - thoughtful

⑤ help - helpful

2 단수형과 복수형이 <u>잘못</u> 짝지어진 것은?

① fish - fish

② woman - womans

③ piano - pianos

④ sandwich - sandwiches

⑤ child - children

3 각 형용사의 비교급, 최상급이 <u>어색한</u> 것은?

① nice - nicer - nicest

② active - activer - activest

③ useful - more useful - most useful

④ late - later - latest

⑤ little - less - least

4 빈칸에 들어갈 순서로 알맞은 것은?

> • How _____ times a month do you eat out?
>
> • How _____ water do you drink every day?

① many - much　　② many - many

③ often - many　　④ much - many

⑤ often - much

5 〈보기〉의 밑줄 친 like와 쓰임이 <u>다른</u> 것은?

> ● 보기 ●
>
> The sky looks <u>like</u> a jelly.

① Jane <u>likes</u> playing badminton.

② She dances <u>like</u> a dancer.

③ Jina looks <u>like</u> her aunt.

④ What does it taste <u>like</u>?

⑤ What's the weather <u>like</u> today?

6 밑줄 친 단어의 뜻이 <u>다른</u> 문장을 고르면?

① The bag looks <u>pretty</u>.

② He likes <u>pretty</u> girls.

③ The movie was <u>pretty</u> boring.

④ I enjoy <u>pretty</u> things.

⑤ I'm so <u>pretty</u>.

7 밑줄 친 부분과 바꿔 쓸 수 있는 것을 <u>모두</u> 고르시오.

> There were <u>many</u> things to play with.

① a few　　　　② lots of

③ some　　　　④ much

⑤ a lot of

8 빈칸에 공통으로 들어갈 단어는?

> • What kind of feeling did you try to show _____ your picture?
>
> • The writer was very poor, but he tried to express hope _____ his book.

① by　　　　② off　　　　③ or

④ into　　　　⑤ through

CHAPTER 05 전치사 · 명사와 관사 · 형용사 · 부사 · 비교급, 최상급 125

9 효정이의 주방이다. 잘못된 묘사 2개를 고르시오.

① An egg is in the box.

② A tomato is on the chair.

③ The cheese is on the table.

④ The bread is on the table.

⑤ There is milk next to the bread.

10 〈보기〉의 밑줄 친 단어와 같은 의미로 쓰인 것은?

> ● 보기 ●
>
> Can you see the player hitting a small, hard ball with a bat?

① Exercise hard if you want to get a good shape.

② He took a rest on a hard mattress.

③ I had an exam last week, so I studied hard for it.

④ She solved a hard question yesterday.

⑤ After hard work he finally bought the computer.

11 빈칸에 들어갈 순서로 알맞은 것은?

> A: May I take your order?
>
> B: I want _____ pasta.
>
> A: Sorry, we don't have _____ now.

① some - some

② any - some

③ some - any

④ any - any

⑤ some - others

12 표와 다른 내용은?

	Steak A	Steak B	Steak C
Price	$8	$16	$24
Size			
Taste	★☆☆	★★☆	★★★

① Steak C is more delicious than Steak B.

② Steak A is more expensive than Steak C.

③ Steak C is smaller than Steak A.

④ The price of Steak A is lower than that of Steak B.

⑤ Steak B is bigger than Steak A.

13 밑줄 친 부분이 어법상 어색한 것은?

① You never listen to me.

② We go often to swimming.

③ He is often busy at the end of the week.

④ He always eats breakfast at 6:30.

⑤ I usually get up late on Sunday.

14 어법상 어색한 것은?

① A: I did my homework last night.

　B: So did he.

② A: He can play the drum.

　B: So am I.

③ A: They can pass through the hole.

　B: So can she.

④ A: I have a headache.

　B: So does my brother.

⑤ A: She is a good student.

　B: So is her sister.

15 어법상 옳은 문장은?

① Sam and I meets in front of the park.
② Banks usually closes at 4:00 p.m.
③ The bag costed me a lot of money.
④ Water boil at 100 degrees Celsius.
⑤ We never washes our dirty bike.

16 밑줄 친 부분 중 어법상 어색한 것은?

① She is <u>bigger than</u> I heard.
② Jenny is <u>more beautiful than</u> I thought.
③ Today is <u>more cool than</u> yesterday.
④ This machine is <u>more useful than</u> I thought.
⑤ The car is <u>faster than</u> I expected.

17 어법상 옳은 것을 모두 고르면?

ⓐ Birds are singing merry.
ⓑ It will be of no use.
ⓒ She looks very health.
ⓓ There is an oxen.
ⓔ Hurry up, or you'll be late for school.
ⓕ They have a lot of sheep.
ⓖ People act different in different weather.

① ⓐ, ⓒ, ⓖ
② ⓑ, ⓔ, ⓕ
③ ⓐ, ⓑ, ⓔ, ⓖ
④ ⓑ, ⓓ, ⓔ, ⓕ
⑤ ⓒ, ⓔ, ⓕ, ⓖ

18 어법상 옳은 문장은?

A: Wow, look at these airplanes.
　① They look greatly.
B: Thanks. ② I made them herself.
A: ③ That are incredible.
　④ How did you make them?
B: ⑤ I just read some book and practiced a lot.

19 문맥상 어울리지 <u>않는</u> 표현은?

How tall are you? Do you want to grow taller? ① <u>Why don't you</u> drink ② <u>a glass of</u> milk? Milk has ③ <u>a lot of</u> calcium, and ④ <u>is good at</u> your bones. You don't like milk? Then, try cheese or yogurt. They're just ⑤ <u>as good as</u> milk.

20 어법상 옳지 <u>않은</u> 것은?

① Julie usually gets up early. ② But tomorrow she will sleep until her dad wakes her up. Tomorrow is Sunday! ③ She always spends her weekend at her aunt's house. ④ She can play tennis and go swimming. ⑤ She will fun.

서술형

1 우리말에 맞게 문장을 완성하시오.

I can't run _____ fast _____ she. (나는 그녀만큼 빨리 달릴 수 없다.)

2 괄호 속에 주어진 단어를 변형하여 문장을 완성하시오.

I think English is much _____ than math. (easy)

3 주어진 단어를 사용해 문장을 완성하시오.

❶ Seven _____ are in the parking lot. (car)

❷ The _____ are turning red and yellow. (leaf)

❸ We have four _____ on Thursday. (class)

❹ Minki has three cute _____. (baby)

❺ The firefighters save many people's _____. (life)

4 〈보기〉의 문장과 같은 의미가 되도록 so를 사용해 문장을 완성하시오.

---• 보기 •---
Amy looks excited today. And Tom looks excited, too.

= Amy looks excited today. _____ _____ _____.

5 틀린 부분을 바르게 고치시오.

❶ I am as prettier as an actress.

_____ → _____

❷ You don't know about math as many as I do.

_____ → _____

❸ John can speak Chinese as good as I do.

_____ → _____

6 괄호 속 단어들을 문맥에 맞게 재배열하시오.

The Antarctic Ice Marathon (the / is / world / marathons / of / toughest / in / one / the).

→ _____.

7 우리말에 맞게 문장을 완성하시오.

그녀는 관습과 전통뿐만 아니라 요리의 비법까지도 배운다.

→ She learns the secrets of cuisine _____ _____ _____ customs and traditions.

8 표를 보고 수진과 제이슨을 비교하는 문장을 완성하시오. (주어진 단어를 활용)

	Sujin	Jason
English grade	95점	88점
Height	162	170

English grade

→ Sujin's grade _____.
   (good)

Height

→ Jason _____. (tall)

9 주어진 단어를 사용해 영작하시오.

> 이 기계 장치를 어린아이들의 손에 닿지 않는 곳에 두십시오.
> (this / reach / out / device / the / keep / of)

→ _____

of young children.

10 반 여학생들 사이에 인기 있는 간식에 대한 설문 조사 결과이다. 그래프를 보고 다음 질문에 대한 내용을 순서대로 작성하시오.

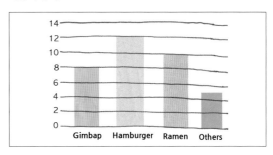

> ### Female Students' Favorite Snacks
> The most popular snack among the female students in Jane's class is hamburger.
> ❶ Q: How many students say they like hamburger most?
>
>   A: _____.
> ❷ Q: What is the second most popular snack?
>
>   A: _____.
> ❸ Q: What is the third most popular snack?
>
>   A: _____.

1 명사의 단수형과 복수형이 잘못 짝지어진 것은?

① child - children

② tooth - teeth

③ sandwich - sandwiches

④ question - questions

⑤ life - lifes

2 형태가 바르게 짝지어지지 않은 것은?

① invent - invention

② attract - attraction

③ display - displation

④ discuss - discussion

⑤ participate - participation

3-4 〈보기〉의 밑줄 친 부분과 의미가 같은 것은?

3

> ● 보기 ●
>
> If you buy a hamburger, you will get a
> free coke.

① This is sugar free.

② You are free to go home.

③ I play chess in my free time.

④ Please call me when you are free.

⑤ We give free computer lessons to old
   people.

4

> ● 보기 ●
>
> It takes about 20 minutes.

① Alice doesn't care about her friends.

② We should talk about this.

③ Let's think about these problems.

④ I have about ten dollars now.

⑤ I tell you about my plan.

5 빈칸에 올 수 없는 것은?

> I have _____ more books than you.

① even　　　　　② still

③ a lot　　　　　④ very

⑤ far

6 우리말을 영어로 잘못 옮긴 것은?

① 대신에 고구마를 먹어라.

　　→ Try sweet potatoes instead.

② 너는 더 집중을 잘하게 될 것이다.

　　→ You will become less focused.

③ 나는 키가 더 크고 싶어서 우유를 마신다.

　　→ I want to grow taller, so I drink milk.

④ 나는 단 것을 먹고 싶을 때 사탕과 초콜릿을 먹는다.

　　→ When I want something sweet, I eat
   candy and chocolate.

⑤ 한 줌의 견과류로 여러분은 다시 놀 준비가 될 것이
   다.

　　→ With a handful of nuts, you'll be ready
   to play again.

7 빈칸에 공통으로 들어갈 말을 고르시오.

> • I got up late, _____ I was late for
>   school.
> • She is _____ busy that she can't
>   help you.

① as　　　　② so　　　　③ but

④ such　　　⑤ too

8-9 빈칸에 알맞은 것은?

8

> **A:** Griffin didn't have a car.
> **B:** Neither _____ I.

① am   ② do   ③ done
④ was   ⑤ did

9

> This summer, I will go swimming as _____ as possible.

① many   ② more   ③ most
④ often   ⑤ more often

10 빈칸에 들어갈 순서로 알맞은 것은?

> The air pockets make the orange _____ than the water, so it floats.
> Without them, it sinks because the orange is now _____ than the water.

① heavier - dense   ② lighter - lighter
③ lighter - denser   ④ denser - heavier
⑤ denser - lighter

11-12 ⓐ~ⓒ에 들어갈 단어를 바르게 나열한 것은?

11

> They made it ⓐ_____ plastics.
> They change the plastics ⓑ_____ small pieces and turn them ⓒ_____ something new.

① out of - into - at
② for - into - at
③ out of - into - into
④ for - in - into
⑤ out of - in - into

12

> • Look ⓐ_____ the board and choose your favorite pet.
> • Every day I walk ⓑ_____ Jane in the park.
> • Many people say hello ⓒ_____ her.

① on - in - with
② at - to - on
③ on - at - on
④ at - with - to
⑤ with - with - with

13-15 13-15 어법상 옳지 <u>않은</u> 것은?

13

① There are empty glasses on the table.
② There are cookies on the floor.
③ There is a cat and a dog on the sofa.
④ Every garbage can is full.
⑤ My mother yelled at me angrily, "This place is a mess!"

14

① He is 160 centimeters tall.
② The river is 10 meters wide.
③ I bought a three-meters-long rope.
④ The Nile is 6,437 kilometers long.
⑤ There used to be a ten-meter-deep river.

15

① Jimin is taller than I.
② You are richer than Jisuk.
③ He is more handsome than I expected.
④ This bag is expensiver than I expected.
⑤ The computer game is more interesting than I expected.

16-17 어법상 옳은 것은?

16

① He has three leafs in his bag.
② Bob bought ten potatos and two melons.
③ Wendy has two children and four sheeps.
④ Those man are four.
⑤ I caught some fish yesterday.

17

① She go to the library.
② John plays the violin well.
③ My mom and dad cooks well.
④ My sister doesn't likes books.
⑤ He visit his father once a week.

18 밑줄 친 표현 중 옳은 것은?

① There are <u>three bottles of waters</u>.
② Would you like <u>a cups of coffee</u>?
③ Glue the heart and the card onto <u>a piece of heavy paper</u>.
④ Can you give me <u>five pieces of banana</u>?
⑤ He ate <u>four slice of pizzas</u>.

19-20 어법상 옳은 것은?

19

① Sora is middle school students. ② Her school starts in March 2nd. ③ Once a month, Sora's family goes hiking. ④ In March, they go hiking in the 19th. ⑤ And there is one more events in March.

20

> **A:** My trunk is ① long and wrinkle. It looks ugly.
>
> **B:** No. ② I always have thought your trunk is cool. When you sprinkle water on your back with your trunk, you look great. ③ Beside, you can carry things ④ by using your trunk. I think ⑤ you should proud of it.

---

3 It is ~ that ... 구문으로 장소를 강조하여 주어진 단어를 모두 사용해 문장을 완성하시오.

> lives / next / a / star
> my / to / movie / house

→ _____ .

---

4 빈칸에 알맞은 말을 쓰시오. (3단어)

> Sora is very tall. Minju is taller than Sora. But Minju is _____ Jihun. Jihun is the tallest of them.

→ _____ _____ _____

📑 **서 술 형**

1 빈칸에 알맞은 말을 쓰시오.

> • My mom looks ⓐ _____ because she got mo.
>
> (엄마는 '모'가 나와서 흥분하신 것 같다.)
>
> • That looks ⓑ _____ a lot of fun.
>
> (그것은 정말 재미있어 보인다.)

ⓐ _____ ⓑ _____

---

5 괄호 안의 단어를 변형하여 문맥에 맞게 문장을 완성하시오.

Winter is _____ season of the year. (cold)

---

2 〈보기〉의 세 문장을 한 문장으로 바르게 쓰시오.

> ─────────── 보기
> • A town is smaller than a city.
> • A city is larger than a village.
> • A village is smaller than a town.

→ A town is _____ than a village but _____ than a city.

---

6 표를 보고 질문에 대한 대답을 완전한 문장으로 쓰시오. (5단어)

	Sujin	Jane
height	163	163
weight	50	48
age	18	17

Q: Who is younger, Sujin or Jane?

A: _____ .

통 합 유 형

7 주어진 단어를 사용해 영작하시오.

나는 Tom만큼 운동을 좋아하지 않는다.
(don't / as, 8단어)

→ _____ .

8 주어진 단어를 모두 사용하되 필요한 경우 단어를 변형하거나 추가하여 문장을 완성하시오.

I / get / confuse / more

→ The more I think about the puzzle,

_____ .

9 〈보기〉와 같은 뜻이 되도록 문장을 완성하시오.

━━● 보기 ●━━
Nothing is more important than hard work.

→ Hard work is _____ _____

_____ of all.

10 〈보기〉와 같은 뜻이 되도록 대화를 완성하시오

━━● 보기 ●━━
Tom and Jenny, both of them are very hungry.

Tom: I'm very hungry.

Jenny: _____ _____ _____ .

통 합 5-3 유 형

1-2 두 단어의 관계가 나머지와 <u>다른</u> 것은?

1

① do - deed
② service - serve
③ choice - choose
④ decision - decide
⑤ satisfaction - satisfy

2

① Korea - Korean
② France - French
③ Japan - Japanese
④ China - Chinese
⑤ the UK - England

3-4 ⓐ~ⓒ에 들어갈 말을 바르게 나열한 것은?

3

- I have a meeting ⓐ_____ Thursday.
- She usually has breakfast ⓑ_____ 7:30.
- It rains a lot ⓒ_____ the summer.

① at - on - in
② at - on - of
③ on - at - in
④ on - in - at
⑤ on - at - of

4

I don't have ⓐ_____ money because I spent ⓑ_____ money on snacks or comic books. My sister didn't save ⓒ_____ money, either.

① some - any - any
② any - some - any
③ any - any - some
④ any - some - some
⑤ some - any - some

5 ⓐ~ⓓ에 들어갈 전치사를 바르게 나열한 것은?

There was a house ⓐ_____ 1,000 mirrors. A happy little dog learned ⓑ_____ this place and decided to visit it. He arrived ⓒ_____ the house and jumped happily ⓓ_____ the stairs to the house.

① at - of - to - to
② at - to - at - up
③ of - of - at - up
④ of - about - at - in
⑤ with - about - to - down

6 ⓐ~ⓒ에 들어갈 말을 바르게 나열한 것은?

- I'm a guitarist in the school band, ⓐ_____ my guitar is really important to me. My guitar is ⓑ_____ Germany. I also have a new cellphone.
- My mom isn't very friendly ⓒ_____ other people, but she loves me.

① so - of - to
② so - of - with
③ so - from - to
④ because - from - with
⑤ because - of - to

7 빈칸에 들어갈 순서로 알맞은 것은?

> • My friend likes it, _____.
>
> • He did not do the homework,
>   _____.

① either - also   ② either - too

③ too - either   ④ too - neither

⑤ too - also

8 빈칸에 들어갈 말이 <u>다른</u> 것은?

① _____ _____ a glass of water in my room.

② _____ _____ a lot of restaurants in this building.

③ _____ _____ some orange juice on the table.

④ _____ _____ no fork in her lunch box.

⑤ _____ _____ lots of money in my pocket.

9 빈칸에 들어갈 순서로 알맞은 것은?

> Their eyes may be _____ than yours, or their faces may be _____ than yours.

① big - dark   ② bigger - darker

③ bigger - darkest   ④ biggest - darker

⑤ biggest - darkest

10 우리말과 같은 뜻이 되도록 빈칸에 알맞은 것은?

> 한국에서는 점점 더 많은 사람들이 해외여행을 하고 있다.
>
> = _____ people are travelling abroad in Korea.

① More and more   ② Most of

③ Very many   ④ Many and many

⑤ Almost all

11 빈칸에 알맞은 것 <u>2개</u>를 고르면?

> _____ time and effort from you can be helpful to others.

① A lot of   ② A few

③ Few   ④ Little

⑤ A little

12 주어진 문장과 의미가 같은 것은?

> No boy in my class is smarter than I.

① No boy in my class is more foolish than I.

② I am smarter than any other boy in my class.

③ I am smarter than boys in my class.

④ I am as smart as my friends.

⑤ I am the second smartest boy in my class.

13 어법상 옳은 문장은?

① Do you know he loves you?

② I knew that would he return.

③ They just need strong somebody.

④ Is there wrong anything with this project?

⑤ Let's find wonderful something for his

14 밑줄 친 부분의 쓰임이 옳은 것은?

① John can drive and <u>so do I</u>.

② I am very tall and <u>so does my sister</u>.

③ Julia lives in New York and <u>so do Robert</u>.

④ Ann has finished her homework and <u>so has Mary</u>.

⑤ Mike would like to travel abroad, and <u>so does Anne</u>.

15-17 어법상 옳은 것은?

15

① Welcome to home.

② My brother is carefuler than me.

③ We love her because of her honesty.

④ My English score is better than you.

⑤ She stayed in Busan during three days.

16

① She is prettyer than Jane.

② Sumi is more beautiful than Yura.

③ The bag is expensive than I thought.

④ It is one of the famous thing of Bangkok.

⑤ Love is most important thing in the world.

17

① I need two spoon of sugar.

② Who are going to cut the eggs?

③ I'm really looking forward to see you again.

④ I'm going to bring a bag of balloons and a can of tuna.

⑤ Cover with another 4 slices of bread and then cut each sandwiches in half.

18 어법상 어색한 것을 <u>모두</u> 고르시오.

① Do often you go to the cinema?

② I will always be honest and kind.

③ He doesn't usually work on Sundays.

④ She seldom read English books last year.

⑤ A lot of people come from every countries.

19 대화의 밑줄 친 부분 중 어색한 것 2개를 고르시오.

A: Do you have ① <u>many</u> pens in your bag?

B: No, I don't have many pens. I have ② <u>a few</u> pens and ③ <u>a little</u> sweets.

A: Do you have ④ <u>much</u> money in your pocket?

B: No, I don't have much money. I have some money and ⑤ <u>a few</u> chocolate.

20 어법상 옳은 문장을 모두 묶은 것은?

ⓐ Jihyun runs faster than Sora.

ⓑ James is the best swimmer of us.

ⓒ Let's consider this problem serious.

ⓓ When is a happier time in your life?

ⓔ Jason has the more books in his class.

ⓕ I need to buy a nicer car than this one.

---

① ⓐ, ⓑ, ⓕ   ② ⓐ, ⓑ, ⓒ, ⓕ

③ ⓐ, ⓒ, ⓔ   ④ ⓑ, ⓔ, ⓕ

⑤ ⓒ, ⓓ, ⓔ

서 술 형

1 빈칸에 a, an, the 중 알맞은 것을 쓰시오. (필요 없으면 x 표시)

Mrs. Kim went to _____ bed at ten.

_____ strange noise woke her up at

_____ dawn. She went to _____

living room. Suddenly _____ young

man and a dog ran out of _____

kitchen. _____ dog was very big.

---

2 두 문장이 같은 의미가 되도록 빈칸에 알맞은 말을 쓰시오.

He sings well.

= He is a _____ _____.

3-4 두 문장을 하나로 연결할 때 빈칸에 알맞은 말을 쓰시오.

3

- Thomas has three hundred books.
- Jane has one hundred books.

→ Thomas has _____ _____

_____ many books _____

Jane.

4

- I am sixteen years old.
- You are thirteen years old.

→ You are three years _____

_____ I.

5 같은 의미가 되도록 문장을 완성하시오.

Nothing is more important than good attitude in life.

= Good attitude is _____

_____ _____

_____ in life.

6 우리말에 맞게 영작하시오. (7단어)

그녀는 나만큼 나이가 들어야 해요.

→ _____.

7 밑줄 친 부분을 영작하시오. (단, 주어진 단어를 반드시 포함하고 단어를 추가하여 8~11 단어로 써야 함. 단어 중복 사용 가능)

I guess that 지폐의 역할은 점점 더 작아지게 될 거야.
(paper money / smaller / the / of / will)

→ _____

8 우리말과 같은 의미가 되도록 주어와 동사를 갖춘 완전한 문장을 쓰시오. (빈도부사를 반드시 사용할 것. 미사용 시 오답)

그는 책 읽는 것을 좋아하지 않기 때문에 좀처럼 도서관에 가지 않는다.
→ Because _____.
(to the library / reading books)

→ _____
_____.

9 〈조건〉을 참조하고 주어진 단어를 활용해 우리말에 맞게 영작하시오.

〈조건〉
1. 도치 구문으로 쓸 것.　2. 6단어로 쓸 것.

그 책상 아래에는 고양이 두 마리가 있다.

→ _____.
(under)

10 주어진 단어를 사용해 영작하시오.

우리가 지구에 더 많은 해를 끼칠수록 우리의 삶은 더 악화됩니다.
(the more / the worse / we do / harm / our lives / to the Earth / get)

→ _____
_____.

chapter

06

통합실전
문   제
1~10

1 단어의 관계가 나머지와 다른 2개는?

① friend - friendly

② serious - seriously

③ happy - happily

④ beautiful - beautifully

⑤ height - highly

2 밑줄 친 두 단어의 뜻이 같은 것은?

① Street dogs go <u>around</u> the street.
   This is <u>around</u> 20 dollars.

② Don't <u>throw</u> a thing like that.
   Tom <u>throws</u> stones at the river.

③ I live on the second <u>floor</u> of the
   apartment.
   Students are cleaning the <u>floor</u>.

④ I don't like <u>fish</u> for a meal.
   Let's go <u>fishing</u> tomorrow.

⑤ Would you like something <u>cold</u> to drink?
   She has a bad <u>cold</u>.

3 ⓐ와 ⓑ에 공통으로 들어갈 말로 알맞은 것은?

- Tom thinks ⓐ_____ his girlfriend
  is pretty.
- Susie believes ⓑ_____ the
  concert will be very interesting.

① what   ② which   ③ there

④ why   ⑤ that

4 빈칸에 알맞은 것은?

My mom cooks very well.
She _____ has a nice smile.
She is so generous.

① and   ② too   ③ now

④ also   ⑤ but

5 〈보기〉의 밑줄 친 것과 같은 용법으로 쓰인 것은?

● 보기 ●

<u>It</u> takes an hour from here by bus.

① What time is <u>it</u>?

② <u>It</u> is my lunch bag.

③ <u>It</u>'s on the second floor.

④ Did you find <u>it</u> on your desk?

⑤ <u>It</u> is very thin.

6 빈칸에 알맞은 것은?

I think my backpack is out of fashion and
_____. What can I do?

① boring   ② to bore   ③ bore of

④ bore   ⑤ bored

7 빈칸에 들어갈 순서로 알맞은 것은?

- Tom used to be _____ China.
- Susie is always late _____ work.
- Is there a shop _____ your house?

① of - to - next   ② on - to - next

③ for - from - next to ④ in - for - next

⑤ in - for - next to

8 ⓐ~ⓒ에 들어갈 말을 바르게 나열한 것은?

> I tried ⓐ_____ the problem without
> ⓑ_____ at an answer sheet, but it
> was difficult. So I decided ⓒ_____
> the answer in the answer sheet.

① to solve - to look - to find
② solving - to look - finding
③ to solve - looking - to find
④ solving - to like - to find
⑤ to solve - looking - find

9 〈보기〉의 밑줄 친 studying과 쓰임이 다른 것은?

보기
> Studying English is easy for me because
> I like it.

① His only hobby is traveling.
② The boys like playing soccer.
③ Tom enjoys playing computer games.
④ Watching a sports game is exciting.
⑤ There is a sleeping baby in the room.

10 밑줄 친 부분의 쓰임이 다른 것은?

① I used to study hard when I was in high
   school.
② When it is sunny, we usually go to the
   park.
③ When is his birthday?
④ Mom was cooking when I came home.
⑤ When I left my office, it started raining.

11-12 어법상 옳은 문장은?

11
① Tom and I meets in the shopping mall.
② The library usually closes at 10:00 p.m.
③ My backpack costed a lot of money.
④ Water boil at 100 degrees Celsius.
⑤ She never wash the dishes.

12
① We goes to church every Sunday.
② Does your father has a brother?
③ Do Tom and Susie like English?
④ Does your dog has a house?
⑤ We doesn't have a great guitar.

13 어법상 옳지 않은 것은?
① My father showed me some old
   pictures.
② She gave this book to me.
③ My boyfriend sent me some flowers.
④ Mom bought a toy to me.
⑤ He tells me an exciting story every
   night.

14-16 어법상 자연스러운 문장은?

14
① My parents doesn't sing well.
② She doesn't like math, too.
③ Everyone is handsome.
④ He can must do it.
⑤ Your are not tall.

15

① The yellow bag is't mine.

② I'am not tall but my brother is tall.

③ You cannot studying here.

④ Her mother and my father aren't friends.

⑤ This's not a book for you.

16

① She is not in the second grade.

② My house doesn't near the park.

③ Tom and Susie is very kind to me.

④ My mom isn't wash the dishes in the morning.

⑤ Does he going back home?

17 어법상 옳은 문장을 2개 고르시오.

① I doesn't go to school on Sunday.

② Did they come from Korea?

③ Susie don't go fishing with her father.

④ Does Tom live with his grandparents?

⑤ Does he wake up at 7 yesterday?

18 어법상 옳지 않은 문장을 2개 고르시오.

① Jane or he are good students.

② Where are you from?

③ A teacher and doctor come here.

④ Tom and Susie are classmates.

⑤ Is she your teacher?

19 어법상 옳지 않은 문장은?

① She asked what I wanted.

② He walked slowly because of his bad leg.

③ He speaks German and play handball and soccer.

④ He watched the kids playing in the yard.

⑤ The Athletic Games were held in his honor.

20 어법상 옳은 문장을 고르시오.

> ⓐ I has a lot of work to do.
>
> ⓑ Questions have answered privately by teachers of the blog.
>
> ⓒ Ms. Kim is a very kind doctor.
>
> ⓓ When we saw it, we knew we will love it.
>
> ⓔ Tom and Susie is tall and smart.
>
> ⓕ As soon as the summer vacation starts, I will go to the beach.
>
> ⓖ I am not from Canada.

① ⓒ, ⓓ, ⓕ   ② ⓒ, ⓕ, ⓖ

③ ⓐ, ⓑ, ⓒ   ④ ⓐ, ⓑ, ⓓ

⑤ ⓑ, ⓓ, ⓔ

📋 서술형

1 의문문으로 바꾸시오.

He read an interesting book yesterday.

→ _____?

2 질문에 알맞은 대답을 영어로 쓰시오.

Q: Isn't it in your backpack?

A: _____. (응, 없어.)

3 부가의문문을 쓰시오.

You will go back to LA to study,

_____?

4 괄호 안에서 알맞은 것을 고르시오.

I am hoping (travel / traveling / to travel) to Europe this summer.

5 간접목적어를 주어로 한 수동태 문장으로 만드시오.

Mom always gives me a lot of money.

→ _____.

6 두 문장을 한 문장으로 연결하시오. (접속사 and나 but, 관계대명사 that은 사용할 수 없음. 답은 두 가지 이상 기재 가능)

❶ • The boy likes Susie.
  • The boy is wearing red pants.

→ _____.

→ _____.

❷ • I visited a big shopping mall.
  • The shopping mall opened on May 16th.

→ _____.

→ _____.

7 두 문장의 의미가 같도록 빈칸에 알맞은 말을 쓰시오.

He came to America four years ago. And he still lives here.

= He _____ in America _____ four years.

8 어법상 옳지 <u>않은</u> 단어를 찾아 바르게 고쳐 쓰시오.

Yesterday, I met the famous singer in my house. I said to him, "I've heard of you many times and I'm very happy seeing you. What an honor to have you in my house! Maybe, my friends won't believe that I talked with the famous world star, Rain, in my house."

_____ → _____

9 2개의 시계를 비교하시오.

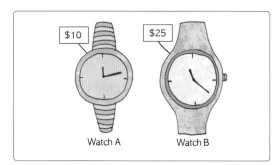

$10

$25

Watch A   Watch B

→ Watch A _____.

10 우리말에 맞게 주어진 단어를 사용해 문장을 완성하시오.

나는 건강해지려고 매일 조깅을 한다.
(every day / be healthy / go jogging)

→ I _____.

1 동사의 -ing형으로 옳지 <u>않은</u> 것은?

① buy - buying ② try - trying

③ smile - smiling ④ stop - stoping

⑤ solve - solving

2 단어의 관계가 나머지와 <u>다른</u> 것은?

① happy : happily

② love : lovely

③ beautiful : beautifully

④ kind : kindly

⑤ final : finally

3 질문과 대답으로 알맞지 <u>않은</u> 것은?

① Q: Is she tired?

A: Yes, she is.

② Q: Is this food hot?

A: No, it's not.

③ Q: Does he have a dog?

A: No, he doesn't.

④ Q: Does he like bread?

A: Yes, he do.

⑤ Q: Do you like English?

A: Yes, I do.

4 밑줄 친 부분의 쓰임이 나머지와 <u>다른</u> 것은?

① I believe <u>that</u> she is honest.

② I am sure <u>that</u> you will pass the exam.

③ My mother knows <u>that</u> I skipped the breakfast.

④ Tom says <u>that</u> he is very smart.

⑤ Don't you think <u>that</u> is right?

5 빈칸에 알맞은 것은? (2개)

> My mom _____ me practice the piano.

① had ② wanted ③ made

④ asked ⑤ told

6 빈칸에 들어갈 수 <u>없는</u> 것은?

> • They are happy _____ the result.
> • I need to go out _____ a change.
> • I can go fishing with you _____ July 1st.
> • I love fruit _____ bananas and apples.

① on ② like ③ with

④ in ⑤ for

7 빈칸에 들어갈 말이 나머지와 <u>다른</u> 것은?

① You should _____ quiet in the public place.

② She will _____ back soon.

③ The view will _____ very beautiful.

④ Let's _____ about it.

⑤ Don't _____ late for the party.

8 〈보기〉의 밑줄 친 to make와 같은 용법으로 쓰인 것

> ● 보기 ●
> His goal is to make friends at a new school.

① There is something to eat on the dinner table.
② I was excited to go to the concert.
③ Does she have a job to make money?
④ My mom wants me to get up early.
⑤ I need a pen to write with.

9 〈보기〉의 밑줄 친 've seen과 같은 용법으로 쓰인 것

> ● 보기 ●
> I've seen that movie many times.

① I have never visited my uncle's house.
② We have been together since 2010.
③ She has lived in Paris for 10 years.
④ He has gone to America to study English.
⑤ He has written five letters today.

10 두 문장의 뜻이 서로 같지 <u>않은</u> 것은?

① Susie is taller than Tom.
  → Tom is shorter than Susie.
② This car was more expensive than his car.
  → His car was cheaper than this car.
③ I am smarter than him.
  → He is as smart as I am.
④ Wealth is not more important than health.
  → Wealth is less important than health.
⑤ This house is bigger than your house.
  → Your house is smaller than this house.

11-12 어법상 옳은 것은?

11
① I'm very happy because of I can go to school.
② Is your children polite?
③ I amn't a student.
④ Are Tom and Susie from Paris?
⑤ There's wrong something with the TV.

12
① Her house doesn't near the school.
② Wear sunglasses, and you will look fashionably.
③ I am not in the first grade.
④ Read a lot of books, or you will become smarter.
⑤ Do you going to school today?

13 어법상 <u>어색한</u> 문장을 <u>모두</u> 고르면?

① He goes to the museum with his girlfriend.
② They live usually together and help each other.
③ They do the same thing every day.
④ Tom and Susie speak English well.
⑤ If I will get my allowance, I will buy a new computer.

14 어법상 옳은 것은?

① She can't not play the piano.

② I doesn't can come to school.

③ He can speaking Korean.

④ Mom can cooks Bulgogi very well.

⑤ Owls can see well at night.

15 ⓐ~ⓔ 중 어법상 옳지 <u>않은</u> 것은?

Today ⓐ <u>is</u> the first day of the school festival. Tom and Susie ⓑ <u>are</u> good ⓒ <u>friend</u>. ⓓ <u>They're</u> very happy and ⓔ <u>excited</u> here!

① ⓐ   ② ⓑ   ③ ⓒ   ④ ⓓ   ⑤ ⓔ

16-18 어법상 옳은 것을 <u>모두</u> 고르면?

16

ⓐ Pandas is animals.

ⓑ I'm afraid of speak in front of many people.

ⓒ My homework is there on the table.

ⓓ Hurry up, and you will late for school.

ⓔ Her shoes are on the floor.

ⓕ A butterfly is an insect.

ⓖ Look outside. There's no cloudy in the sky.

① ⓐ, ⓔ   ② ⓓ, ⓔ   ③ ⓔ, ⓕ

④ ⓑ, ⓒ, ⓓ   ⑤ ⓓ, ⓔ, ⓕ, ⓖ

17

ⓐ You spend much time playing soccer.

ⓑ He sends his mom to some beautiful flowers.

ⓒ Why are they copy your answers?

ⓓ Put the bottles in the red bin.

ⓔ My sister teaches English to me.

ⓕ Tom likes music and play the guitar.

ⓖ Does Susie and Henry go swimming every day?

① ⓐ, ⓓ, ⓔ   ② ⓐ, ⓓ, ⓕ   ③ ⓐ, ⓔ, ⓖ

④ ⓑ, ⓓ, ⓕ   ⑤ ⓔ, ⓕ, ⓖ

18

ⓐ Doesn't we go to the party?

ⓑ Susie doesn't usually sleep until late.

ⓒ How about meeting at the mall after lunch?

ⓓ My dream is became a famous actor.

ⓔ Does Mr. & Mrs. Kim go fishing on Sunday?

① ⓐ, ⓑ   ② ⓑ, ⓒ   ③ ⓒ, ⓓ

④ ⓐ, ⓒ, ⓔ   ⑤ ⓑ, ⓓ, ⓔ

19 다음 중 어법상 잘못된 것을 고르면?

A: Hi. ① <u>Are you from Korea?</u>

B: ② <u>No, you're not.</u> I'm from Japan.

A: Oh, I see. ③ <u>Is listening to music your favorite hobby?</u>

B: ④ <u>No, it's not.</u> ⑤ <u>Listening to music isn't my favorite hobby.</u> I like reading books.

A: Really? Reading books is my favorite, too.

20 ⓐ~ⓔ 중에서 문법적으로 옳은 것은?

ⓐ You smell and taste badly. ⓑ When birds try eat a bug, they realize that it has a terrible taste. They never want to try again. ⓒ Your special looks help birds to remember the terrible taste. ⓓ So, doesn't think badly about your looks. ⓔ Your looks is your good quality.

① ⓐ　　② ⓑ　　③ ⓒ　　④ ⓓ　　⑤ ⓔ

📋 서 술 형

1 부정문으로 바꾸어 쓰시오.

She plays the piano every day.

→ _____.

2 그림을 보고 주어진 단어를 사용하여 질문에 답하시오.

play / soccer

A: What are they doing?
B: _____.

---

3 주어진 단어를 바르게 배열하여 문장을 완성하시오.

He decided to take a taxi (arrive / on time / to).

→ He decided to take a taxi

_____.

4 관계대명사를 사용하여 한 문장으로 쓰시오.

Tom has a big house. + It is too big for him to live alone.

→ _____.

5 주어진 주어로 시작하는 문장으로 바르게 고쳐 쓰시오.

He wrote this poem.
→ This poem _____.

6 우리말에 맞게 영작하시오. (4단어)

수업 중에 말하지 마시오.

→ _____.

150

7 주어진 단어를 사용해 영작하시오.

> 너는 1주일 이내에 그 책들을 반납해야 한다. (8단어)

→ _____ .

8 주어진 문장을 감탄문으로 바꿔 쓰시오.

> It is a very interesting movie.

→ _____ !

9 주어진 단어를 사용해 영작하시오. (단어 형태 변경 가능)

> 나는 설거지를 잘해요.
> (am / wash the dishes / good / I / at)

→ _____ .

10 밑줄 친 부분을 현재완료를 사용해 영작하시오.

> I got a phone call from Susie just now. She said she couldn't come to my party. 왜냐하면 그녀는 3일 동안 죽 아팠대 (그리고 지금도 아프대).

→ Because _____

_____ .

1 단어의 관계가 나머지와 다른 것은?

① cookie - bread ② meal - dinner

③ color - black ④ instrument - drum

⑤ furniture - table

2 빈칸에 들어갈 말이 다른 것은?

① What _____ you reading?

② _____ you hungry?

③ How tall _____ you?

④ _____ you take an English lesson?

⑤ _____ you a student?

3 빈칸에 들어갈 알맞은 말은?

> You should take a shower before _____ to bed.

① went ② going ③ to go

④ go ⑤ having gone

4 대화의 빈칸에 들어갈 알맞은 것은?

> **A:** He likes music, _____?
> **B:** Yes, he does. He can play all kinds of instruments.

① aren't you ② doesn't he ③ does he

④ shall we ⑤ are you

5 〈보기〉의 밑줄 친 right와 같은 의미로 쓰인 문장은?

> ● 보기 ●
> He dropped it <u>right</u> on the roof!

① Is this the <u>right</u> way to the city hall?

② He was standing <u>right</u> behind her.

③ Keep on the <u>right</u> side of the road.

④ Put your <u>right</u> hand on the desk.

⑤ I hope we are doing the <u>right</u> thing.

6 빈칸에 들어갈 수 있는 단어 2개를 고르면?

> They saw Tom and Susie _____ at each other quietly.

① looked ② to look

③ looking ④ having looked

⑤ look

7 밑줄 친 부분 중 생략할 수 없는 것은?

① You can get advice <u>that</u> you need.

② Tom said <u>that</u> being on time is important.

③ Everyone believes <u>that</u> he is a great actor.

④ Don't say anything and choose the one <u>that</u> you want.

⑤ I don't think <u>that</u> book is yours.

8 ⓐ와 ⓑ에 들어갈 말을 바르게 나열한 것은?

> Tom has been the leader of our school band ⓐ_____ March.
> Susie took a picture ⓑ_____ me.

① for - to ② for - of

③ since - of ④ since - on

⑤ for - on

9 빈칸에 들어갈 순서로 알맞은 것은?

> - You can go to the grocery store and
>   _____ some vegetables.
> - My parents enjoy listening to music
>   and _____ books.

① to buy - reading   ② buy - reads
③ to buy - read   ④ buy - reading
⑤ buy - read

10 to leave와 그 쓰임이 <u>다른</u> 것은?

> I was excited <u>to leave</u>, but saying good
> bye to my friends was sad.

① I decided <u>to lose</u> weight.
② Did Tom go to America <u>to study</u>?
③ He practiced hard <u>to win</u> the game.
④ I was happy <u>to hear</u> that.
⑤ We tried hard, only <u>to fail</u> in the final
exams.

11-14 어법상 옳은 것은?

11
① Cats usually doesn't sleep on the bed.
② They can't play the soccer.
③ When the phone rang, we are all ready
to go shopping.
④ She's smiling because of she did well on
the test.
⑤ Susie cannot swim very well.

12
① My parents were shocking to find that I
would leave them.
② There is a boy looked at you.
③ Studying hard means that I have a
chance to go to a good college.
④ When I got home from school,
everybody has already gone to bed.
⑤ I wanted to know how your life was like
in America.

13
① Are you interested in have a party?
② Why don't you doing our homework
together?
③ Did you finding answers in the books?
④ How about going shopping today?
⑤ I'm looking forward to meet you!

14
① Does Tom and Susie is washing their
car?
② She often plays tennis with me in the
park.
③ I'm very pleased to meeting you.
④ They sometimes ride a bikes every
weekend.
⑤ My friend and I am cleaning the window.

15 어법상 옳지 <u>않은</u> 문장을 <u>모두</u> 고르시오.

① Tom and Henry are twins.

② My teachers are always kind to me.

③ Susie and Andy's school are around here.

④ His friends thought that some problems must solve by their leader.

⑤ Our teachers are so cool.

16 어법상 옳은 문장을 <u>2개</u> 고르면?

① He and I were very upset yesterday.

② Is Tom's friends surprised at the presents?

③ I didn't do well on the math test since I had a stomachache during the test.

④ Math and science are bored.

⑤ Minsu and Suji has lots of homework.

17 어법상 옳은 문장은?

① My family doesn't has breakfast.

② Does Tom and Susie go and see a doctor?

③ Teddy has not a banana.

④ What kind of sports does your brother like?

⑤ Does Henry listens to music?

18 다음 중 옳은 문장이 몇 개인지 고르시오.

- My father play soccer on Sundays.
- He play not soccer on Sundays.
- Study hard, and you will fail in the exam.
- He reads the textbook from cover to cover yesterday.
- Do your parents watch TV at night?
- I will going shopping after work.
- Susie and I am going to school.

① 1개   ② 2개   ③ 3개   ④ 4개   ⑤ 5개

19 밑줄 친 ⓐ~ⓔ 중 어법상 옳지 <u>않은</u> 것은?

I ⓐ <u>talk to my family a lot</u>, but I talk to my mother ⓑ <u>most</u>. I ⓒ <u>hardly see my father at home on weekdays</u> ⓓ <u>because</u> he comes home lately at night. I talk to him ⓔ <u>only on weekends</u>.

① ⓐ   ② ⓑ   ③ ⓒ   ④ ⓓ   ⑤ ⓔ

20 어법상 옳은 것은?

ⓐ "I'm so exciting!" said Tom. "Tomorrow is my first day of school. ⓑ <u>I can't wait to make friends and seeing new teachers.</u>" "School is not fun." said his sister, Susie. "You know what? Three years ago, I ⓒ <u>arrived</u> at school and ⓓ <u>enter</u> the classroom. ⓔ <u>There were no one</u> I knew."

① ⓐ   ② ⓑ   ③ ⓒ   ④ ⓓ   ⑤ ⓔ

📖 서 술 형

1 의문문으로 바꾸시오.

He takes a shower after playing soccer.

→ _____ _____

_____ a shower after playing

soccer?

2 우리말에 맞게 주어진 단어를 사용해 문장을 완성하시오.

> 햄버거가 서양 문화와 함께 한국으로 들어왔던
> 반면, 불고기는 우리 문화와 함께 다른 나라들로
> 전파되고 있다.
> (come into / while / spread, 동사의 과거
> 형과 현재진행형을 각 1회 사용)

→ _____ hamburger _____

_____ Korea _____

western culture, Bulgogi _____

_____ _____

_____ our culture.

3 표를 보고 키에 대해서 빈칸에 적절한 말을 쓰시오.

Name	Age	Height (cm)	weight (kg)
Tom	15	165	60
Susie	15	170	72
Henry	17	180	80

Henry is _____ of the three

students.

4 어법에 맞게 문장을 다시 쓰시오.

How good she speaks English!

→ _____ !

5 두 문장을 관계대명사를 이용해 한 문장으로 만드시오.

> • The food was very delicious.
> • My family loved it.

→ _____ .

6 단어를 바르게 배열하여 문장을 완성하시오.

> the sound / surprised / me / made

→ _____ .

7 ⓐ, ⓑ 중 그림과 일치하지 <u>않는</u> 문장의 기호를 쓰고 바르게 고쳐 쓰시오.

> ⓐ The bat is shorter than the umbrella.
> ⓑ The picture is larger than the
> window.

❶ 일치하지 않는 문장 기호: _____

❷ 바르게 고친 문장

_____ .

8 수동태로 바꾸시오.

I will fix the machine tomorrow.

→ The machine ＿＿＿＿＿＿ ＿＿＿＿＿＿

＿＿＿＿＿＿ ＿＿＿＿＿＿

＿＿＿＿＿＿ tomorrow.

9-10 Tom의 부모님이 외출할 때 남긴 쪽지를 보고 물음에 답하시오.

⟨해야 할 일⟩	⟨안 해도 될 일⟩
do the dishes	mop the floor

⟨조건⟩
· 모두 have to 표현을 활용할 것. (필요 시 적절하게 변형할 것)
· 완전한 영어 문장으로 작성할 것.

9 Tom이 해야 하는 일

＿＿＿＿＿＿＿＿＿＿＿＿＿＿＿＿＿.

10 Tom이 안 해도 될 일

＿＿＿＿＿＿＿＿＿＿＿＿＿＿＿＿＿.

1 두 단어의 관계가 나머지와 다른 것은?

① play - player   ② cook - cooker

③ dig - digger   ④ paint - painter

⑤ teach - teacher

2 빈칸에 들어갈 순서로 알맞은 것은?

- Today is the best day _____ my life.
- I walk _____ the park _____ my boyfriend.
- I take a piano lesson _____ school.

① in - after - with - to

② in - after - to - with

③ of - to - with - after

④ of - after - to - with

⑤ of - to - after - in

3 빈칸에 공통으로 들어가는 말끼리 짝지어진 것은?

ⓐ _____ she go to school on foot?

ⓑ _____ they learn English from him?

ⓒ _____ your friends take a picture well?

ⓓ _____ his mom practice every day?

ⓔ _____ her brother like horror movies?

① ⓐ, ⓒ, ⓓ   ② ⓐ, ⓒ, ⓔ

③ ⓐ, ⓓ, ⓔ   ④ ⓑ, ⓓ, ⓔ

⑤ ⓒ, ⓓ, ⓔ

4 밑줄 친 부분 중 동명사가 아닌 것은?

① She is looking forward to <u>meeting</u> him again.

② <u>Knowing</u> him, I decided to lose weight.

③ Let's keep <u>contacting</u> each other.

④ She doesn't feel like <u>having</u> dinner tonight.

⑤ Honestly, I am tired of <u>listening</u> to him.

5 ⓐ~ⓒ에 들어갈 말을 바르게 나열한 것은?

He solved the problems ⓐ_____.
There are ⓑ_____ other ways to approach them, if I think ⓒ_____ enough.

	ⓐ	ⓑ	ⓒ
①	differently	probably	hardly
②	different	probable	hard
③	different	probably	hardly
④	differently	probably	hard
⑤	differently	probable	hard

6 빈칸에 알맞은 것은?

_____ late. (늦지 마시오.)

① Never   ② Do   ③ Don't you

④ Don't   ⑤ Don't be

7 그림에 대한 설명으로 옳지 <u>않은</u> 것은?

① The ball is in the box.
② The book is on the desk.
③ The cat is in front of the door.
④ The dog is under the bed.
⑤ The cap is on the piano.

8 밑줄 친 부분의 쓰임이 같은 것은?

① People should keep the rules <u>like</u> waiting in line.
   What do the animals look <u>like</u>?
② <u>English</u> is spoken in many countries.
   He must be <u>English</u>, and I know it from his accent.
③ Turn <u>left</u>, and you will see the bank.
   I <u>left</u> my key in the car.
④ Susie asked her father <u>if</u> she can go to the party.
   They can come to my party <u>if</u> they want.
⑤ Tom believes <u>that</u> he will become successful.
   I think <u>that</u> student is the leader of the class.

9 밑줄 친 부분의 쓰임이 <u>다른</u> 것은?

① Some people don't like <u>to eat</u> alone.
② Mom always wants me <u>to study</u> hard.
③ All I want <u>to do</u> is to be successful.
④ I came here <u>to try</u> some new food.
⑤ <u>To be</u> on time at school is important.

10 글을 읽고 빈칸에 들어갈 내용을 순서대로 나열한 것은?

> Tom is taller than Mike, but he is shorter than Jack.

	ⓐ	ⓑ	ⓒ
①	Tom	Mike	Jack
②	Tom	Jack	Mike
③	Mike	Jack	Tom
④	Mike	Tom	Jack
⑤	Jack	Tom	Mike

11 어법상 옳은 문장은?

① Did your father surprised at the news?
② Are all the pets cute?
③ She and I were very excited at the show.
④ Making dinner are interesting.
⑤ My mother usually take a walk after lunch.

12-14 옳은 문장 2개를 고르시오.

12

① I felt sleep.

② My friends look friendly.

③ It has a short legs and a long tail.

④ She will can solve the problem.

⑤ They're having dinner at home.

13

① My parents don't very strict.

② I and Susie doesn't do our homework.

③ You don't need to worry about it.

④ John, or I is the famous star.

⑤ We aren't friends anymore.

14

① Will Susie goes to the concert?

② She is not lying in her room.

③ Why do you running?

④ My parents likes go fishing together.

⑤ They're not in the library.

15-16 다음 중 어법이 옳지 않은 것은?

15

① Is Tom in a debate club?

② Does your father work at the bank?

③ Their leader seemed to be looking for something.

④ Does he has any pets?

⑤ I had to pick it up when I first saw it.

16

> ⓐ I love traveling. I am not rich but ⓑ I try to save money to go to different places. Last year, I went to Japan for five days. ⓒ There is many countries that I plan to go to. ⓓ Traveling is exciting ⓔ because I can see many new things.

① ⓐ   ② ⓑ   ③ ⓒ   ④ ⓓ   ⑤ ⓔ

17 어법상 옳은 것을 모두 고른 것은?

> ⓐ Who is our new English teacher?
> ⓑ He isn't late for the work.
> ⓒ Is Henry a famous musician?
> ⓓ She is thirteen and good student.
> ⓔ Is Tom and Susie in the room?

① ⓐ, ⓑ, ⓒ   ② ⓐ, ⓒ, ⓓ

③ ⓑ, ⓒ, ⓓ   ④ ⓑ, ⓓ, ⓔ

⑤ ⓒ, ⓓ, ⓔ

18 밑줄 친 ⓐ~ⓔ 중 쓰임이 옳은 것은?

> **Tom:** Where ⓐ are our music classroom?
> **Susie:** It ⓑ has upstairs, Room 3.
> **Tom:** Who ⓒ are our music teacher?
> **Susie:** Ms. Lee. She looks nice.
> Tom and Susie ⓓ are already good friends. They ⓔ is very happy and excited here!

① ⓐ   ② ⓑ   ③ ⓒ   ④ ⓓ   ⑤ ⓔ

19 밑줄 친 ⓐ~ⓔ에서 형태가 옳지 <u>않은</u> 것을 <u>2개</u> 고르시오.

Every night before going to bed I keep a diary: I ⓐ <u>went</u> to the zoo with my friends. We ⓑ <u>seen</u> some monkeys hanging on the trees. They ⓒ <u>run</u> very fast and ⓓ <u>jumped</u> to other trees. They were smiling at us. They ⓔ <u>wanted</u> bananas.

① ⓐ   ② ⓑ   ③ ⓒ   ④ ⓓ   ⑤ ⓔ

20 어법상 옳지 <u>않은</u> 것을 고르면?

Henry: Hi, Jenny. ⓐ <u>You are from China, are you?</u>

Jenny: ⓑ <u>No, I am not.</u> I'm from Philippines.

Henry: Oh, I see. ⓒ <u>Is swimming your favorite hobby?</u>

Jenny: ⓓ <u>No, it's not.</u> ⓔ <u>Swimming isn't my favorite hobby.</u> I like to sing and dance.

Henry: Really? Singing and dancing is my favorite, too.

① ⓐ   ② ⓑ   ③ ⓒ   ④ ⓓ   ⑤ ⓔ

  서 술 형

1 괄호 안의 단어들을 사용하여 <u>현재진행형</u> 문장을 영작하시오.

❶ (study / library)

He _____.

❷ (take / English lesson)

They _____.

❸ (have / dinner)

I _____.

2 괄호 안의 단어를 바른 순서로 배열해 질문을 완성하시오.

A: _____?

(TV / many / there / shows / interesting / are / on)

B: Yes, there are.

3 두 문장을 관계대명사를 이용하여 한 문장으로 연결하시오.

- This is a book.
- It tells us many interesting stories.

→ _____.

4 두 문장을 동격을 이용해 한 문장으로 바꿔 쓰시오.

Lee Juil was a famous comedian. He showed a lot of interesting actions to audience.

→ _____

_____.

5 그림을 보고, 주어진 표현을 사용하여 준호에게 제안하는 말을 쓰시오.

why / stop / computer games / you / don't

→ _____

6 주어진 단어를 사용해 문장을 완성하시오.

그들은 무엇을 하고 있었니?
(doing / what / they / were)

→ _____ ?

7 같은 의미가 되도록 빈칸에 알맞은 말을 쓰시오.

William Shakespeare wrote many great plays.

= Many great plays _____

_____ _____ William Shakespeare.

8 주어진 단어를 사용해 문장을 완성하시오.

그녀의 눈은 별만큼 빛난다.
(bright / are as / star / as / a / eyes)

→ Her _____ .

9 문장을 각각 What과 How로 시작하는 감탄문으로 만드시오. (How 포함하여 5단어, What 포함하여 6단어로 쓸 것)

It is a very expensive car.

❶ What _____ !
❷ How _____ !

10 〈보기〉에서 알맞은 단어를 골라 어법에 맞게 고쳐 쓰시오. (주어진 단어는 한 번만 사용)

●━━ 보기 ━━●
taste / look / feel / sound

❶ I like pineapples. It _____ sour and sweet.
❷ They touched the sheepskin coat. It _____ smooth.

1 단어의 관계가 나머지와 다른 것을 고르시오.

① advise - advice   ② think - thought

③ ease - easy   ④ act - action

⑤ behave - behavior

2 밑줄 친 It의 쓰임이 다른 하나를 고르시오.

① It is Sunday.

② It is sunny and cool.

③ It is hard to learn English.

④ It is getting dark.

⑤ It is going to snow this weekend.

3 〈보기〉와 쓰임이 같은 것을 2개 고르면?

> ● 보기 ●
> I want a nice jacket to wear.

① Tom wants to be a teacher.

② I needed hot water to drink.

③ He exercises hard to pass the finals.

④ We are out of snacks to eat.

⑤ You have to do your best.

4 〈보기〉의 May와 같은 용법으로 쓰인 것은?

> ● 보기 ●
> May I go home now?

① He may be wrong.

② It may be sunny tomorrow.

③ They may be different.

④ The story may not be true.

⑤ You may take food from this basket.

5 밑줄 친 부분의 쓰임이 〈보기〉와 다른 것은?

> ● 보기 ●
> Her hobby is collecting coins.

① He enjoys reading a magazine.

② Thank you for inviting to your party.

③ Watering the plants is important.

④ Tom is good at playing the guitar.

⑤ She was dancing in front of many people.

6 빈칸에 들어갈 단어가 다른 것은?

① This food was made _____ him.

② Please be home _____ five.

③ This picture was taken _____ Mi-na.

④ Tom was loved _____ her.

⑤ The mountain was covered _____ snow.

7-8 ⓐ~ⓒ에 들어갈 말을 바르게 나열한 것은?

7

> I went to America two years ago with my family. We visited the Empire States Building, the Statue of Liberty, and did a lot of shopping in New York. Then we flew to Las Vegas. I was ⓐ_____ to find out that there ⓑ_____ many places to gamble. My parents enjoyed ⓒ_____. My father was happy to win some money.

	ⓐ	ⓑ	ⓒ
①	surprised	is	gambling
②	surprising	are	gambling
③	surprising	is	gambling
④	surprised	are	gambling
⑤	surprised	is	to gamble

8

> • She wrote a letter ⓐ_____ me.
> • May I ask a favor ⓑ_____ you?
> • I made a birthday card ⓒ_____ Tom.

	ⓐ	ⓑ	ⓒ
①	to	to	for
②	to	of	to
③	to	of	for
④	to	to	of
⑤	of	to	for

9 대화의 빈칸에 들어갈 말이 알맞게 짝지어진 것은?

> **A:** _____ are you doing?
> **B:** I'm baking some cookies.
> **A:** I didn't know that you can bake cookies. Can I try it?
> **B:** Sure. Go ahead. _____ is it?
> **A:** It tastes really good.

① When - Where   ② When - How
③ What - When   ④ What - How
⑤ How - What

10 밑줄 친 a beautiful을 '가장 아름다운'의 뜻으로 바르게 옮긴 것은?

> The children started singing a beautiful song.

① very beautiful   ② more beautiful
③ the more beautiful   ④ the most beautiful
⑤ the best beautiful

11 어법상 옳은 문장은?

① Tom is a my best friend.
② My mom is 42 year old.
③ Susie wears glass.
④ They are twins.
⑤ I drink often soda.

12 대화 중 어법에 맞는 문장은?

① A: You are very rich, wasn't it?
   B: Yes, I am.
② A: He doesn't have a car, does he?
   B: No, he didn't.
③ A: You can play the violin, can't you?
   B: Yes, I can.
④ A: You like English, do you?
   B: No, I don't.
⑤ A: Susie plays baseball now, isn't she?
   B: Yes, she does.

13 어법상 어색한 문장은?

① Mom makes the dog to carry her bag.
② I want my brother to hold my coat.
③ My mother doesn't let me watch TV at night.
④ My father had me fix his car.
⑤ She doesn't want to let her children eat sweets.

14 어법상 자연스러운 문장은?

① His voice sounds beautifully.
② You look palely. You should see a doctor.
③ They look very useful things.
④ You looked like very gorgeous in that dress.
⑤ You look like your mother when you say that.

15 어법상 <u>틀린</u> 문장은?

① My job is fixing a car.

② Thank you for helping me with this.

③ Get up early seems very difficult for him.

④ Is she interested in gardening?

⑤ You can't solve the problem without making mistakes.

18

① You need healthy something to eat.

② Tom and Susie was wearing a school uniform.

③ Do you remember when he left?

④ Were she baking just for fun?

⑤ We go shopping together yesterday.

16-18 어법상 옳은 문장은?

16

① He remembered lock the door.

② Thank you very much for make delicious food.

③ I'm going to going shopping with my boyfriend.

④ Why don't you turn off the TV and do your homework?

⑤ I turned off the water when I'm brushing my teeth.

19 문법적으로 맞는 문장을 <u>2개</u> 고르시오.

① I hate to eat the raw fish.

② They finished to painting a wall.

③ Would you mind to turn off the radio?

④ We started singing for Mom's birthday.

⑤ I expected passing the finals.

17

① Cats and dogs are friend.

② They were not very friendly to me.

③ Was you teacher disappointed with the news?

④ Are his sister pretty?

⑤ Watching TV are boring.

20 밑줄 친 문장 중 옳지 <u>않은</u> 것을 고르시오.

ⓐ <u>There are many different types of museums.</u> ⓑ <u>I enjoy to visit art museums</u> and ⓒ <u>seeing famous works of well known artists like Picasso.</u> ⓓ <u>I also like visiting history museums</u> ⓔ <u>because I can learn a lot about history.</u>

① ⓐ   ② ⓑ   ③ ⓒ   ④ ⓓ   ⑤ ⓔ

서술형

1 두 문장을 until을 사용해 한 문장으로 완성하시오.

- She found her ring.
- She looked for her ring.

→ _____ .

2 괄호 안에서 알맞은 단어를 고르시오.

❶ Have you ever (eat / ate / eaten / eating) Indian food?

❷ He gave some money to the person (sit / sat / sitting / sits) on the street.

3 밑줄 친 단어의 바른 형태를 쓰시오.

He threw the ball to the girl <u>wear</u> a red cap.

→ _____

4 문장에서 어법이 틀린 부분을 고쳐 다시 쓰시오.

❶ I was also afraid of be laughed at.
❷ If I will have a garden, I will make it beautifully.

❶ _____ .

❷ _____ .

5 다음 표를 보고 빈칸에 적절한 단어를 쓰시오.

Name	Age	Height (cm)	weight (kg)
Anna	14	160	55
Kevin	14	170	65
Sally	15	163	50

Kevin is _____ Anna.

(Age에 대해서)

6 어법이 옳지 <u>않은</u> 부분을 찾아 바르게 고쳐 쓰시오. (2개)

- His dad bought a new bike of him.
- His mom made him cookies.
- His sister wrote a congratulation card to him.
- His grandma gave pocket money for him.

❶ _____ .

❷ _____ .

7   주어진 단어를 사용해 문장을 완성하시오.

> 일부 사람들은 지구가 인간 활동에 의해 손상을
> 입고 있다고 말한다. (damage)

→ Some people say that the earth
_____ _____ _____ by human
activity.

8   관계대명사를 이용하여 주어진 두 문장을 한 문장으로
바꾸시오.

> I lost the umbrella. My mother gave it
> to me.

→ _____.

9-10 주어진 단어를 한 개씩 활용하여 우리말에 맞게 문
장을 완성하시오.

> live / feel / sound

9   모든 것이 거짓말처럼 들린다.

→ Everything _____.

10 그녀의 손은 따뜻하게 느껴졌다.

→ Her hands _____.

1 단어의 관계가 〈보기〉와 같은 것은?

> ● 보기 ●
> forget - remember

① always - sometimes
② happy - pleased
③ above - against
④ ask - answer
⑤ lost - missing

2 ⓐ에 들어갈 적절한 것은?

> A: Do I have to give a ticket to you?
> B: ⓐ_____

① No, you are.
② No, you don't.
③ No, you aren't.
④ No, you doesn't.
⑤ Yes, you do don't.

3 빈칸에 들어갈 적절한 표현은?

> Your final exam is just around the corner.
> You _____ study hard to get some
> good grades.

① should
② shouldn't
③ would
④ won't
⑤ don't have to

4 빈칸에 옳지 <u>않은</u> 것은?

> There are _____ on the table.

① three pencils
② many books
③ a bag
④ two rulers
⑤ two photo frames

5 빈칸에 들어갈 알맞은 관계대명사가 순서대로 나열된 것은?

> ● Tom is the last person _____ I can
>   believe.
> ● I have a pet dog _____ name is
>   Mong.

① who - that
② that - which
③ that - that
④ who - which
⑤ that - whose

6 〈보기〉의 밑줄 친 부분과 용법이 같은 것은?

> ● 보기 ●
> Susie <u>hasn't finished</u> it yet.

① I <u>have read</u> the book twice.
② She <u>has lived</u> in London for three years.
③ She <u>has lost</u> her bag.
④ They <u>have</u> always <u>visited</u> the kingdom.
⑤ He <u>has</u> just <u>done</u> working today.

7 의미가 <u>다른</u> 문장은?
① You should not bring your kids to the
   party.
② You don't have to bring your kids to the
   party.
③ You're not allowed to bring your kids to
   the party.
④ Don't bring your kids to the party.
⑤ You must not bring your kids to the
   party.

8 문장의 밑줄 친 부분의 쓰임이 다른 것은?

① You should focus on it <u>when</u> you study.
<u>When</u> I am tired, I go to bed early.

② It was raining <u>when</u> I came home.
I don't know <u>when</u> his birthday is.

③ <u>When</u> he becomes a student, he will study hard.
<u>When</u> she has free time, she usually reads a book.

④ <u>When</u> you use sharp tools, be careful.
Time went out so fast <u>when</u> I was busy.

⑤ <u>When</u> I was sick, I didn't eat anything.
Let me know <u>when</u> you have a problem.

9 괄호 안에서 알맞은 것을 고르시오.

My family holds a party every ⓐ (month / months). It ⓑ (is not / not is) big, but we have fun gathering together. Why don't you ⓒ (join / joining) us? You can be a party member, too.

	ⓐ	ⓑ	ⓒ
①	month	is not	join
②	months	is	notjoin
③	months	not is	joining
④	month	is not	joining
⑤	month	not is	joining

10 문장을 감탄문으로 바르게 바꾼 것은?

Tom is a very honest person.

① How Tom honest is!
② What honest Tom is!
③ How honest Tom student is!
④ What an honest person Tom is!
⑤ How a very honest person Tom is!

11 밑줄 친 쓰임이 어색한 것을 고르시오.

① I opened the box, <u>and</u> I took it out.
② He looks very rich <u>but</u> he is poor.
③ You have to buy oranges <u>or</u> lemons for this food.
④ He never had his own car, <u>but</u> he has one now.
⑤ His name is Tom <u>but</u> he is your roommate.

12 문법상 틀린 문장은?

① Tell me why you are here.
② I wonder there are places to buy food.
③ I want to know where you live now.
④ She wanted to know where to go.
⑤ What do you think of her?

13 문법상 옳은 문장은?

① This's not a stone.
② You're not a baby anymore.
③ The girl standing over there is't a new student.
④ I'm not short but my sister is small.
⑤ His mother and my father isn't cousins.

14-15 어법상 옳지 <u>않은</u> 것은?

14

① Susie plays computer games well.
② Tom go fishing with his father on Sundays.
③ She is not upset.
④ My mother reads a newspaper every morning.
⑤ What do you want to buy?

15

① There is a picture of me and my sister.
② My friends are very tall and strong.
③ He play soccer after school.
④ I'm a class leader.
⑤ Tom ran fast to catch the bus.

16-17 어법상 옳은 것은?

16

① He is in the third grade.
② Does he going to school?
③ My house doesn't near your house.
④ Ted and Sophia is very kind to me.
⑤ My sister isn't wash the dishes after dinner.

17

① Can Tom makes bread?
② He don't have any money.
③ My boyfriend doesn't like bread.
④ Do your father play golf?
⑤ Susie cans sing and dance well.

18-20 ⓐ~ⓔ 중 어법에 맞지 <u>않는</u> 것은?

18

A: Hey, Tom. ⓐ How are you?
B: Good. ⓑ I has an English class today. It's my favorite subject.
A: Oh, do you like languages?
B: ⓒ Yes. I do. ⓓ I take a Korean lesson on Sundays. What's your favorite subject?
A: I like Korean, too. ⓔ Let's study and practice together.
B: That sounds great!

① ⓐ　　② ⓑ　　③ ⓒ　　④ ⓓ　　⑤ ⓔ

19

I got to the meeting place ⓐ by subway and ⓑ it took me about an hour. There isn't any bus ⓒ that directly take me here from my house. ⓓ I was lucky to get here on time ⓔ because there was an accident on the road, and the traffic jam was really bad.

① ⓐ　　② ⓑ　　③ ⓒ　　④ ⓓ　　⑤ ⓔ

20

Jeju Island ⓐ is located in the southern part of Korea. You can take a plane ⓑ or a ship there. ⓒ It takes about one hour from here. You can see many palm trees and ⓓ strangely shaped volcanic rocks there. ⓔ It feels a foreign country.

① ⓐ　　② ⓑ　　③ ⓒ　　④ ⓓ　　⑤ ⓔ

서 술 형

1 빈칸에 적절한 말을 쓰시오.

_____ about the

writer is his age.

(그 작가에 관해 가장 놀라운 점은 그의 나이이다.)

2 문장을 수동태로 바꾸시오.

> My mother made this creative food
> with apples.

→ _____.

3 단어들을 이용하여 선생님이 학생들에게 할 수 있는 명령문을 <u>2개</u> 만드시오.

> wash / in class / quiet / your hands /
> before / be / lunch

❶ _____.

❷ _____.

4 주어진 단어들을 바르게 배열하여 완전한 문장을 완성하시오.

> excited / the / made / concert / them

→ _____.

5 밑줄 친 부분을 우리말에 맞게 알맞은 형태로 쓰시오.

> 오늘의 점심이 어제보다 더 맛있다.
> Today's lunch <u>delicious</u> yesterday's
> lunch.

→ _____

6 우리말을 영어로 옮기시오.

> 너는 그 책을 읽어 본 적 있니?

→ _____?

7 어법상 <u>틀린</u> 곳을 찾아 바르게 고쳐 쓰시오.

> **W:** Does you sister clean your house
> sometimes?
> **M:** Sure. She does housework because
> my mother makes her to do that.
> **W:** Really? What does she usually do?
> **M:** She mops the floor.

→ _____.

8 주어진 단어를 활용하여 우리말을 영어로 옮기시오.

> 내가 이 책을 읽는 데 약 5시간이 걸렸어.
> (it / take)

→ _____ .

9 문장을 읽고 **틀린** 부분을 바르게 고치시오.

❶ The Central Park in New York is one of the larger park in U.S.

→ _____ .

❷ I was been tired because I didn't slept well last night.

→ _____ .

10 밑줄 친 ⓐ~ⓔ를 과거형으로 바꾸시오.

> Two years ago, I ⓐ <u>buy</u> a smartphone. It ⓑ <u>doesn't</u> cost me anything because the phone company ⓒ <u>give</u> it to me for free. It usually costs much so I was happy that I didn't have to pay any money. People always ⓓ <u>use</u> mobile phones for many reasons. They ⓔ <u>take</u> care of their business or talked to friends on the phone.

ⓐ _____

ⓑ _____

ⓒ _____

ⓓ _____

ⓔ _____

1 빈칸에 공통으로 들어갈 말은?

- This is a private area. You _____ go in there.
- When you make a speech, you _____ see the script. It's a rule.
- You _____ eat this plant. It has poison.

① have to   ② must
③ cannot be   ④ don't have to
⑤ must not

2 빈칸에 들어갈 말이 알맞은 것은?

Put your one hand on the red line and _____ hand on the blue line.

① two   ② others
③ other   ④ the other
⑤ another

3 〈보기〉의 밑줄 친 것과 쓰임이 같은 것을 고르시오.

● 보기 ●
<u>When</u> the shop was about to close, there's nothing left.

① <u>When</u> will it begin to snow?
② <u>When</u> did you meet Tom?
③ <u>When</u> he finished doing his homework, his mom called him.
④ <u>When</u> is the party held?
⑤ <u>When</u> do you think he will come?

4 〈보기〉의 밑줄 친 if와 쓰임이 같은 것은?

● 보기 ●
I wonder <u>if</u> this project will succeed.

① <u>If</u> you know his phone number, please let me know.
② I'm not sure <u>if</u> Tom can sing well.
③ You can come in <u>if</u> you want.
④ <u>If</u> I were you, I would tell him honestly.
⑤ Can I go shopping with my friends <u>if</u> I finish doing homework?

5 재귀대명사가 들어간 문장 중 옳은 문장은?
① They enjoyed <u>theyselves</u>.
② Find out the truth <u>youself</u>.
③ Susie looked at <u>herself</u> in the mirror.
④ She fixed the toy <u>sheself</u>.
⑤ We wanted <u>ourself</u> to do better.

6 밑줄 친 to부정사의 명사적 용법 중 나머지와 <u>다른</u> 것은?
① I needed <u>to buy</u> red pants.
② His future goal is <u>to be</u> a teacher.
③ They want <u>to see</u> me now.
④ She decides <u>to learn</u> Korean.
⑤ They like <u>to take</u> a walk with their dog.

7 우리말에 맞게 빈칸에 들어갈 알맞은 말을 고르시오.

> 이 길로 가는 것은 위험하다.
> _____ is dangerous _____ this road.

① It - take
② This - take
③ It - to take
④ This - take to
⑤ The - to take

8 대화의 빈칸에 알맞은 문장은?

> **A:** Many people are studying in the library.
> **B:** _____

① You should not.
② You should talk so loud.
③ You should be talking so loud.
④ You should not talk so loud.
⑤ You should not talking so loud.

9 문장의 형식이 <u>다른</u> 하나를 고르시오.

① They found the concert exciting.
② My son call the toy BeBe.
③ Our family called the dog Pup.
④ The guitar made the song beautiful.
⑤ I believe that he will pass the exam.

10 빈칸에 들어갈 말을 바르게 나열한 것은?

> - She _____ to America to study three years ago.
> - We have known each other _____ three years.
> - Tom _____ this movie before.

① went - since - has seen
② has gone - since - has seen
③ has gone - for - saw
④ went - for - has seen
⑤ went - since - saw

11 관계대명사의 쓰임이 <u>다른</u> 하나는?

① That is the office <u>which</u> I used to work in.
② There is a cat <u>which</u> my family raised.
③ Tom is looking at the picture <u>which</u> you gave him.
④ The toy truck <u>which</u> is on the floor is my baby's.
⑤ The ring <u>which</u> he brought is expensive.

12 밑줄 친 부분을 생략할 수 있는 것은?

① He is the wise boy about <u>whom</u> they talked.
② I know the man <u>that</u> is standing at the gate.
③ She entered the house <u>whose</u> door was red.
④ He can't join the party <u>which</u> you hold.
⑤ He is the only friend <u>that</u> really understands her.

13 어법상 옳은 것은?

① My friend asks who is he.

② The runner ran quickly and quiet.

③ I want to know what did you do yesterday.

④ He knows when is Tom going to arrive.

⑤ The men will have fun and concentrate on this special project.

14 문장의 밑줄 친 부분이 옳지 않은 것은?

① Don't eat snacks <u>made</u> with too much butter.

② There is a <u>destroyed</u> playground next to my house.

③ The boy <u>run</u> with his dog is Tom.

④ The novel was <u>written</u> by my teacher.

⑤ They are <u>watching</u> TV.

15 어법상 옳은 것은?

① I had my mom cutted my hair.

② How often do you go fishing with your father?

③ Did he have you to do his task?

④ We don't have you copied the book.

⑤ My sister had me ran an errand sometimes.

16 어법이 옳지 <u>않은</u> 문장은?

① I can't make the kids have vegetables.

② I helped mom to set the table.

③ Don't ask me to come home early.

④ Look at the baby to smile at me.

⑤ They had a stranger take a picture of them.

17-19 어법상 옳은 문장을 <u>모두</u> 고른 것은?

17

ⓐ My daughter go to bed late at night.

ⓑ Tom learns English every weekends.

ⓒ My father often stays at home on Sundays.

ⓓ My children always study hard.

ⓔ We don't play basketball after school.

ⓕ Doctors works in a hospital.

① ⓐ, ⓒ, ⓓ   ② ⓑ, ⓒ, ⓕ

③ ⓒ, ⓓ, ⓔ   ④ ⓑ, ⓒ, ⓓ, ⓕ

⑤ ⓐ, ⓑ, ⓔ, ⓕ

18

ⓐ The musical is really exciting.

ⓑ Where is the couch in your room?

ⓒ Are your friend middle school students?

ⓓ Susie usually do her homework after dinner.

ⓔ Does your mom goes jogging every morning?

① ⓐ, ⓑ   ② ⓐ, ⓒ

③ ⓒ, ⓓ   ④ ⓐ, ⓒ, ⓔ

⑤ ⓑ, ⓓ, ⓔ

19

ⓐ I watched my computer to fix by him.

ⓑ He looks greatly when he exercises.

ⓒ Mr. Kim stopped smoking ten years ago.

ⓓ Buheung Middle school has been here for 1996.

ⓔ She looks friendly like our school's English teachers.

① ⓐ, ⓑ   ② ⓒ, ⓔ

③ ⓐ, ⓒ, ⓔ   ④ ⓒ, ⓓ, ⓔ

⑤ ⓐ, ⓑ, ⓒ, ⓓ

20 어법상 옳지 <u>않은</u> 것을 <u>2개</u> 고르면?

I meet new people every day ⓐ <u>because I am a hairdresser.</u> ⓑ <u>I usually enjoy meeting them,</u> but sometimes it can be hard ⓒ <u>because there is many strange people out there.</u> The other day, one of my customers came and I told her that ⓓ <u>it was not wise for her to have it permed.</u> Suddenly, she started ⓔ <u>yelling at me.</u>

① ⓐ   ② ⓑ   ③ ⓒ   ④ ⓓ   ⑤ ⓔ

📋 서 술 형

1 미술관 입구에 게시된 표지판 문구를 문장으로 완성하시오. (5단어 이상)

NO FOOD or DRINK.

→ We want you _____ inside.

2 지문을 읽고 질문에 완전한 문장으로 답하시오.

I am in the school music club. Our club members go to an orphanage every Sunday. If you want to join us, come to our office.

Q: When do the club members go to an orphanage?

A: _____.

3 괄호 안의 단어를 사용해 문장을 완성하시오.

I take a swimming lesson. (will / next year)

→ _____.

4 우리말 문장에 맞게 밑줄 친 단어를 바꾸어 문장을 다시 쓰시오.

치타가 말보다 더 빨리 달린다.

→ The cheetah runs <u>fast</u> than the horse.

→ _____.

5 관계대명사를 사용하여 같은 뜻을 갖도록 고쳐 쓰시오.

> I like these shoes, and my wife bought them for me yesterday.

→ _____.

6 그림 속 상황에 맞게 대화를 완성하시오.

A: My back hurts.

B: Make _____ _____

_____ _____ heavy

things.

(너는 무거운 것들을 들지 않도록 하렴.)

7 두 문장의 의미가 같도록 빈칸을 채우시오.

> • He began to solve the problems two hours ago.
> • He is still solving the problems.

→ He _____.

(8단어)

8 주어진 단어를 사용해 문장을 완성하시오.

> 나의 꿈은 세계를 여행하는 것이다.
> (around the world / is / traveling / my dream)

→ _____.

9 틀린 곳을 찾아 문장을 바르게 고치시오.

❶ He went to the bookstore buying some school textbooks.

→ _____.

❷ If you don't practice hard, you are fail in the finals.

→ _____.

10 ⓐ~ⓔ 중 어법상 어색한 곳의 기호를 적고 바르게 고쳐 완전한 영어 문장으로 쓰시오.

> Jane is a writer. ⓐ She lives in Boston City and is really into Korean culture. ⓑ She goes to Korean traditional villages, and watches Korean dramas. ⓒ These days, she enjoys making Korean food like Bibimbap and Galbitang. ⓓ It was difficult of her to learn to make those dishes. However, ⓔ Jane tells us about her first try cook Korean food.

❶ 기호: _____

바르게 고친 문장

_____.

❷ 기호: _____

바르게 고친 문장

_____.

1 밑줄 친 단어의 뜻이 서로 같은 것은?

① How do you <u>like</u> the food I made?
  She looks <u>like</u> her mom.
② My friend <u>made</u> me a birthday card.
  They sold everything and <u>made</u> 100,000
  won.
③ I forgot to <u>water</u> the plants.
  There is no <u>water</u> in the cup.
④ If you <u>miss</u> the first train, you'll be late
  for work.
  Don't <u>miss</u> the opportunity to get a job.
⑤ Please give me a <u>hand</u> with this box.
  Put your <u>hand</u> on the table.

2 밑줄 친 접속사가 적절한 것은?

① Eat breakfast, <u>or</u> you will be healthier.
② Protect trees, <u>and</u> birds will lose their
  homes.
③ Come home by six, <u>and</u> your mom will
  be angry.
④ Don't give up, <u>or</u> you can make it in your
  study.
⑤ Look at the sky at night, <u>and</u> you can
  guess tomorrow's weather.

3 빈칸에 들어갈 알맞은 말은?

| 나는 오늘 내 자전거를 도둑맞았다. |
| I had my bicycle _____ today. |

① steal   ② stealing
③ stole   ④ stolen
⑤ to steal

4 밑줄 친 to help와 쓰임이 같은 것끼리 짝지어진 것은?

| You can still volunteer <u>to help</u> him. |

| ⓐ You should study hard <u>to get</u> a good |
| grade. |
| ⓑ They were excited <u>to win</u> the game. |
| ⓒ It's time <u>to go</u> home and rest. |
| ⓓ I went to the pet shop <u>to buy</u> some |
| snacks for my dog. |
| ⓔ Mom wanted me <u>to set</u> the table. |

① ⓐ, ⓓ   ② ⓐ, ⓔ
③ ⓑ, ⓓ   ④ ⓐ, ⓓ, ⓔ
⑤ ⓑ, ⓒ, ⓓ

5 ⓐ~ⓒ에 들어갈 말을 바르게 나열한 것은?

| Friends are important because you |
| can share the joys and the sorrows |
| ⓐ _____ your life with each other. |
| When my friends bring good news |
| ⓑ _____ me, I am happy |
| ⓒ _____ them, and when they |
| share their sorrow, I try to be supportive |
| and be with them. |

① of - to - for   ② in - to - from
③ in - from - of   ④ with - out - in
⑤ of - out - from

6 빈칸에 들어갈 인칭대명사를 순서대로 나열한 것은?

> I have a sister. _____ name is Susie.
> I like _____ very much. She has
> birds and fish. They are very cute, so I
> like _____.

① She - her - they
② She - her - him
③ Her - her - them
④ Her - her - their
⑤ Her - her - theirs

7 〈보기〉의 May와 같은 용법으로 쓰인 것은?

> ● 보기 ●
> May we take a rest here?

① You may be wrong.
② It may be cloudy tomorrow.
③ He may be very honest.
④ The report may be mine.
⑤ You may listen to the radio when you
   study.

8 밑줄 친 it의 쓰임이 나머지와 다른 것은?

① It is in my pocket.
② It is rude to talk back to your mom.
③ It is easy to solve this problem.
④ It was difficult to say goodbye to you.
⑤ It is important to make a good decision.

9 밑줄 친 말이 어색한 것은?

① You should love yourself.
② She hid herself behind a car.
③ They are drawing itself in art class.
④ I myself grow the plants.
⑤ Henry looked at himself in the mirror.

10 〈보기〉의 밑줄 친 that과 쓰임이 같은 것은?

> ● 보기 ●
> I think that having breakfast is important.

① Look at that dog! It's so cute.
② I don't think you are that tall.
③ Where did you find that bag?
④ I am not that interested in music.
⑤ I believe that he will be a leader.

11 문법상 옳지 않은 문장은?

① Not eat too much junk food.
② Go swimming every day.
③ Go to bed early at night.
④ Lock the door when you leave.
⑤ Don't run around in the restaurant.

12-14 다음 문장 중 어법상 옳은 것은?

12
① How far does it take from here to your
   house?
② Look inside. There's a stranger.
③ Run fast, or you will late for work.
④ Susie has a big family. There is eight in
   her family.
⑤ Tom is quiet. He don't speak at all in
   class.

13
① I want to earn many money.
② Susie goes often to the concert.
③ My brother plays the soccer well.
④ Mom cleans the living room every
   Sundays.
⑤ My mother woke me up late.

14

① Susie will goes shopping this Friday.

② You not can swim in the sea at night.

③ Can Tom does his homework by himself?

④ You can't use something important.

⑤ They will hang out not again.

15 어법상 옳지 <u>않은</u> 부분은 <u>모두</u> 몇 개인가?

I spent time with my friends this weekends. We did many thing together. For example, Tom and I played computer games. Susie and Henry watch TV. Then we ride bikes together.

① 없음   ② 1개   ③ 2개

④ 3개   ⑤ 4개

16 ⓐ~ⓔ 중 어법상 옳은 문장은?

ⓐ I go often fishing with my father. ⓑ My dad and I sets up a tent. ⓒ we cook dinner with the fish we caught. ⓓ We sing song together. At night I look at the stars in the sky. ⓔ Sometimes I see fireflys.

① ⓐ   ② ⓑ   ③ ⓒ   ④ ⓓ   ⑤ ⓔ

17-19 어법상 옳은 문장을 <u>모두</u> 고른 것은?

17

ⓐ Tom feeding his cat.

ⓑ It rains a lot in summer.

ⓒ He was going to home.

ⓓ Are you running after me?

ⓔ It's sunny and warm outside.

ⓕ The men in the white suit is my uncles.

① ⓐ, ⓒ, ⓓ   ② ⓐ, ⓔ, ⓕ

③ ⓑ, ⓒ, ⓔ   ④ ⓑ, ⓓ, ⓔ

⑤ ⓒ, ⓓ, ⓕ

18

ⓐ What is he do?

ⓑ Susie love to go swimming.

ⓒ I am not waiting for him.

ⓓ She is lying in her bed.

ⓔ My family is having dinner at home.

ⓕ Our father stoped smoking for us.

① ⓐ, ⓒ, ⓓ   ② ⓑ, ⓒ, ⓕ

③ ⓑ, ⓓ, ⓔ   ④ ⓒ, ⓓ, ⓔ

⑤ ⓒ, ⓓ, ⓕ

19 어법상 옳은 문장은 모두 몇 개인가?

① They knew that she writes the novel.

② Mr. Kim whose father is the manager of a company helped me to get a job.

③ Tom was thirsty so that he drank a bottle of water.

④ Is it true that Jina got a perfect score on SAT essays?

⑤ Turn on the light so that we can see him.

⑥ Speak so loudly that they can hear you.

⑦ Do you know the woman that Tom is talking to?

① 2개   ② 3개   ③ 4개   ④ 5개   ⑤ 6개

20 어법상 옳지 <u>않은</u> 것은?

The small bird and the huge alligator help ① each other. The bird eats insects that ② bother in an alligator's mouth. The bird also warns the alligator ③ about enemies. The alligator gives ④ to the bird a safe place. When there is danger, the bird ⑤ hides on the back of the alligator.

📋 **서 술 형**

1 현재완료진행형 문장으로 고치시오.

He bakes some cookies in the kitchen.

→ He _____ some cookies in the kitchen.

2 〈보기〉의 세 문장을 한 문장으로 바꿀 때 빈칸에 적절한 말을 쓰시오. (형태 변경 가능)

● 보기 ●

Tom is younger than Henry.

Henry is older than Susie.

Tom is younger than Susie.

Susie is ⓐ _____ than Henry but ⓑ _____ than Tom.

ⓐ: _____   ⓑ: _____

3 주어진 단어를 사용해 영작하시오.

만약 내일 날씨가 좋다면, 나는 공원에 산책할 것이다.

(if / take a walk / park / fine)

→ _____.

4 주어진 단어를 사용해 영작하시오.

우리가 함께한지 1년이 되었다.

(for / been / year / have / we / a / together)

→ _____.

5 같은 의미가 되도록 빈칸에 알맞은 말을 쓰시오.

Is it okay If I take pictures in this natural science museum?

= Would you mind _____

_____ pictures in this natural science museum?

6-7 우리말에 맞게 주어진 단어를 사용해 문장을 완성하시오.

> who / which

6 그녀는 춤출 수 있는 인형을 원했다.

She wanted a doll _____

_____.

7 나는 의사가 된 동생이 한 명 있다.

I have a brother _____

_____.

8 〈보기〉의 표현을 사용해 특정 장소에 가려는 목적을 영작하시오.

> ● 보기 ●
> exercise / ride a bike / open a bank
> account / buy sneakers

❶ I go to a park _____.

❷ I go to a shopping mall

_____.

❸ I go to the bank _____.

❹ I go to a gym _____.

9 제시된 〈조건〉과 우리말에 맞게 영작하시오.

> 〈조건〉
> 1. once를 사용할 것.
> 2. 10단어로 쓸 것.
> 3. decide, give up를 사용할 것.

> 일단 그녀가 무엇인가를 살 결정을 하면, 그녀는 결코 포기하지 않는다.

→ _____.

10 우리말에 맞게 영작하시오.

A: How _____

_____?

(나의 엄마에 의해 요리된 불고기는 어땠어?)

B: It was _____

_____.

(그것은 지금까지 내가 먹어 본 가장 맛있는 음식이었어.)

1 밑줄 친 단어의 의미가 같은 것끼리 짝지어진 것은?

① His face <u>turned</u> pale when he heard the news.

The weather has <u>turned</u> cool.

② Because of hot weather, the milk <u>turned</u> bad.

You should <u>turn</u> right here.

③ Come on. It's my <u>turn</u>.

She <u>turned</u> red when she met his boyfriend.

④ Whose <u>turn</u> is it to make a speech?

<u>Turn</u> left at the second corner.

⑤ <u>Turn</u> right, and it's next to the bank.

Wait for your <u>turn</u> to get food.

2 감탄문 중 옳은 표현을 2개 고르면?

① What cute dog she is!

② How tall tree it is!

③ What boring movies they are!

④ How delicious the food is!

⑤ What shocking!

3 우리말로 바꿨을때, 영어로 바르게 표현한 것은?

> 만약 내게 이것 같은 연장이 있다면, 그것을 고칠 텐데.

① If I had a tool like this, I would fix that.

② If I had a tool like this, I will fix that.

③ If I had a tool like this, I fix that.

④ If I have a tool like this, I would fix that.

⑤ If I have a tool like this, I will have fixed that.

4 ⓐ와 ⓑ에 들어갈 말이 바르게 나열된 것은?

> I don't understand ⓐ_____ she is saying. But I should tell her that it's my point of view and that's ⓑ_____ I should take a rest.

① that - what

② that - how

③ what - how

④ how - why

⑤ what - why

5 〈보기〉의 문장과 의미가 같은 것은?

> ● 보기 ●
>
> She speaks so fast that I can't understand her.

① She speaks to fast too understand her.

② She speaks slow enough to understand her.

③ She speaks too fast for me to understand.

④ She speaks fast enough to understand.

⑤ She speaks very fast.

6 〈보기〉의 밑줄 친 who와 쓰임이 같은 것은?

> ● 보기 ●
>
> He was a famous musician <u>who</u> played in the orchestra.

① I know <u>who</u> he is.

② <u>Who</u> will be the leader in my class?

③ Tom asked me <u>who</u> is my favorite actor.

④ Susie is the girl <u>who</u> will be my partner.

⑤ He was not sure about <u>who</u> is coming here.

7 빈칸에 들어갈 알맞은 말은?

> Keep _____ until you finally make it.

① try
② trying
③ to try
④ tried
⑤ have trying

8 문장 중 의미가 <u>다른</u> 한 쌍은?

① You must not talk loud here.
   → You don't have to talk loud here.
② Mom is good at baking.
   → Mom can bake well.
③ My teacher always gives us much homework.
   → My teacher always gives much homework to us.
④ Will you buy me a new cellphone?
   → Will you buy a new cellphone for me?
⑤ Can you help me?
   → Can you give me a hand?

9 빈칸에 들어갈 말을 바르게 나열한 것을 고르시오.

> Yesterday, I went for a movie with my cousin, Tom. I think the movie was so _____. So I really enjoyed the movie. But Tom said, "I don't like the movie. I was so _____."

① exciting - bored
② interesting - boring
③ interesting - excited
④ excited - boring
⑤ interested - bored

10 ⓐ~ⓒ에 들어갈 말을 바르게 나열한 것은?

> Some of the elderly people were so happy that they even forgot ⓐ_____ their lunches. I was really ⓑ_____. I have never made so much money ⓒ_____.

① eaten - exciting - before
② to eat - exciting - ago
③ to eat - excited - before
④ eating - excited - ago
⑤ eating - exciting - yesterday

11 밑줄 친 관계대명사 중 <u>어색한</u> 것은?

① Do you know the student <u>whom</u> Jenny will teach?
② The concert <u>whom</u> I'm watching is very exciting.
③ Swimming is the only sport <u>that</u> I don't like.
④ Tell me about the book <u>that</u> you read yesterday.
⑤ I can't understand the picture <u>which</u> you painted.

12 어법상 가장 옳은 것은?

① If she ask me, I will help her.
② I will not go fishing if it rains tomorrow.
③ If you come to my party, I am so happy.
④ If she won't like red color, I will buy her a red dress.
⑤ It will take more than an hour if she will go by bus.

13-14 어법상 옳지 <u>않은</u> 것은?

13

① Susie is a good lawyer.

② There are many clothes in my closet.

③ I am not a good cook.

④ She and I usually goes to school together.

⑤ Do you remember me?

14

① When Galileo said the earth is round, people wanted to kill him.

② His eyes were saying that he didn't like the stranger.

③ They climbed higher so that they get a better view.

④ I hoped you would get well soon.

⑤ I'll never forget the day which I first met you on.

15 주어진 문장을 고친 부분이 <u>잘못된</u> 것을 고르시오.

① He and she is teachers.

  → He and she are teachers.

② This is my brother. It's eyes are big.

  → This is my brother. Its eyes are big.

③ Do they your brothers?

  → Are they your brothers?

④ She does not a doctor.

  → She is not a doctor.

⑤ These are my students. I love him very much.

  → These are my students. I love them very much.

16 어법상 어색한 문장을 <u>모두</u> 고르시오.

① Tom is practice hard now.

② Will you to the party today?

③ Is your sister writing an article?

④ Susie will visits my house next week.

⑤ The teacher won't give us homework on holiday.

17 어법상 옳지 <u>않은</u> 것은?

My favorite thing is this comedy movie. ① I made a small comedy movie with my friend, Susie ② She acted the scene, and I filmed the action. ③ This movie is about two friend. ④ They are very funny and smart. ⑤ Our comedy movie is so cool.

18 ⓐ~ⓔ 중 어법상 옳지 <u>않은</u> 것은?

Some people ⓐ <u>don't</u> like vegetables, but I ⓑ <u>like</u> vegetables a lot. I planted some vegetables in my garden. There ⓒ <u>are</u> carrots, tomatoes and broccoli in my garden. My children also ⓓ <u>love</u> to eat vegetables. How about you? Do you like vegetables, ⓔ <u>either</u>?

① ⓐ　　② ⓑ　　③ ⓒ　　④ ⓓ　　⑤ ⓔ

19 어법상 옳은 문장은?

① We perform a play for poor children in the orphanage.

② Tom became a eye doctor for people who has poor eyesight.

③ A top singer, Susie, teach music.

④ Henry doesn't write anything, but he have creative thinking.

⑤ We sings along with the students.

20 어법상 옳은 것을 <u>모두</u> 고르시오.

ⓐ I was made a key holder by him.

ⓑ A postcard sent to him from Italy by Mary.

ⓒ Many questions were asked of her by Tom.

ⓓ We were taught baseball by our P. E. teacher.

ⓔ A computer was given to him as a gift by his dad.

ⓕ An old car was bought to my brother by my mother.

① ⓐ, ⓑ, ⓔ   ② ⓐ, ⓒ, ⓓ

③ ⓑ, ⓒ, ⓕ   ④ ⓒ, ⓓ, ⓔ

⑤ ⓒ, ⓔ, ⓕ

📋 **서 술 형**

1 두 문장을 한 문장으로 바꿔 쓰시오.

My father hurried in the morning. He didn't want to be late for work.

= My father hurried in the morning

_____ _____

_____ _____ for work.

2 '너 화난 거 아니지, 그렇지?'라는 의미가 되도록 〈보기〉에서 골라 문장을 쓰시오.

보기
upset / is / was / are / you / not / do / does

→ _____ ?

3 주어진 두 문장을 같은 의미가 되도록 하나의 문장으로 쓰시오.

- She began to take a swimming lesson a year ago.
- She is still taking a swimming lesson.

→ _____ .

4 우리말에 맞게 밑줄 친 부분을 바꿔 전체 문장을 쓰시오.

가족이 일보다 더 중요하다.

→ Family is <u>important</u> work.

→ _____ .

5 밑줄 친 우리말을 영어로 쓰시오. (단, to를 꼭 사용할 것)

> 너는 <u>여름 방학 때 입을 수영복</u>이 필요하구나.

→ You need a _____

_____ .

6 틀린 표현 <u>2개</u>를 찾아 바르게 고쳐 쓰시오.

> If you will keep walking to use your phone on the street, you will be in trouble or accident.

❶ _____ → _____

❷ _____ → _____

7 관계대명사를 이용하여 두 문장을 연결하시오.

> • The shopping mall is huge.
> • It is near my house.

→ _____ .

8 5단어를 추가하여 밑줄 친 부분을 영어로 쓰시오.

로봇의 역할이 <u>점점 더 커지게 될 거야</u>. (big / get)

→ The role of the robot _____

_____ .

9 어법상 틀린 곳 <u>3개</u>를 찾아 바르게 고쳐 쓰시오.

> The most serious result of global warming would be the sea level rising because the ice in Greenland are melting. For the past 100 years, the sea level has rise about 23 centimeters, and the ice is melting faster than the past because warmer weather.

❶ _____ → _____

❷ _____ → _____

❸ _____ → _____

10 밑줄 친 부분을 주어로 하는 수동태 문장으로 바꿔 쓰시오.

❶ She gave <u>me</u> some cookies.

→ _____ .

❷ Father bought my brother <u>a new bicycle</u>.

→ _____ .

1 빈칸에 생략된 말로 가장 적절한 것은?

> I know _____ my dad hates animals but I want to raise a dog.

① whose　　② what　　③ who
④ that　　　⑤ which

2 다음 밑줄 친 -ing의 쓰임이 다른 하나는?

① I don't like <u>arguing</u> with you.
② Look at the people <u>fighting</u> over there.
③ The girl <u>standing</u> next to me is my sister.
④ He writes about people <u>raising</u> animals.
⑤ Who's that men <u>walking</u> down the street?

3 〈보기〉의 밑줄 친 부분과 용법이 같은 것은?

> ● 보기 ●
> <u>Have</u> you ever <u>made</u> a pancake?

① They <u>have lost</u> the tickets.
② She <u>has gone</u> to China.
③ We <u>have known</u> each other since I was 20.
④ I <u>have studied</u> it for three years.
⑤ She <u>has read</u> the novel many times.

4 우리말을 영어로 바르게 옮긴 것 2개는?

> 너는 나영이에게 전화할 필요가 없어.

① You should not call Nayoung.
② You must not call Nayoung.
③ You don't have to call Nayoung.
④ Do not call Nayoung.
⑤ You need not call Nayoung.

5 그림을 묘사한 것 중 어법상 가장 올바른 것은?

① Jason heard a phone ringing.
② Jane listened to a bird sung.
③ Allen saw a handsome man to run.
④ July smelled something have burn.
⑤ John saw a dog being smile at a cat.

6 주어진 말을 사용해 가주어 it구문에 맞게 쓴 문장은?

> exciting / a motorcycle / ride

① To ride is exciting motorcycle it.
② It is motorcycle to ride exciting.
③ It is exciting to ride a motorcycle.
④ To exciting ride it is motorcycle.
⑤ It is to ride exciting motorcycle.

7 〈보기〉에 쓰인 as의 의미와 같은 것을 2개 고르시오.

> ● 보기 ●
> He didn't go to the party <u>as</u> he was sick in bed.

① He has potential <u>as</u> a teacher.
② They invited him <u>as</u> a specialist.
③ <u>As</u> I didn't study hard, I couldn't pass the test.
④ He watched the TV show <u>as</u> he ate snacks.
⑤ <u>As</u> the train will start soon, you should hurry up.

8 〈보기〉의 밑줄 친 부분과 쓰임이 같은 것을 고르시오.

> ──────────────── 보기 ────
> The problem was difficult to solve.

① He needs something to eat.
② You should go to see a doctor.
③ To master English is not easy.
④ My goal is to become a lawyer.
⑤ The article was not easy to understand.

9 빈칸에 들어갈 수 없는 것 2개는?

> Do you want to _____ ?

① take a shower   ② playing games
③ watch the movie   ④ some cookies
⑤ drink some water

10 ⓐ~ⓒ에 들어갈 말을 바르게 나열한 것은?

> When the performance ⓐ _____,
> thousands of people in Carnegie Hall
> stood up and gave a big hand. The
> audience ⓑ _____ and happy. Jo Youngpil
> is one of the most famous singers in
> Korea. His music has given many people
> deep impression. Since he made a
> successful debut in Carnegie Hall in 1980,
> he ⓒ _____ for 35 years in Korea.

	ⓐ	ⓑ	ⓒ
①	has finished	were excited	has been singing
②	finished	were excited	is singing
③	finished	were exciting	has been singing
④	finishes	were exciting	is singing
⑤	finished	were excited	has been singing

11 문장 전환이 어색한 것 2개를 고르시오.

① Father gave Mom the ring.
  → Father gave the ring to Mom.
② He bought me a new computer.
  → He bought a new computer to me.
③ He was rude to talk like that to his mom.
  → It was rude for him to talk like that to his mom.
④ To learn a swimming skill is useful.
  → It is useful to learn a swimming skill.
⑤ To solve the case on your own is important.
  → It is important to solve the case on your own.

12 밑줄 부분이 옳은 것은?

① Mom told me clean my desk.
② Our math teacher told us solving the problems.
③ Susie asked me return her paper.
④ He wants me stopping playing games.
⑤ My sister asked me to help her with this.

13 어법상 옳은 것은?

① Shopping with friends makes me happy.
② A test result make my brother angry.
③ Baseball games make my dad exciting.
④ Washing the dishes make me carefully.
⑤ Too many homework make students tired.

14 문법상 옳지 <u>않은</u> 문장은?

① The story made me surprised.

② I had the repairman fix my computer.

③ He will make you tell the truth.

④ She will allow me go camping.

⑤ Exercising every day can make you feel healthy.

15 밑줄 친 부분이 옳은 문장을 고르시오.

① Tom is a <u>15-years-old</u> boy.

② The photo <u>took</u> by Henry.

③ I am <u>very bigger</u> than you.

④ This is the smallest animal <u>who</u> I have ever seen.

⑤ There are three flavors <u>which</u> I want to taste.

16 문법상 옳은 것 <u>3개</u>를 고르시오.

① That is a house to live in.

② You and your brother doesn't have to come home.

③ You need not spend too much time on games.

④ If it will be sunny tomorrow, I'll go fishing with you.

⑤ The child and the dog that live together are good friends.

17-18 다음 중 어법상 옳지 <u>않은</u> 문장은?

17

① I usually get up early in the morning to go to school. ② But I will sleep until my mom wake up me tomorrow because tomorrow is Saturday. ③ I always spend my time at my friend's house on Saturday. ④ I can play games and go shopping with my friend. ⑤ It is very fun.

18

① I had a rabbit when I was young. ② My parents got him at a pet shop. ③ I took care of him by feeding him carrots, ④ which was his favorite. I also cleaned his cage every day. He was important to me ⑤ because he was my first pet.

19 형태가 바르지 <u>않은</u> 것은?

ⓐ I am not good at cooking. ⓑ I have been living alone for a long time, ⓒ but never had any chance to learn how to cook properly. ⓓ My mother is a very good cook, so I call her when I need cooking advice, ⓔ but I don't think that I do talented in cooking.

① ⓐ ② ⓑ ③ ⓒ ④ ⓓ ⑤ ⓔ

20 밑줄 친 @~ⓔ 중 옳은 문장은 <u>모두</u> 몇 개인가? ?

> @ Last year, all the family members on my mother's side gather for my grandmother's birthday. ⓑ We went to a buffet restaurant and have a family party. ⓒ We enjoyed many foods. ⓓ It was nice to see everyone ⓔ and to celebrate my grandmother's birthday together.

① 1개　② 2개　③ 3개　④ 4개　⑤ 5개

서 술 형

1 괄호 안의 말을 바르게 배열하여 문장을 완성하시오.

Taking a warm bath (me / feel / made / relaxed).

→ Taking a warm bath _____.

2 우리말에 맞게 빈칸에 한 단어씩 써서 문장을 완성하시오.

> 빨리 달려가. 그러면 마지막 기차를 잡을 수 있을 거야.
> ①_____ fast, ②_____ you'll catch the last train.

❶ _____　　❷ _____

3 단어를 바르게 배열하여 감탄문을 만드시오.

> kind / stranger / the / is

→ How _____ _____ _____
_____!

4 주어진 두 문장을 관계대명사를 사용하여 하나의 문장으로 완성하시오.

> • Our club members got the first prize in a debate competition.
> • They talked well on the topic.

→ _____
_____.

5 두 문장의 의미가 같아지도록 문장을 완성하시오.

❶ He was told the story by his mom.

→ His mom _____.

❷ Susie takes care of the birds.

→ The birds _____ by Susie.

6 두 문장을 동격을 이용해 한 문장으로 바꿔 쓰시오.

Jun is my best friend. He loves playing computer games very much.

→ _____.

7 문장에서 <u>어색한 부분</u>을 찾아 바르게 고쳐 쓰시오.

❶ You are happy, isn't it?

_____ → _____

❷ She liked ice cream, doesn't he?

_____ → _____

❸ Let's go shopping to the shop, will you?

_____ → _____

8 어법상 <u>틀린</u> 문장을 <u>2개</u> 골라 기호를 쓰고 그것을 바르게 고쳐 쓰시오.

> ⓐ My brother had me do his homework.
> ⓑ I saw Susie dancing on the stage.
> ⓒ My baby made this toy broke.
> ⓓ She listened to her name called.
> ⓔ I got the man carry my backpack.
> ⓕ The teacher helped me find the answer.

_____

_____

9-10 물음에 답하시오.

Susie	Tom
나이: 20	나이: 24
키: 170 cm	키: 165 cm
몸무게: 50 kg	몸무게: 65 kg

> young / old / tall / short
> heavy / popular

9 상자 속 단어를 참고해 Susie를 주어로 Tom과 나이를 비교하는 문장을 만드시오.

Susie is _____.

10 상자 속 단어를 참고해 Tom을 주어로 Susie의 키와 몸무게를 비교하는 문장 <u>2개</u>를 만드시오.

❶ _____.

❷ _____.

chapter

07

최신 신경향 기출

서 술 형

100

최신 신경향 기출 **서술형 100제**

chapter 01

1　주어를 G. Dragon으로 바꾸고 의문문으로 쓰시오.

I sing very well.

→ _____?

2　문장을 부정문으로 바꾸어 쓰시오.

My mother teaches English.

→ _____.

3　어법상 어색한 문장 2개를 찾아 바르게 고치시오.

Hi, I am Tom. I have a pet dog. She
name is Happy. We is good friends.

❶ _____.

　→ _____.

❷ _____.

　→ _____.

4　우리말에 맞게 문장을 완성하시오.

그것은 얼마나 아름다운 그림인가!

_____ _____ _____

_____ _____ _____!

5　주어진 단어를 사용해 문장을 완성하시오.

네 가방을 오늘만 빌릴 수 있을까?

→ _____?

(bag / I / today / your / borrow / just /
can / for)

6　괄호 안 단어를 활용해 B의 제안을 완성하시오.

A: I want to speak English well.
B: Why don't you _____?
　(talk / in English / your friends / to)
A: That's a good idea!

→ _____

7　다음과 같이 질문하는 친구에게 할 조언을 빈칸을 채워
완성하시오.

What do you think is the best way to
make friends?

Listen to your friends, _____ you
will make friends.

8　그림을 보고 친구에게 '금지'를 나타내는 부정 명령문을
쓰시오.

→ _____ in the classroom.

9 〈보기〉를 참조하여 틀린 부분을 찾아 2개의 문장을 다시 쓰시오. (제시된 단어를 사용할 것)

> ● 보기 ●
> • Birds fly in the ground.
> → Birds don't fly in the ground. They fly in the air.

> in the sea / in the ground / in the air

A fish swims in the ground.

→ _____ .

→ _____ .

10-11 어법에 어긋난 두 곳을 찾아 고쳐 쓰시오. (각각 한 단어로 쓸 것)

10

> It's late fall here. It's get colder day by day. The leaf are turning yellow, red and brown. My favorite season is summer because I love going camping.

❶ _____ → _____

❷ _____ → _____

11

> It's the second day outside the school. We enjoy our time. In the evening all of us come to a big room. It is full of student. Then, a girl with brown hair cry and some teachers run to her. Teachers look after the students.

❶ _____ → _____

❷ _____ → _____

---

12 어법상 틀린 문장을 2개 찾아 틀린 부분만 바르게 고치시오.

> ⓐ Does Mr. & Mrs. Kim go to church every Sunday?
> ⓑ Jenny enjoys listening to music.
> ⓒ I didn't answer the phone when I heard the ring.
> ⓓ Are you interested in dancing?
> ⓔ Are they love each other?

❶ _____ → _____

❷ _____ → _____

---

13 어법상 틀린 문장을 3개 찾아 틀린 부분만 바르게 고치시오.

> ⓐ What did you do last weekend?
> ⓑ This is my brother and her eyes are big.
> ⓒ She becomes sick because of the dirty air.
> ⓓ Do you like play computer games?
> ⓔ He doesn't gets up early on Sundays.
> ⓕ Do you have any special plans for summer vacation?

❶ _____ → _____

❷ _____ → _____

❸ _____ → _____

14 그림을 보고 어법에 맞게 ⓐ~ⓓ에 알맞은 말을 쓰시오.

❶ Kelly shows Thomas ⓐ_____

_____. (2단어) He thinks that it

is wonderful.

❷ Ms. Lee reads ⓑ_____

a book (2단어). She thinks that

ⓒ _____. (4단어)

15 표를 보고 단어를 자유롭게 연결하여 긍정문, 부정문, 의문문 형태의 완전한 문장을 만드시오. (단, be동사는 주어에 맞게 바꿀 것)

not	be	Korea
from	Korea	be
Korea	they	be

❶ 긍정문

_____.

❷ 부정문

_____.

❸ 의문문

_____?

chapter 02

16 〈보기〉를 참조하여 그림을 묘사하는 영어 문장을 5개의 단어로 쓰시오. (현재진행형)

→ _____.

17 문장을 be going to를 사용해 미래의 뜻이 되도록 쓰시오.

She sings her favorite songs.

→ _____.

18 우리말에 맞게 영작하시오.

나는 거기에서 많은 흥미 있는 것들을 볼 거야.
(be going to / lots of 사용)

→ _____.

19 어법상 어색한 부분을 찾아 고쳐 전체 문장을 쓰시오.

Gongmin was the captain of our baseball
team since January.

→ _____

_____.

20 주어진 단어로 시작하여 같은 뜻이 되게 쓰시오.

He teaches us English.

→ English _____.

→ We _____.

21 제시된 〈조건〉에 맞게 영어로 바르게 쓰시오.

〈조건〉
1. 9단어로 쓸 것.
2. an interesting story를 주어로 하는 수동태로 바꿀 것.

He told us an interesting story.

→ _____.

22 '그녀는 나만큼 나이가 들어야 해요.'를 영어로 쓰시오.
(8단어, as / has를 이용)

→ _____.

23 어법상 틀린 부분을 3개 찾아 바르게 고치시오.

Jane bought some cookies and a scarf
on the Internet. The cookies smelled
well and tasted deliciously. The scarf felt
soft. Jane looked happily.

❶ _____ → _____

❷ _____ → _____

❸ _____ → _____

24 어법상 틀린 부분을 2개 찾아 바르게 고치시오.

Here are some safety rules. First, don't
use your cellphone when you walk on
the street. You may fall down and get
injured. Second, don't jaywalk even if
you are busy. You may hit by a car. Third,
when you ride a bike, wearing a helmet
will protect you from a dangerous
situation. These rules will make you
safely.   *jaywalk 무단횡단하다

❶ _____ → _____

❷ _____ → _____

25 밑줄친 동사를 문맥에 맞게 고치시오.

In 1979, he <u>give</u> the Magsaysay Award,
known as the Asian Nobel Prize.

_____ → _____

26 주어진 단어를 사용해 문장을 완성하시오. (형태 변경 가능)

너 새로 생긴 미술관 가 본 적 있니?
(the new art museum)

→ Have _____?

27 그림에서 두 사람이 각각 무엇을 하고 있는지 문장을 완성하시오.

→ Ben is _____.

→ Kate is _____.

28 어법상 <u>틀린</u> 부분을 <u>2개</u> 찾아 바르게 고치시오.

Yesterday I visited a museum that opened last month. At the museum, I saw a vase which looked for a bird. A woman was explaining something special about the vase. A group of people who were wearing the same uniform was listening to her.

❶ _____ → _____

❷ _____ → _____

29 우리말에 맞게 문장을 완성하시오.

Tom은 14살 때부터 H 중학교에서 공부하고 있다.

→ Tom _____ at H Middle School since he was 14.

30 어법상 <u>틀린</u> 부분을 <u>2개</u> 찾아 바르게 고치시오.

Boys and girls! I believe I should be the president of Songpa Middle School for our future. If I will become the school president, I will make you happily. I can make our school full of hope. Make the right choice and vote me as your school president.

❶ _____ → _____

❷ _____ → _____

31 밑줄 친 부분을 영작하시오.

<u>우리가 초등학교를 졸업한 그날 이후로 나는 그녀를 결코 본 적이 없다.</u> (6단어로)

→ I have never seen her _____

_____.

32 어법상 <u>틀린</u> 부분을 <u>3개</u> 찾아 바르게 고치시오.

Hippo looked for his eye. He dug at the river bottom. The river became very muddy. Poor Hippo couldn't found his eye. Hippo saw Crocodile and asked for his help. Crocodile said, "You'll find your eye. Just wait." But Hippo dug and dug. He grew tired and stop digging. After a while, the river became clearly again. Hippo could see the river bottom.

❶ _____ → _____

❷ _____ → _____

❸ _____ → _____

33 밑줄 친 listen의 단어 형태를 바르게 고쳐 쓰시오.

Jinsu is not all ears. It means that he is not a good listener. He is bad at <u>listen</u> to other people.

→ _____

34 〈보기〉와 의미가 같도록 빈칸을 채우시오.

> • 보기
> Yong enjoys reading books.

→ Yong thinks that _____

_____ is fun.

35 주어진 단어를 사용해 문장을 완성하시오.

그는 가지고 쓸 펜이 하나 있나요?

→ Does _____?
(write)

36 주어진 단어를 활용하여 '시도해 보지도 않고 절대 포기하지 말아라'를 쓰시오. (5~6단어 사용, 형태 변형 가능)

→ _____.

(give / try / never)

37 사역동사 make를 사용하여 영작하시오.

아버지께서 나에게 아버지의 컴퓨터를 고치라고 시키셨어.

→ My father _____ me fix

_____.

38 우리말에 맞게 문장을 완성하시오.

너는 이 젓가락을 어떻게 사용해야 하는지 아니?

→ Do you know _____

_____ _____ these

chopsticks?

39 그림과 같은 의미가 되게 문장을 완성하시오.

→ Bonnie wants Jake not _____

_____.

→ Narah wants Henry _____

_____.

40-42 주어진 단어를 사용해 문장을 완성하시오.

40

그가 영어로 책을 쓰는 것은 쉬운 일이 아닐지도 모른다.
(a book / for / to / in / write / him / English)

→ It may not be easy _____

_____.

41

> 앉을 의자를 하나 찾아 봅시다. (sit)

→ Let's _____ .

42

> 우리는 학교에서 휴대전화로 게임하면서 시간을
> 보내서는 안 된다.
> (should / our / spend, 10단어)

→ We _____

_____ at

school.

43 괄호 안에 주어진 동사를 문맥에 맞게 알맞은 형태로 바
꾸어 쓰시오.

❶ Jane is good at _____(sing) as

well as _____(dance).

❷ Tom enjoys not only _____(cycle)

but also _____(car race).

44 그림을 보고 내가 할 일에 대한 문장을 주어진 동사를
이용해 완성하시오.

→ I will have my brother _____

_____ _____ . (repair)

45 〈보기〉에서 필요한 단어를 골라 영작하시오.

> ● 보기 ●
> she / too / so / is / that / young / can / a
> car / drive / to

그녀는 운전을 하기에 너무 어리다. (그녀는 너무 어려
서 운전을 할 수 없다.)

→ _____ .

46 주어진 단어를 사용해 문장을 완성하시오. (주어진 단어
는 한 번씩만 사용하되 모두 사용할 것)

> 너는 다시는 속이지 않겠다고 약속해야 한다.
> (not / promise / cheat again / to / should)

→ You _____ .

47 주어진 단어를 사용해 문장을 완성하시오.

> 학생들은 영어 공부하는 것을 꺼려하면 안 된다.
> (mind)

→ The students _____ .

48 같은 의미가 되도록 다음 빈칸을 채우시오.

❶ I just hope to meet a famous
Hollywood star.

→ My dream _____

_____ .

❷ We are going to go fishing tomorrow.

→ Our plan _____

_____ .

49 사역동사 have를 사용해 밑줄 친 문장을 영작하시오.

> 어머니께서 아버지에게 세탁기를 고치라고 시키셨어. (the washing machine / repair)

→ Mother _____

_____ .

50 두 문장을 so that을 이용하여 한 문장으로 연결하여 쓰시오.

> - I stopped talking on the phone.
> - People in the library could study.

→ I stopped talking on the phone

_____ .

51 어법상 어색한 곳을 찾아 고쳐 쓰시오.

❶ My father made me cleaning his car.

_____ → _____

❷ She was very satisfied by the present.

_____ → _____

52 어법상 옳지 않은 부분을 바르게 고쳐 쓰시오.

❶ He chose overcoming his limitations by keep doing his best.

_____ → _____

_____ → _____

❷ He refused to give up master daily tasks.

_____ → _____

53 어색한 문장을 찾아 번호를 적고, 바르게 고쳐 쓰시오.

> ① Juyoung is a middle school student. ② Her school starts on March 2nd. ③ Juyoung's family goes to hiking once a month. ④ There are one more event in March. ⑤ It is father's birthday on the 25th.

→ _____ .

→ _____ .

54 어법상 옳지 않은 것을 찾아 바르게 고치고 틀린 이유를 쓰시오.

> ⓐ It'll be nice to ride a roller coaster and have fun.
> ⓑ My mom had me do the dishes.
> ⓒ Jason watches his friends plays basketball.

❶ 번호 _____

❷ 틀린 부분 → 바른 형태

_____ → _____

❸ 어법상 바르지 않은 이유

_____

55 틀린 문장을 <u>2개</u> 찾아 바르게 고쳐 쓰시오.

> ⓐ She enjoys to learn foreign languages.
> ⓑ He hopes to visit his uncle during the vacation.
> ⓒ They avoided getting into trouble with their friends.
> ⓓ I just finished to read an English poem.
> ⓔ He expects to make many experiences at his new office.

❶ _____ → _____

❷ _____ → _____

56 밑줄 친 부분 중 옳지 <u>않은</u> 것을 <u>3개</u> 찾아 바르게 고쳐 쓰시오.

> Erin, my little sister had her arm <u>broke</u> yesterday. So she had his arm <u>examined</u> at the hospital. But she was <u>worried</u> about her car more than her arm. So, my dad <u>had</u> a repairman <u>fixed</u> her car. Erin also wanted to have it <u>painting</u> to look like a new one.

❶ _____ → _____

❷ _____ → _____

❸ _____ → _____

chapter 01

57 우리말에 맞게 문장을 완성하시오.

→ The door opened _____.
(문이 저절로 열렸다.)

58 ⓐ와 ⓑ를 바르게 연결하여 〈보기〉와 같은 형태의 문장 <u>2개</u>를 만드시오.

• 보기 •

> Because it was a little dark outside, I didn't go out.

> ⓐ
> it works well
> he helps other people
> you don't have to go tomorrow
> many people are playing in the park

> ⓑ
> it is sunny
> he is poor
> you are not ready
> the radio is very old

❶ _____.

❷ _____.

59-60 우리말에 맞게 문장을 완성하시오.

59

> Alice 뿐만 아니라 James도 미국 출신이다.

→ _____ as well as _____

_____ from America.

60

> 내 친구들 중 몇 명은 Sydney에 살고 있다.

→ _____ .

61 두 문장을 both 또는 either를 이용하여 한 문장으로 바꿀 때 빈칸에 알맞은 말을 쓰시오.

❶ She was thirsty. She was hungry.

→ She was _____ .

❷ She would like to eat a pizza and a cake. But she can't eat both of them at the same time.

→ She can _____ .

62 우리말에 맞게 문장을 완성하시오.

> 만일 내일 그녀가 파티에 오지 않으면, 난 슬플 거야.

→ _____ to the party tomorrow, I will be sad.

63-64 관계대명사를 사용해 두 문장을 한 문장으로 쓰시오.

63

> • The teacher is very famous.
> • All the students like him.

→ _____ .

64

> • The cats are now four years old.
> • I raised them in my backyard.

→ _____

_____ .

65 관계대명사 that이 생략된 부분 두 군데를 찾아 표시하시오.

> Choose any place you want and plant any vegetables you like.

66 관계대명사와 주어진 단어를 사용해 문장을 완성하시오.

> ● 보기 ●
> 옆집 사는 그 남자는 친절하다.
> (live / the / friendly / man / next / door / be)

→ _____ .
　　(8단어, 형태 변화 가능)

67 주어진 단어와 관계대명사를 사용해 영작하시오.
(Juliet 제외 9단어)

> Juliet은 Romeo와 사랑에 빠진 그 소녀입니다.
> (fall in love with)

→ Juliet _____ .

68 우리말에 맞게 문장을 완성하시오.

> 그의 계획에는 중요한 무언가가 있다.

→ There is _____ _____ in his plan.

69 수동태를 사용해 문장을 완성하시오.

> A: This princess doll is a present. I will give it to my girlfriend.
> B: Excuse me?
> A: This princess doll _____.
> B: I envy your girlfriend who will get the princess doll.

→ _____

70 두 문장을 한 문장으로 쓰시오. (and 사용 불가)

> • This is the gym.
> • I often exercise at the gym.

→ _____.

71 주어진 단어를 사용해 문장을 완성하시오. (단어 추가, 변형 및 중복 사용 가능)

> 나는 매우 궁금해져서 그 문자 메시지들을 읽기로 결심했다.
> (so / that / the text messages / curious)

→ I _____
_____.

chapter 05

72 두 문장에 공통으로 들어갈 단어를 쓰시오.

> • Mina is _____ing plants with her family.
> • Jason is drinking _____.

→ _____

73 그림을 보고 해당 주어의 위치를 설명하는 영어 문장을 완성하시오.

❶ A table is _____.
(5단어)

❷ Two dogs are _____.
(3단어)

74-75 우리말에 맞게 문장을 완성하시오.

74

> 고성에서 Tom의 가족은 양파와 토마토 같은 채소를 기른다. (onion and tomato: 복수형 사용)

→ In Gosung, _____
_____.

75

> 감기가 들면, 물을 많이 마셔라. (lots of)

→ When you _____.

76 자연스럽지 <u>않은</u> 것을 찾아 고쳐 쓰시오.

> **A:** Are you still looking ⓐ <u>at</u> the club activities homepage? Do you have any clubs ⓑ <u>in</u> mind?
> **B:** Yes. I'm thinking ⓒ <u>about</u> joining the dance club this year.
> **A:** Shall we watch those clubs' sites then?
> **B:** Sure.
>
> *Welcome ⓓ to our sites.*
> *Are you interested ⓔ from dancing?*

→ _____

77 그림을 보고, 예시와 같이 동물의 위치를 묘사하시오.

(예시) About the cat:
　　　 Under the table are two cats.

About the dog:

_____ the dog.

78 괄호 안의 낱말들을 알맞은 순서대로 배열하여 문장을 완성하시오.

> This experiment (as / as / is / one / the last / easy / not).

→ This experiment _____

　　 _____.

79 우리말에 맞게 문장을 완성하시오. (5단어)

> 엄마는 내게 가능한 한 일찍 집에 돌아오라고 말씀하셨다.

→ Mom told me to come back home

　　 _____.

80 어법상 잘못된 <u>두 곳</u>을 찾아 바르게 고쳐 쓰시오.

> People all around the world love to eat street food. Street food looks good and tastes deliciously. It's cheap, too! Let's find out about street food to different countries.

❶ _____ → _____

❷ _____ → _____

81 주어진 단어를 사용해 대답을 영작하시오.

> **A:** I love bread. How about you?
> **B:** 나도 그래. (so)

→ _____

82 주어진 단어를 사용해 문장을 완성하시오. (필요 시 형태 변형)

> 그 소식에 충격을 받은 사람들은 거의 없었다.
> (shock / people)

→ There _____

　　 at the news.

83 어법상 틀린 단어 2개를 찾아 바르게 고쳐 쓰시오.

When you talk to your friends, they listen to you well. They are understanding and generous. ⓐ You can share your feelings with them. It's good to have such friends. ⓑ They not only listen to you, but also give you an advice. ⓒ They encourage you and are fun to play with. ⓓ They enjoy talking and spend time with people. ⓔ Opposite friends have different interests, but you can get along with them.

❶ _____ → _____

❷ _____ → _____

84 주어진 단어를 모두 사용하여 장소를 강조하는 문장을 쓰시오.

is / the hotel / behind the city hall / which / stay at / will / you

→ _____.

➕ **통합문제**

85 주어진 단어를 모두 배열하여 문장을 완성하시오.

I went to the library _____

_____.

(about / traveling / a book / to / find)

86 빈칸에 들어갈 동사를 〈보기〉에서 골라 형태를 바르게 고쳐 쓰시오.

━━━━━━━━━━━━━━━ ● 보기 ●

put / come / learn / teach / beat / take

❶ Mr. Watson has _____ us English since last year.

❷ _____ a walk is a good exercise.

87 밑줄 친 단어의 형태를 바꾸시오.

Rabbit and Turtle had a race. Rabbit ran fast. But it got tired. It stopped ① run and started ② sleep. Turtle ③ pass the ④ sleep Rabbit. After all, Turtle won the race.

❶ _____

❷ _____

❸ _____

❹ _____

88 우리말에 맞게 문장을 완성하시오.

빨간 모자를 쓰고 있는 그 남자는 나의 동생이다.

The man _____ _____

_____ _____ is my brother.

89 각 문장에서 어법상 **틀린** 부분을 찾아 바르게 고쳐 쓰시오.

① Kate asked me whether I would like my chocolate ice cream in a cup and a cone. ② I chose eating for a cone.
③ She said to me I was lucky because of there was only one cone left.

❶ ＿＿＿＿＿＿ → ＿＿＿＿＿＿

❷ ＿＿＿＿＿＿ → ＿＿＿＿＿＿

❸ ＿＿＿＿＿＿ → ＿＿＿＿＿＿

90 틀린 부분을 찾아 바르게 고쳐 쓰시오.

ⓐ Julia bear in Boston, U.S.
ⓑ She wrote about working horses which were treated bad in the 1870s.
ⓒ Many people were moved by this story. ⓓ Julia was very weak when she was young, and she could not walk very well. ⓔ But she was good at ride a horse, and she loved animals.

❶ ＿＿＿＿＿ → ＿＿＿＿＿

❷ ＿＿＿＿＿ → ＿＿＿＿＿

❸ ＿＿＿＿＿ → ＿＿＿＿＿

91 우리말에 맞게 문장을 완성하시오.

나는 음식을 더 많이 먹지 않는 게 좋겠다.

→ I ＿＿＿＿＿ ＿＿＿＿＿

＿＿＿＿＿ ＿＿＿＿＿

＿＿＿＿＿ food.

92 어법상 **틀린** 부분 **2개**를 찾아 바르게 고쳐 쓰시오.

I am not going to go to school next Friday. I want to spent my time wisely that day. If it rains, I will stay home and read books. I will also help my mom. She wants me to help her with cook. If it's sunny, I will go outside. My dad wants me to go fishing with him.

❶ ＿＿＿＿＿＿ → ＿＿＿＿＿＿

❷ ＿＿＿＿＿＿ → ＿＿＿＿＿＿

93 주어진 단어를 모두 사용해 영작하시오.

여러분의 부모님께서는 여러분이 정말로 하고 싶은 일들을 하게 허락하실 것이다.
(let / will / things / which / want / really)

→ ＿＿＿＿＿＿＿＿＿＿＿

＿＿＿＿＿＿＿＿＿＿＿.

94 어색한 부분을 찾아 바르게 고쳐 쓰시오.

- 틀린 것을 찾아서 제대로 표시하여 작성한 경우 답이 맞지 않아도 1점을 부여함.
- 시제는 과거임.

Today was my friend Nayoung's thirteenth birthday. I wanted making her happy. So, I bought two movie tickets and some flower. Then, we went to the movies and it was moving. But, some parts made us sadly. After the movie, we met Sungjun to have a birthday party for Nayoung.

❶ ＿＿＿＿＿＿ → ＿＿＿＿＿＿

❷ ＿＿＿＿＿＿ → ＿＿＿＿＿＿

❸ ＿＿＿＿＿＿ → ＿＿＿＿＿＿

95 주어진 우리말을 영어로 쓰고, 이 두 문장을 관계대명사를 사용해 하나의 문장으로 쓰시오.

❶ 저 학생은 Kelly임에 틀림없다.

_____.

❷ David는 그 학생과 산책하고 있다.

_____.

❸ _____

_____.

96 어법이 틀린 부분을 모두 찾아 바르게 고쳐 쓰시오.

Each students picked another student's names and wrote good something about him or her.

❶ _____ → _____

❷ _____ → _____

❸ _____ → _____

97 문법적으로 어색한 부분을 찾아 고쳐 쓰시오.

Do you love animals? If you do, has you ever wanted to work with animals in a pet shop, a zoo, or even Africa? Here are some people who loves animals and work with them for their jobs.

❶ _____ → _____

❷ _____ → _____

98 문법적으로 어색한 부분 3개를 찾아 바르게 고쳐 쓰시오.

Today, many art works often look similar to the ones that made a long time ago. But they make us feel very different. The person in the old work looks uneasy and sad. The person in the poster looks funny and cute. I think that today's art uses the image of old art because of both of them look very similar.

❶ _____ → _____

❷ _____ → _____

❸ _____ → _____

99 주어진 단어를 모두 사용해 문장을 완성하시오.

인라인 스케이트를 타는 사람들은 어려운 묘기들을 하기 위해 만들어진 특수한 인라인 스케이트를 신는다.
(doing / for / difficult tricks / made)

→ Inline skaters put on special inline skates

_____.

100 대화가 자연스럽도록 우리말에 맞게 영작하시오.

A: Jenny likes Korean music a lot.
B: ① 그녀의 동생도 좋아해. (4단어: 도치구문으로)
   They often buy Korean song albums.
A: I see. By the say, did you do your project?
B: No, I didn't. How about you?
A: ② 나도 안 했어. (3단어: 도치구문으로)
   Why don't we do our project together?
B: That's a good idea.

❶ _____.

❷ _____.

정답
Answers

1 <u>Do you</u> have a radio?

2 <u>Does he get</u> up at six?

3 <u>Does</u> Su-jin <u>like</u> soccer?

4 Does Mike have a bicycle?

5 Yes, <u>they do</u>.

6 No, he <u>doesn't</u>.

7 No, she <u>doesn't</u>.

8 Yes, <u>he does</u>.

9 They <u>don't</u> use spoons.

10 Mr. Baker <u>doesn't</u> teach English.

11 Su-mi <u>doesn't have</u> a piano.

12 My father <u>doesn't work</u> in a bank.

13 He has two buses.

14 They have three boxes.

15 A dog has four legs.

16 There are seven apples in the box.

17 Ten trees are in the garden.

18 동사

19 인칭대명사 (소유격으로 schoolbag을 수식하는 형용사 역할)

20 인칭대명사

21 명사

22 지시형용사 (book을 수식)

23 명사

24 부정관사 (형용사 역할)

25 지시대명사

26 <u>What a nice teacher</u> she is!

27 <u>What large balls</u> they are!

28 <u>How strong</u> he is!

29 <u>How fast</u> she <u>runs</u>!

30 The girl has many books, <u>doesn't she</u>?

31 My sister went to the movies, <u>didn't she</u>?

32 You can speak English, <u>can't you</u>?

33 She looks very happy.

34 The music sounds sweet.

35 The dinner smells good.

36 Please <u>be</u> quiet.

37 <u>Let's</u> eat lunch.

38 <u>Don't</u> sit on the desk.

39 What a beautiful dress this is!

40 How tall you are!

통합유형 1-1   pp.21-25

1 ③	2 ①	3 ③	4 ④	5 ②
6 ④	7 ⑤	8 ④	9 ⑤	10 ①
11 ⑤	12 ③	13 ②	14 ①	15 ④
16 ①, ⑤	17 ①	18 ②	19 ①, ⑤	20 ⑤

📋 서 술 형

1 Mr. Kim doesn't like to go hiking.

2 Are his parents professors?

  → No, <u>they aren't</u>.

3 ⓑ Does she study English hard?

  ⓒ Do you like Gimbap?

  ⓓ Do you live in Busan?

  ⓔ Does Boa play the piano?

4 <u>Sing in a loud</u> voice.

5 A lot of children are at the playground.

6 They are not elementary school students any longer.

7 ①Jane bought a basketball him.

  → Jane bought a basketball for him.

② Tommy gave a book him about American culture. → Tommy gave a book to him about American culture.

③ Jane made a pencil case him.
→ Jane made a pencil case for him.

④ All the people at the party has a wonderful time. → All the people at the party had a wonderful time.

8 Jenny and Mina go to school by bus.

9 Mina doesn't go to school by bicycle(=bike).

10 ① Jason sent <u>a letter to Juni</u>.
② Thomas bought <u>a basketball for Kelly</u>.
③ Juni gave <u>a book to Thomas</u>.

해설

1 ③
①, ②, ④, ⑤ 반의어 / ③ 유의어

2 ①
fast : faster 형용사 원급:비교급 / help : helper 동사:명사

3 ③
①, ②, ④, ⑤ ~이다 / ③ ~이 있다

4 ④
일반동사 go의 현재형 의문문에 주어가 3인칭 단수(Minwha)인 경우 Does 사용 / 주어가 3인칭 단수(your friend)의 현재진행형 의문문에서 be동사 is가 앞으로 감 / 일반동사 like의 현재형 의문문에 주어가 3인칭 단수(his teacher)인 경우 Does 사용

5 ②
I에 어울리는 be동사 현재형은 am / My hair에 어울리는 be동사 현재형은 is

6 ④
일반동사 like의 현재형 의문문에 주어가 복수인 경우 Do 사용

7 ⑤
① don't / ② This is의 줄임 표현 없음 / ③ isn't / ④ It's

8 ④
감탄문 어순 What (a) 형용사+명사+주어+동사! / How+형용사(부사)+주어+동사! / 명사 books가 있기 때문에 What ~!

9 ⑤
ⓐ Do / ⓑ Do / ⓒ Does / ⓓ Does / ⓔ Does

10 ①
① Do / ②~⑤ Are

11 ⑤
부가의문문에서 does를 사용했기 때문에 앞부분에서는 일반동사의 부정문을 사용해야 하므로 doesn't like

12 ③
보기: like ~처럼 / ①, ②, ④, ⑤ ~처럼 / ③ 좋아하다

13 ②
감각동사 feel, look, sound, taste, smell + 형용사 / smoothly(부사) → smooth(형용사)

14 ①
① make = become ~이 되다 / ② exciting → excited / ③ angrily → angry / ④ sadly → sad / ⑤ to → for

15 ④
do you → did you

16 ①, ⑤
① for → to / ⑤ poor people → to poor people

17 ①
ⓑ Is → Are / ⓓ was → were / ⓔ were → was

18 ②
ⓑ are → is, some advice가 주어

19 ①, ⑤
② increase → decrease / ③ go to the bed → go to bed / ④ take → have

20 ⑤

for → to

통합유형 1-2 pp.26-30

pp.26-30

1 ②   2 ③   3 ④   4 ④   5 ②
6 ①   7 ③   8 ⑤   9 ④   10 ③
11 ①   12 ⑤   13 ③   14 ①   15 ③, ④
16 ②, ④   17 ①   18 ①   19 ②   20 ③

서술형

1 ① He didn't watch his favorite TV show then.

② Did he watch his favorite TV show then?

2 ① <u>Be</u> nice to your parents.

② <u>Don't</u> touch! It's very hot.

3 ① Mrs. Lee <u>speaks</u> German, <u>doesn't she</u>?

② Don't <u>act</u> like a child, <u>will you</u>?

③ Jenny <u>had</u> good grades on the exams,
<u>didn't she</u>?

4 ① Who will you give it to?

② What will you write on the card?

5 I can't understand <u>why you need it</u>.

6 What did your family tell you to live like?

7 Is there anything else I can help you with?

8 ① I will give a book to Nayoung.

② I will buy a bag for Nayoung.

9 How kind(=nice) you are!

10 It will keep them warm.

해설

1 ②

①, ③, ④, ⑤ 동사 – 명사 / ② 명사 – 형용사

2 ③

③ A:B 동의어 = C:D 반의어

3 ④

①, ②, ③, ⑤ be동사의 축약형 / ④ John의 소유격

4 ④

①, ②, ③, ⑤ 3인칭 단수 주어 / ④ 3인칭 복수 주어

5 ②

①, ③, ④, ⑤ 일반동사 do / ② 조동사 do

6 ①

ⓐ Jenny is (이다) / ⓑ we weren't (없었다) /
ⓒ Her parents (그녀의 부모님)

7 ③

Jane and Tom → they, 일반동사 go의 현재형 의문
문으로 do 사용

8 ⑤

주어(Jinhui)가 3인칭 단수, 일반동사 has의 현재형 부정
은 doesn't have

9 ④

대답을 does로 할 수 있는 일반동사 현재형 의문문,
Yes, she does이므로 주어는 여성(Kelly)

10 ③

①, ②, ④, ⑤ are / ③ is

11 ①

5형식 make+목적어+목적격 보어(명사, 형용사), ① 부
사 / ②, ③, ⑤ 형용사 / ④ 명사

12 ⑤

Don't speak in a loud voice. = 큰 소리로 말하지
말아라.

13 ③

① aren't they / ② can't he / ④ don't you /
⑤ do they

14 ①

② to 삭제 / ③ to me / ④ for → to / ⑤ to Jenny

15 ③, ④

① well 형용사(건강한) / ③ kindly → kind /
④ warmly → warm

16 ②, ④

　② Goes → Go / ④ looks → look

17 ①

　think different → think differently / can

　plays → can play / swiming → swimming /

　Does he reads → Does he read

18 ①

　ⓐ gets → get / ⓓ studys → studies / ⓔ plays

　→ play

19 ②

　lately 최근에 → late 늦게

20 ③

　Looking → Look / studys → studies / do →

　does / took → takes

통합유형 1-3

 pp.31-35

1 ⑤	2 ④, ⑤	3 ⑤	4 ③	5 ①
6 ⑤	7 ⑤	8 ⑤	9 ⑤	10 ③
11 ③	12 ④	13 ④	14 ④	15 ④, ⑤
16 ②, ④	17 ④	18 ③	19 ①	20 ④, ⑤

서술형

1 The river is no longer clean.

2 Are there many big parks in our city?

3 ① My mother makes a cake for our friends.

　② I sent a cake to my friend.

　③ I ask an important favor of you.

4 Don't give ice cream or chocolate to a dog.

5 Can you tell me what Judy wants?

6 ① ⓒ Dad, Mom, two brothers, five sisters,

　　and I.

　② ⓓ We have two dogs, too.

　③ ⓔ My dogs' names are Happy and Sen.

7 She took a walk and wrote a poem.

8 She didn't study math and didn't learn English.

9 Take a walk every day, ⓐ and ⓑ you will be

　healthy.

10 Carry this box carefully, ⓐ or ⓑ you will

　break things inside.

해설

1 ⑤

　①~④ 상위 – 하위 개념 / ⑤ 수도 – 네덜란드

2 ④, ⑤

　④ 단수 : 복수 / ⑤ 동의어

3 ⑤

　①~④ 축약에 쓰인 ' / ⑤ 소유격에 쓰인 '

4 ③

　run 달리다, 작동하다

5 ①

　~하게 들리다 sounds / ~하게 느껴지다 feels

6 ⑤

　① was / ② Is / ③ Are / ④ are – be동사 /

　⑤ Do/Did – 조동사

7 ⑤

　전치사 from과 어울리는 형용사 different

8 ⑤

　진수가 버스를 타고 갔기 때문에 No, he didn't.로 답하

　는 게 맞음

9 ⑤

　조동사 will의 부정형 will not의 축약형은 won't

10 ③

　everything 단수 취급 is / different teachers 복

　수주어 are / your classmates 복수주어 are

11 ③

　ⓐ I am (이다) / ⓑ Mr. Oh is (이다) / ⓒ They are

　(이다)

12 ④

Your differences will make your friendship better.

13 ④

① for → of / ② me → to me / ③ of → to / ⑤ to → for

14 ③

일반동사 eat의 부정명령문(~하지 마라)은 Don't를 사용

15 ④, ⑤

① does → is / ② don't → doesn't / ③ is 삭제

16 ②, ④

① starts → start / ③ studys → studies / ⑤ watches → watch

17 ④

ⓑ Do → Does / ⓒ is → are / ⓔ watches → watch

18 ③

go → goes / start → starts / ate → eat

19 ①

ⓑ help not → don't help / ⓓ Let's go not → Let's not go

20 ④, ⑤

ⓓ isn't → can't / ⓔ is → has

---

chapter 02 조동사 · 시제 · 수동태

기 본 실 력 다 지 기 ○━━━━ pp.44-45

1 ① worked   ② lived   ③ washed
   ④ came   ⑤ went   ⑥ stood

2 ① hearing   ② sitting   ③ coming
   ④ writing   ⑤ stopping   ⑥ making
   ⑦ eating   ⑧ running

3 will be

4 be

5 going

6 No, I won't.

7 Yes, you may.

8 No, he can't.

9 너는 최선을 다해야 한다.

10 우리는 일요일엔 학교에 갈 필요가 없다.

11 그녀는 아픈 게 틀림 없다.

12 그는 곧 돌아올지도 모른다.

13 They lived here last year.

14 He plays tennis every day.

15 Did you talk with your teacher yesterday?

16 What did you have for dinner yesterday?

17 I am going to play tennis with my mother.

18 They are not going to go to the party this evening.

19 I'm drawing a picture.

20 In-su was studying English.

21 The doctor was sent for by her.

22 It was called a flower by them.

23 A letter will be written (to) his parents by him.

24 완료

25 결과

26 계속

27 경험

28 The vase was broken by me.

29 She was loved by everybody.

30 His house was built in the woods last year.

31 The movie was made by Leigh Film Co.

32 The room was filled with smoke.

33 The mountain will be covered with snow in winter.

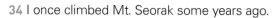

34 I once climbed Mt. Seorak some years ago.

35 I will not go there, either, if it rains
    tomorrow.

36 They <u>had</u> <u>to</u> catch the first train.

37 He <u>doesn't</u> <u>have</u> <u>to</u> hurry up.

38 She <u>must</u> be busy.

39 He <u>is</u> <u>going</u> <u>to</u> be a doctor.

40 Mary <u>is</u> <u>going</u> <u>to</u> meet her friend.

통합유형 2-1   pp.46-50

1 ②	2 ①	3 ⑤	4 ⑤	5 ④
6 ④	7 ③	8 ④	9 ③	10 ②
11 ④	12 ③	13 ⑤	14 ③	15 ①, ④
16 ③, ⑤	17 ④	18 ①	19 ④	20 ①

서술형

1 ① Both <u>study</u> math on Thursday.

   ② Tom <u>reads</u> a book on Friday.

   ③ Jenny <u>does</u> exercise on Saturday.

   ④ But, Tom <u>does</u> his homework on Saturday.

2 have known

3 This novel <u>was written by Tom.</u>

4 Jane reads a comic book.
   → Jane read a comic book.

5 ① She is running in the park.
   ② She was running in the park.

6 Jenny <u>has</u> <u>been</u> to Canada.

7 ① will be going to land → would land
   ② is → was

8 We have just arrived at the park.

9 He should not take the books home.

10 ① Thomas did not take the bus yesterday.

   ② I read the book last week.

   ③ You were thirsty.

해설

1 ②
  ⓓ find - found / ⓔ set - set / ⓖ are - were

2 ①
  보기: last 지속되다 / ① 지속되다 / ② 마지막의 / ③ 지난 / ④ 마지막으로 / ⑤ 마지막의

3 ⑤
  3인칭 단수 주어(a dog)의 현재진행형은 is coming이 맞음

4 ⑤
  복수 주어인 bags가 Jenny Kim에 의해서 디자인되었기 때문에 수동태 were designed

5 ④
  아무도 몰랐기 때문에 didn't know, 몇 명과 이야기했었기 때문에 talked

6 ④
  의무 have to와 바꿔 쓸 수 있는 표현은 must

7 ③
  그녀가 없었던 과거에 그리워했었다는 missed, 전치사 by 뒤에 수업을 빠지지 않음으로써의 동명사 missing

8 ④
  미래시제 will / 당위, 추측 should

9 ③
  10년 동안 살아왔기 때문에 현재완료시제 has lived, for ~ 동안, since ~ 이후로

10 ②
  ⓐ 성인들은 들을 수 없다, 능동태 hear / ⓑ 그 장치는 '모스키토'라고 불렸다, 수동태 was named / ⓒ 몇몇 상점 주인들이 '모스키토'가 매우 유용하다고 생각했다, 능동태 found

11 ④

ⓐ 13살 이후로 계속 먹어왔기 때문에 현재완료시제 have eaten / ⓑ 지난주에 맘껏 먹은 것은 과거 사실이기 때문에 과거시제 helped / ⓒ 쿠키가 나를 신나게 했다이므로 동사 excite의 과거시제 excited

12 ③

ⓐ, ⓑ 거짓말하다 lie의 현재분사형 lying / ⓒ liar 거짓말쟁이

13 ⑤

① cans → can / ② angrily → angry / ③ going → go / ④ happily → happy

14 ③

① warmly → warm / ② will do → does / ④ had → will have / ⑤ very → with *with difficulty 겨우

15 ①, ④

② stayed → stay / ③ be 삭제 / ⑤ has나 last night 삭제

16 ③, ⑤

③ has left → has나 two days ago 삭제 / ⑤ cutten → cut

17 ④

ⓐ health → healthy / ⓒ is eating → eats / ① exciting → excited

18 ①

ⓒ has → had / ⓓ had → has / ⓔ has → had

19 ④

can't catch → couldn't catch

20 ①

What do you do → What did you do

통합유형 2-2 — pp.51-55

| 1 ① | 2 ③ | 3 ① | 4 ④ | 5 ① |
| 6 ① | 7 ⑤ | 8 ⑤ | 9 ⑤ | 10 ① |

| 11 ⑤ | 12 ③ | 13 ③ | 14 ④ | 15 ① |
| 16 ①, ② | 17 ①, ③, ④ | 18 ② | 19 ⑤ | 20 ④, ⑤ |

서술형

1 ① I will write a new grammar book.

② I have been writing a new grammar book.

2 ① On Saturdays, James plays basketball with his friends.

② On Sundays, James helps old people.

3 You should return books within a week.

4 James likes watching soccer games and enjoys playing basketball.

5 I have lived in Seoul for ten years.

6 This letter was written by our teacher a few days ago.

7 A new bag was bought for Jenny by him.

8 The pictures show us how the money will be used.

9 ① inviting → invited

② exciting → excited

③ although → because

10 ① ⓐ Our teacher told us that Columbus discovered the New Continent.

② ⓒ He hasn't talked to me all day.

③ ⓓ If it rains tomorrow, our school will not go on a picnic.

④ ⓘ Have you ever caught a big fish?

해설

1 ①

beat – beat – beaten

2 ③

① 물을 주다, 물 / ② 연주하다, 연극 / ③ 속이다 / ④ 지속되다, 마지막의 / ⑤ 휴식, 나머지

3 ①

② is eating / ③ is taking / ④ is cutting / ⑤ is walking

4 ④

보기: 완료 / ①, ②, ③, ⑤ 계속

5 ①

보기: 허가 / ① 추측

6 ①

보기: 의지 / ②, ③, ④, ⑤ ~할 것이다

7 ⑤

보기: 5형식 (목적어가 ~한 상태가 되도록 하다) / ① 5형식 (사역동사: 목적어가 ~하게 하다) / ② 3형식 / ③ 4형식 / ④ 2형식 / ⑤ 5형식 (목적어가 ~한 상태가 되도록 하다)

8 ⑤

현재완료시제 has taught와 since, for는 어울리는 표현, 10년 전이라는 ten years ago는 과거시제와 어울림

9 ⑤

몸 상태가 좋지 않은 상대방에게 충고할 수 있는 표현은 '병원에 가보라'는 ⑤번

10 ①

to 삭제

11 ⑤

ⓐ 내가 문 열쇠를 가지고 있다면 도둑들은 내 집에 들어갈 수 없다. have / ⓑ 내가 그렇게 불쌍한 사람들을 해친다면 나는 수치심을 느낄 것이다. will be shamed / ⓒ 그 바보들이 나중에 '어리석은 지혜'라고 불리게 될 것이라는 것을 그는 몰랐다. would be called

12 ③

현재완료시제 용법 중 ①, ②, ④, ⑤는 경험 / ③ 완료

13 ③

① was 삭제 / ② was 삭제 / ④ are 삭제 / ⑤ is taken → took

14 ④

① lost → lose / ② 과거시제 ate과 tomorrow는 어울리지 않음 / ③ doesn't → didn't / ⑤ have you cooked → did you cook

15 ①

② shy → be shy / ③ plays → play / ③ be 삭제 / ⑤ will visit → visited

16 ①, ②

③ rose → rises / ④ happen → happens / ⑤ hear → heard

17 ①, ③, ④

① to exercise → exercises / ③ was polluted → pollutes / ④ have met → met

18 ②

ⓒ will be → am / ⓓ for us → to us / ⓔ will come → come

19 ⑤

you to come → that you will come

20 ④, ⑤

④ see → saw / ⑤ were frightening → were frightened

통합유형 **2-3** ————— pp.56-60

1 ⑤	2 ①	3 ⑤	4 ①	5 ③
6 ④	7 ②	8 ②	9 ③	10 ①
11 ④	12 ④	13 ②	14 ④	15 ④, ⑤
16 ③, ④	17 ④	18 ③	19 ④	20 ①, ⑤

📋 서술형

1 I am taking a shower.

2 Suji takes a dancing lesson and goes to sing songs to the concert hall on Friday.

3 The boxes were moved to the school by our students.

4 My parents have been married for 15 years.

5 I <u>have</u> <u>written</u> books on English reading <u>for</u> <u>three</u> <u>years</u>.

6 Jenny ① <u>likes</u> English, but ② <u>doesn't like</u> math. James and I ③ <u>like</u> music, but we ④ <u>don't like</u> science.

7 Korean history <u>should be taught to every</u> <u>student</u>.

8 He <u>spent</u> 10,000 won <u>for</u> games and only <u>saved</u> 10,000 won in the bank.

9 ① since → for

② attend not → not attend

③ will snow → snows

10 It <u>has been almost two months since I</u> <u>started my trip around the world</u>.

해설

1 ⑤

보기: 작동하다 / ① 운영, 제공하다 / ② 달리다 / ③ ~하게 되다 / ④ 운영하다 / ⑤ 작동하다

2 ①

looking at your family picture

3 ⑤

①~④ 다음주 일요일이라는 가까운 미래에 '~할 예정이다'를 대용하는 진행시제 / ⑤ '지금하고 있다'는 의미의 진행시제

4 ①

보기: 단정(~임에 틀림없다) / ① 단정 / ②~⑤ 의무

5 ③

보기: (현재완료의 쓰임 중) 계속 / ① 경험 / ② 완료 / ③ 계속 / ④ 경험 / ⑤ 결과

6 ④

능동태 과거시제 cleaned를 수동태로 바꾸면 was cleaned

7 ②

ⓑ 지시형용사 / ⓐ, ⓒ, ⓓ, ⓔ 접속사

8 ②

since ~한 이후로, 뒤가 과거면 앞은 현재완료. 주어가 3인칭 단수이므로 has been

9 ③

어제 처음 본 것이 마지막이 아니라면 한 번만 본 적이 있는 것은 아님

10 ①

어제 휴일이었기 때문에 그는 학교에 갈 필요가 없었다.

11 ④

ⓐ woke up 일어났다 / ⓑ didn't bring 가져오지 않았다 / ⓒ fell down 넘어졌다

12 ④

had better not+동사원형, ~하지 않는 게 좋다

13 ②

① makes → made / ③ Get → Getting / ④ will can → will be able to / ⑤ will 삭제

14 ④

① puts → put / ② begun → began / ③ ate → eat / ⑤ studyed → studied

15 ④, ⑤

④ will 삭제 / ⑤ have you done → did you do

16 ③, ④

① broked → broke / ② donates → donate / ⑤ felted → felt

17 ④

ⓐ rains → rain / ⓒ Because → Because of / ⓔ am still not feeling → don't still feel

18 ③

ⓑ are → do / ⓒ visits → visit / ⓔ comes → come / ① stayed → stay

19 ④

ⓐ taken → took / ⓒ was bought → bought /

ⓔ sweetly → sweet

20 ①, ⑤

ⓐ remembers → remembered / ⓔ filled →

were filled

chapter **03** 부정사 · 동명사 · 분사

기 본 실 력 다 지 기 ———————○ pp.68~70

1 나는 학교에 지각하고 싶지 않다.

2 그는 나에게 일찍 잠자리에 들라고 말했다.

3 나는 그가 일요일에 교회에 가는 걸 봤다.

4 나는 그가 그 방을 청소하게 했다.

5 그가 영어로 편지를 쓰는 것은 어렵다.

6 그렇게 말하다니 네가 친절하구나.

7 잠시 동안 내가 널 기다려도 괜찮겠니?

8 그는 정말 그녀가 학교에 지각하는 걸 좋아하지 않는다.

9 경찰관은 술 취한 남자를 똑바로 걷게 했다.

10 소녀들은 그를 봤을 때 이야기하는 것을 멈췄다.

11 목적어

12 주어

13 보어

14 진주어

15 부사적 용법(목적)

16 명사적 용법(주어)

17 형용사적 용법(명사 수식)

18 명사적 용법(목적어)

19 형용사적 용법(명사 수식)

20 부사적 용법(결과)

21 명사적 용법(보어)

22 부사적 용법(원인)

23 부사적 용법(판단의 이유, 근거)

24 명사적 용법(진주어)

25 The baseball game was very <u>exciting</u>.

26 I am <u>interested</u> in dinosaurs.

27 I saw the beautiful moon through the <u>broken</u> window.

28 I smelled something <u>burning</u> in the kitchen.

29 Have you finished <u>sending</u> e-mails?

30 He can't but <u>fall</u> asleep.

31 동명사

32 현재분사

33 현재분사

34 동명사

35 동명사

36 She is very good at <u>dancing</u>.

37 My father is proud of <u>my(=me)</u> teaching Korean history.

38 <u>On</u> <u>hearing</u> the news, he was shocked.

39 How <u>about</u> <u>going</u> on a picnic?

40 They <u>could</u> <u>not</u> <u>help</u> <u>laughing</u> at the sight.

41 Do you know <u>the</u> <u>gentleman</u> <u>sitting</u> <u>on</u> the sofa?

42 It is important <u>to</u> <u>read</u> <u>hard</u>.

43 Try to get along with your friends.

44 I go to school to study.

45 I heard him sing / singing a song.

46 I want him to go to school now.

47 They had him do it.

48 Did you decide to be a singer?

49 He is ashamed of not being tall.

50 I don't feel like studying now.

51 What do you say to having some break?

52 Riding a horse is not as easy as riding a bicycle.

53 My mother had that coat cleaned.

54 I bought a camera made in Korea.

통합유형 3-1

pp.71-75

1 ④	**2** ⑤	**3** ②	**4** ②, ⑤	**5** ①, ⑤
6 ⑤	**7** ③	**8** ⑤	**9** ⑤	**10** ⑤
11 ④	**12** ③	**13** ④	**14** ③	**15** ①
16 ②	**17** ②	**18** ③	**19** ③	**20** ③

서술형

1 Please give me <u>something cool to drink</u>.

2 ① exciting

  ② excited

  ③ interesting

3 He went to the party <u>to meet her</u>.

4 The man <u>asked him to give</u> her this letter.

5 ① <u>Helping</u> the poor makes us <u>happy</u>.

  ② It's time <u>to go home</u>.

6 She <u>had</u> her computer <u>fixed</u> yesterday.

7 He is <u>too young to</u> watch the movie.

8 We enjoy watching soccer games.

9 It is very <u>dangerous for you to play computer games</u> for a long time.

10 ① ⓐ First, our parents want us to prepare everything before going to school.

  ② ⓑ Next, they tell us to keep a rule of our home.

  ③ ⓒ Our father also advises us not to come home late.

  ④ ⓓ It's because our parents are worried about us.

해설

1 ④

Lieing → Lying

2 ⑤

made는 사역동사로 동사원형을 목적보어로 씀

3 ②

② to join / ①, ③, ④, ⑤는 동명사 / ③은 부정사도 가능

4 ②, ⑤

want, plan + to부정사

5 ①, ⑤

hope, try + to부정사 / 나머지는 동명사

6 ⑤

look forward to ~ing/명사 ~하기를/~를 기대하다

7 ③

finish는 동명사를 목적어로 씀

8 ⑤

① 주어, ② 목적어, ③ 보어, ④ 목적어로 쓰는 부정사의 명사적 용법 / ⑤ 부정사의 형용사적 용법

9 ⑤

①~④는 부사적 용법 중 목적(~하기 위하여) / ⑤ 형용사적 용법

10 ⑤

①~④는 형용사적 용법 / ⑤ 부사 용법 중 목적

11 ④

보기: 주어로 쓰인 동명사 / ① 보어 / ② 목적어 / ③ 전치사의 목적어 / ⑤ 주어로 쓰인 동명사 / ④ 현재분사

12 ③

①, ②, ④, ⑤ 목적어로 쓰인 동명사 / ③ 진행형으로 쓰인 현재분사

13 ④

① going → to go / ② will → would / ③, ⑤ to not → not to (부정사의 부정은 not을 부정사 앞에)

14 ③

① Play → Playing / ② are you → you are /

④ plays → playing(=to play) / ⑤ are → is

15 ①

② buy → buying / ③ shop → shopping / ④
Keep → Keeping / ⑤ saying → say

16 ②

① to go → go / ③ fix → fixed / ④ to wash →
wash / ⑤ working → worked / ② clean도 가능

17 ②

ⓐ 진행형으로 carrying / ⓑ 조동사 뒤 동사원형으로
rain / ⓒ need to + 동사원형 (~할 필요가 있다)

18 ③

say → said 시제 일치

19 ③

(A)는 부사적 용법 중 목적, (B)는 목적어로 쓰인 명사적
용법

20 ③

to move → moving, cars를 수식하는 진행의 의미

통합유형 **3-2** ── pp.76-79

1 ⑤	2 ①	3 ②	4 ②	5 ①
6 ⑤	7 ②	8 ①	9 ②	10 ②
11 ①	12 ②	13 ③	14 ⑤	15 ④
16 ①, ③	17 ④	18 ③	19 ⑤	20 ⑤

📋 서 술 형

1 It is important to have(=eat) breakfast every
day.

2 He wanted her to join a club.

3 He let them go to the birthday party.

4 Do you know a wonderful place to visit?

5 He knew the dancing girl with something
strange.

6 She had him eat breakfast.

7 So he needs a pen to write with.

8 The box was so heavy that she couldn't lift
it.

9 She saw a man come to her.

10 • I like playing soccer but I don't like
watching movies.

• Mia likes playing the piano but she
doesn't like watching baseball games.

해설

1 ⑤

eatting → eating

2 ①

want는 부정사를 목적어로 쓰고 전치사 뒤는 명사나 동
명사를 씀

3 ②

영화가 지루하게 하기에 boring(능동), 그녀가 감동을 받
기에 impressed(수동)

4 ②

② to부정사 / ③, ⑤ 동명사 / ①, ④ 현재분사

5 ①

쓸 펜에서 펜을 가지고 쓰기에 with를 사용

6 ⑤

let은 사역동사라 목적보어는 동사원형을 씀

7 ②

② 목적어로 쓰인 명사적 용법 / 나머지는 형용사적 용법

8 ①

보기와 ①은 부사적 용법의 목적 / ② 목적어로 쓰인 명사
적 용법 / ③ 형용사적 용법 / ④ 명사적 용법 / ⑤ 부사적
용법의 원인

9 ②

보기와 ②는 명사적 용법의 목적어 / ①, ③ 부사적 용법의
원인 / ④ 부사적 용법의 목적 / ⑤ 부사적 용법의 근거

10 ②

② man을 수식하는 현재분사 / ①, ⑤ 목적어로 쓰인 동명사 / ③은 주어, ④는 전치사의 목적어로 쓰인 동명사

11 ①

②~⑤ 목적어로 쓰인 동명사 / ① 주어로 쓰인 동명사

12 ②

ⓐ game은 지루하게 하기에 boring / ⓑ be interested in ~에 흥미가 있다 / ⓒ be surprised at ~에 놀라다

13 ③

① watch / ② annoyed / ④ saving(=to save) / ⑤ washed / ③ to do도 가능

14 ⑤

to making → make(=to make)

15 ④

① see → to see / ② to go → going / ③ gaining → to gain / ⑤ to go → going

16 ①, ③

① to eat → eating / ③ to open → opening

17 ④

cleaned → clean

18 ③

ⓒ to playing → playing / ⓔ feeling → feel

19 ⑤

going → go

20 ⑤

to go → going

통합유형 3-3

pp.80-84

1 ①	**2** ④	**3** ⑤	**4** ⑤	**5** ④
6 ④	**7** ④	**8** ③	**9** ⑤	**10** ⑤
11 ③	**12** ⑤	**13** ④	**14** ①	**15** ④
16 ①, ⑤	**17** ②, ⑤	**18** ④	**19** ④	**20** ④

1 He finished reading and drank some water.

2 He had many(=a lot of) friends to play with.

3 have → having

4 His uncle told him not to play computer games.

5 Their hobby is swimming in the river.

6 Seoul is the best place to visit.

7 She was <u>too</u> <u>sick</u> <u>to</u> go to school.

8 Tom told Sujin to <u>make</u> <u>pizza</u> <u>for</u> him.

9 I watched boys <u>swimming in the river.</u>

10 You <u>must exercise regularly to be healthy.</u>

해설

1 ①

finish는 동명사 목적어를 취한다.

2 ④

siting → sitting

3 ⑤

talented: '재능 있는' 의미의 형용사, touched는 '나는 감동 받았다'의 수동의 의미

4 ⑤

interesting: 재미있게 하는 능동의 의미, excited: 그가 흥분되었으므로 수동의 의미

5 ④

going은 동명사 주어이므로 동사는 is, '담배 피우는 것을 멈추다'이므로 동명사 smoking이 정답 (to smoke; 피우기 위해서)

6 ④

동명사의 부정은 동명사 앞에 not을 쓰므로 by not turning, finish는 동명사를 목적어로 쓰기에 doing이 정답

7 ④

① 능동의 현재분사 / ②, ③, ⑤ 진행의 의미로 쓰인 현재

분사 / ④ like의 목적어로 쓰인 동명사

8 ③

to do는 things를 수식하는 형용사적 용법 / ③ friend를 수식 / ①, ④ 목적어로 쓰인 명사적 용법 / ②, ⑤ 목적으로 쓰인 부사적 용법

9 ⑤

to tell은 목적으로 쓰인 부사적 용법 / ⑤ 만나기 위해서 / ① 부사적 용법의 원인 / ② 부사적 용법의 근거 / ③ 목적어로 쓰인 명사적 용법 / ④ something을 수식하는 형용사적 용법

10 ⑤

⑤ 형용사적용법 / ① 부사적 용법의 원인 / ②, ③ 부사적 용법의 목적 / ④ 부사적 용법의 결과

11 ③

ⓐ 주어 자리므로 동명사 / ⓑ 전치사 뒤이므로 동명사 / ⓒ 주어 girl를 수식하는 역할을 하는 현재분사

12 ⑤

①, ④번 목적어로 쓰인 동명사 / ②, ③ 주어로 쓰인 동명사 / ⑤ someone을 수식하는 현재분사

13 ④

④ give up은 동명사를 목적어로 취하는 동사이므로 to play → playing

14 ①

② could → can / ③ good so that → so good that / ④ nervously → nervous / ⑤ regular → regularly

15 ④

① to clean → clean / ② to wash → wash / ③ help → to help / ⑤ to play → play

16 ①, ⑤

② boring → bored(수동) / ③ bored → boring(능동) / ④ surprising → surprised(수동)

17 ②, ⑤

① to travel → traveling / ③ doing → do(=to

do) / ④ to make → making

18 ④

ⓐ, ⓑ, ⓓ 부사적 용법 원인 / ⓒ, ⓔ 형용사적 용법

19 ④

① to watch (=watching) / ② watched / ③ exciting(능동) / ⑤ plan to + 동사원형: ~할 계획이다

20 ④

ⓒ in order to watch not → in order not to watch / ⓓ talking → to talk

chapter **04**   대명사 · 접속사 · 관계사

기 본 실 력 다 지 기   pp.93-94

1 It rains a lot in summer.

2 There was a strong wind a few days ago.

3 There's a dark cloud in the sky.
  It's going to rain.

4 There's light in this room.

5 A: What is this?

6 A: Where does Ms. Kim live?

7 A: How old is your father?

8 A: Why do you like Susan?

9 A: Whose books are these?

10 A: What day is it today?

11 의문대명사(주어)

12 관계대명사

13 의문대명사(목적어)

14 관계대명사(=the thing which)

15 관계대명사

16 베티가 무척 사랑하는 그 고양이는 아주 작고 귀엽다.

17 이 사람이 네가 어제 공원에서 만났던 그 미국인이니?

18 이건 지금까지 내가 읽은 가장 유용한 책이다.

19 자기 자동차를 도둑 맞은 그 남자는 경찰서로 가버렸다.

20 He has a son <u>whose</u> name is Tom.

21 She is the lady <u>who</u> teaches us music.

22 That is the boy with <u>whom</u> I played tennis yesterday.

23 Is this the girl <u>whom</u> you met in the park?

24 Both the buses <u>and</u> the trains are running late.

25 I know a girl who(=that) can speak English well.

26 That is the boy whose name is Jack.

27 Once there was a king whom(=that) all the people loved in China.

28 Look at the house whose roof is red.

29 This is the key which(=that) I have been looking for.

30 The book which(=that) I bought last week is easy.

31 Please give <u>them</u> to <u>me</u>.

32 Please give <u>it</u> to <u>her</u>.

33 Please give <u>them</u> to <u>her</u>.

34 Please give <u>it</u> to <u>us</u>.

35 Please give <u>it</u> to <u>them</u>.

36 She got out of the bath and dried <u>herself</u> with a towel.

37 When I am alone, I often talk to <u>myself</u>.

38 He fell off the building but he didn't hurt <u>himself</u>.

39 Don't burn <u>yourself</u>.

40 I'm angry with <u>myself</u>.

41 I have two cats; <u>one</u> is black, and <u>the other</u> is white.

42 I have three brothers; <u>one</u> lives in Seoul

and <u>the others</u> live in Busan.

43 Here are four flowers; <u>one</u> is a rose, <u>another</u> is a lily, and <u>the others</u> are tulips.

44 I don't like this cap. Show me <u>another</u>.

45 There are many students in our school. <u>Some</u> students come to school by bus, <u>others</u> come to school on foot.

통합유형 **4-1** ————— pp.95-99

1 ④	2 ④	3 ②	4 ④	5 ②
6 ⑤	7 ③	8 ③	9 ⑤	10 ⑤
11 ④	12 ⑤	13 ③	14 ⑤	15 ②
16 ③	17 ③	18 ①, ⑤	19 ②	20 ④

📝 서술형

1 ① She goes to the park.

② Is she late? No, she isn't.

③ Does she help the unhappy? Yes, she does.

2 She eats breakfast at 8 a.m., but he doesn't eat breakfast.

3 <u>If it rains</u> tomorrow, I will not go on a trip.

4 They enjoyed <u>themselves</u> at the party yesterday.

5 ① Junho plays soccer <u>before he takes a shower</u>.

② <u>After he has dinner</u>, he studies for exams.

6 The tea is <u>so hot that</u> he can't drink it.

7 I know the girl who(=that) is singing in the room.

8 One good tip to the problem is to use the manual which is written in English.

9 I ate some cookies that she made for me.

10 He is the soccer player that they respect.

해설

1 ④

④ 주격 – 소유격 관계, 나머지는 주격 – 목적격

2 ④

the boys는 복수, the boys – they

3 ②

is 앞에 단수가 와야 하므로 누군가를 소개하는 표현인 this is~, 명사 앞에 소유격이 와야 하므로 his

4 ④

④ it은 특정한 사물을 가리키는 대명사(그것), 나머지는 비인칭주어

5 ②

나를 가리키며 명사 앞이라 소유격 my, Jeje를 가리키며 명사 앞이라 소유격 his

6 ⑤

사람을 선행사로 하고, 뒤에 동사가 오므로 주격 관계대명사 who가 와야 함 / ④는 who(m)이 가능

7 ③

결과 + because + 원인 / 원인 + so + 결과

8 ③

③ 문장과 문장을 이어주는 접속사(~할 때), 나머지는 의문사(언제)

9 ⑤

목적어로 명사절을 이끄는 접속사 that: 뒤에 완전한 문장이 와야 함 / ①, ② 지시형용사 / ③ 지시부사 / ④ 지시대명사

10 ⑤

사물을 선행사로 하고 주격인 관계대명사 which / 사람을 선행사로 하고 주격인 관계대명사 who 대신 쓸 수 있는 that

11 ④

that: 지시대명사로 hear의 목적어, say 뒤에서 완전한 문장을 이끌며 목적어로 쓰인 명사절 이끄는 that

12 ⑤

접속사 when: 문장과 문장을 이으며 뜻은 ~할 때 /

what to do: '무엇을 해야 할지'의 의문사 what

13 ③

이유를 묻는 의문부사 why가 어울림

14 ⑤

주어가 she이므로 herself

15 ②

명사 앞에는 소유격을 써야 하므로 his book, he's = he is

16 ③

동사 앞에는 주격 관계대명사가 와야 하므로 who

17 ③

–thing의 부정대명사는 형용사가 뒤에서 수식하므로 something cold

18 ①, ⑤

②, ③, ④ 선행사가 단수 / ② have → has, ③ save → saves, ④ have → has

19 ②

James와 Shilla를 가리키며 명사 앞에 오므로 소유격인 their를 써야 함

20 ④

명사 앞이므로 소유격 her

통합유형 4-2 — pp.100-104

1 ③	2 ⑤	3 ④	4 ①	5 ③
6 ①	7 ②	8 ④	9 ④	10 ①
11 ①	12 ④	13 ②	14 ⑤	15 ④
16 ①	17 ①, ②	18 ③	19 ⑤	20 ①

서술형

1 When he is in the museum, he do not take a picture.

2 Because he got up late, he missed the train.

3 Growing vegetables yourself is good for a healthy life.

4 I'm looking for a house whose color is white.

5 Listen carefully and do exactly as she said.

6 He liked the food which(=that) was made by his mom.

7 ① I have a computer which I can search the information with.

② I have a computer (=that) I can search the information with.

③ I have a computer with which I can search the information.

8 The place which I wanted to visit last year was London.

9 He gave her all the books that he had.

10 He used different techniques so as to create new picture images that anyone had not ever seen before.

1 ③

명사 앞에는 소유격

2 ⑤

it ~ to + 동사원형, 가주어 진주어 구문

3 ④

구체적인 행동과 시간에 대한 답이 주어져 있으므로 what과 when이 와야 함

4 ①

문장과 문장을 이어 주며, 앞문장과 뒷문장이 상반되는 내용이므로 but이 와야 함

5 ③

③ while ~이지만, 반면에 / 나머지는 ~ 동안에

6 ①

전치사 in의 목적어 역할을 하는 목적격 관계대명사 that

/ 관계대명사 앞에 전치사가 위치할 수 있으므로 in which

7 ②

문장과 문장을 이어 주는 접속사 when (~할 때)

8 ④

④ 원인을 나타내는 접속사 because가 와야 함 / 나머지는 when

9 ④

uniform과 bag을 가리키며 need의 목적어 역할을 하는 them / Jisu를 가리키며 명사 room 앞에 와야 하므로 소유격 her

10 ①

앞문장과 뒷문장이 상반되므로 However / 결과를 나타내는 문장이 왔으므로 at last (마침내)

11 ①

because + 원인, 이유 / but+상반된 내용 / unlike + 명사 ~와 달리

12 ④

one of[each of] + 복수명사 + 단수동사, some of + 복수명사 + 복수동사

13 ②

she는 여자를, uncle은 남자를 나타내므로 함께 쓰일 수 없음

14 ⑤

⑤ 지시대명사 / 나머지는 목적어로 쓰인 접속사로 생략 가능

15 ④

①, ②는 주어가 복수이므로 study, play / ③, ⑤는 주어가 단수이므로 watches, has

16 ①

② 목적격 which가 있으므로 it을 삭제 / ③ she → who / ④ whom → who / ⑤ voice 앞의 that을 소유격 관계대명사 whose로 바꿔야 함

17 ①, ②

③ 전치사 to를 문장 끝이나 관계대명사 앞에 넣어야
함 / ④ 하나의 문장이므로 불필요한 that 삭제 / ⑤
which → who, 관계대명사절을 doctor 뒤로 이동

18 ③

보기: 비인칭 주어 / ⓐ~ⓒ 정답 / ⓓ, ⓔ, ① 대명사

19 ⑤

④에서 He and I 언급, ⑤ they가 아닌 we가 와야 함

20 ①

② what → that(접속사) / ③ what → who / ④
or → but / ⑤ but → and

통합유형 4-3

pp.105-109

1 ⑤	2 ④	3 ③	4 ④	5 ④
6 ⑤	7 ④	8 ②	9 ①	10 ①
11 ②	12 ②	13 ②	14 ②	15 ⑤
16 ③	17 ④	18 ②	19 ③	20 ②

📝 **서술형**

1 She wanted to see <u>that</u> he would <u>buy</u> <u>it</u>.

2 ① If he takes the bus, it will take 8 minutes.
② If he rides a bike, it will take 10 minutes.
③ If he gets a ride, it will take 7 minutes.

3 I enjoy movies <u>which(=that)</u> make me cry.

4 That building whose roof is round is my
house.

5 ① Get up early, and you will catch the school
bus.
② Study harder than you used to, and you
will have better scores.
③ Open the window, and you can see the
wonderful lake.

6 The box <u>was so heavy that he couldn't move</u>
<u>it</u>.

7 This is the <u>picture</u> <u>which(=that)</u> shows my
family members.

8 I saw a statue which looked like a bear.

9 The paintings <u>which(=that)</u> <u>he</u> <u>drew</u> <u>were</u>
wonderful.

10 ① The dog which has short ears is mine.
② The bird whose tail is long is white.
③ He knows the girl who carries the book.
(*The book which she carries is thick.)

해설

1 ⑤

it − itself

2 ④

명령문 + or: ~해라, 그렇지 않으면 보기와 나머지는 and

3 ③

where to+동사원형: 어디서 ~해야 할지, how to+동
사원형: 어떻게 ~해야 할지

4 ④

④ who는 the person을 선행사로 하는 주격 관계대명
사, 나머지는 의문사

5 ④

사람이 선행사이고 주격 관계대명사 자리이므로 who 또
는 that / 사물이 선행사이고 주격 관계대명사 자리이므로
which 또는 that

6 ⑤

소유대명사 mine 나의 것 / yours 너의 것

7 ④

as a result 그 결과, still 그럼에도 불구하고,
additionally 게다가

8 ②

쿠킹 클래스에서 어머니의 날을 위해 할 수 있는 내용이 들
어가야 함

9 ①

① know의 목적절로 '~인지 아닌지'의 의미로 쓰인 명사절 접속사, 나머지는 '만약 ~라면'의 의미로 쓰인 완전한 문장과 문장을 이어 주는 부사절 접속사

10 ①

① 주어를 강조하는 강조적 용법의 재귀대명사: 생략 가능, 나머지는 전치사나 타동사 뒤에서 목적어 역할을 하는 재귀적 용법의 재귀대명사: 생략 불가

11 ②

though 비록 ~라 할지라도, However 그러나

12 ②

ⓐ look + 형용사 / ⓑ but: 앞 문장의 different와 뒷 문장의 same이 상반됨 / ⓒ Most of all 무엇보다도

13 ②

① talk 다음에 전치사 to나 with / ③ unless가 '만약 ~하지 않는다면'의 의미이므로 don't 삭제 / ④ if절에서는 현재가 미래를 대신하므로 will take는 takes로 / ⑤ sit 다음에 전치사 on을 써야 함

14 ②

시간을 나타내는 의문사 when이 의미상 적절

15 ⑤

①, ② 주어가 2명, 복수이므로 is → are, doesn't → don't / ③ watch → watches / ④ don't → aren't

16 ③

① or → and / ② it 생략 / ④ 내용상 don't 생략 / ⑤ happily → happy

17 ④

① 주어가 people, 복수 is → are / ② 주어가 단수 are → is / ③ towers → tower / ⑤ 주어가 복수 am → are

18 ②

ⓐ because + 완전한 문장 / ⓑ 주어와 목적어가 같은 대상을 나타내므로 재귀대명사 himself / ⓒ 내용상 방법, 문법적으로 완전한 문장이 따라오므로 의문부사 how

19 ③

however: 앞 문장과 상반되는 내용

20 ②

ⓑ, ⓒ some..., others... 어떤 사람들은… 다른 사람들은… / ⓓ one out of three 셋 중에 하나

chapter 05 전치사 · 명사 · 형용사 · 부사 · 비교

기 본 실 력 다 지 기 pp.119-120

1 ① families ② buses
③ radios ④ boxes
⑤ dishes ⑥ oxen
⑦ cities ⑧ pianos

2 That is <u>an</u> egg.

3 She can play <u>the</u> piano well.

4 Look at <u>the</u> cat on the chair.

5 He plays <u>X</u> tennis every day.

6 I like <u>an</u> honest girl.

7 I'm going to study here for <u>a few</u> days.

8 There is <u>a little</u> water in the well.

9 <u>A few</u> students play baseball after school.

10 B: Yes, but just <u>a little</u>.

11 Is there <u>any</u> surviving family member?

12 He doesn't have <u>any</u> brothers.

13 Will you have <u>some</u> cookies?

14 Min-su has <u>some</u> friends in New York.

15 There is <u>much</u> oil in the bucket.

16 Tom has <u>many</u> friends in Seoul.

17 There is <u>little</u> water in this lake.

18 He came <u>a few</u> minutes later.

19 She has <u>no</u> money.

20 Jane has <u>many</u> pretty dolls.

21 We have <u>much</u> snow in January.

22 The garden <u>has</u> many trees.

23 Bill is <u>as</u> tall as Tom.

24 Washington is not <u>as</u> large as New York.

25 He is not so old <u>as</u> she.

26 Do they play tennis <u>better</u> than we?

27 Which is <u>more useful</u>, a donkey or a horse?

28 This is the <u>most</u> beautiful <u>of</u> all.

29 The Han River is one of the longest <u>rivers</u> <u>in</u> Korea.

30 Seoul is <u>larger</u> than any other city in Korea.

31 Jane is <u>as beautiful</u> as her sister.

32 We had <u>more</u> rain this year than last year.

33 He was as <u>poor</u> as a church mouse.

34 He had <u>less</u> money than she.

35 He became <u>bad(worse)</u> after he took the medicine.

36 That building is <u>much</u> higher than this building.

37 Health is more important than money.

38 He is taller than I.

39 It's the worst movie that I have ever watched.

40 She is the tallest girl in her class.

통합유형 5-1

pp.121-125

1 ④	2 ②	3 ②	4 ①	5 ①
6 ③	7 ②, ⑤	8 ⑤	9 ④, ⑤	10 ②
11 ③	12 ②	13 ②	14 ②	15 ③
16 ③	17 ②	18 ④	19 ④	20 ⑤

서술형

1 I can't run <u>as</u> fast <u>as</u> she.

2 I think English is much <u>easier</u> than math.

3 ① Seven <u>cars</u> are in the parking lot.

② The <u>leaves</u> are turning red and yellow.

③ We have four <u>classes</u> on Thursday.

④ Minki has three cute <u>babies</u>.

⑤ The firefighters save many people's <u>lives</u>.

4 Amy looks excited today. <u>So</u> <u>does</u> <u>Tom</u>.

5 ① prettier → pretty

② many → much

③ good → well

6 The Antarctic Ice Marathon <u>is one of the toughest marathons in the world</u>.

7 She learns the secrets of cuisine <u>as</u> <u>well</u> as customs and traditions.

8 • Sujin's grade <u>is better than Jason's grade</u>.

• Jason <u>is taller than Sujin</u>.

9 <u>Keep this device out of the reach</u> of young children.

10 ① Twelve students say they like hamburger most.

② Ramen is the second most popular snack.

③ Gimbap is the third most popular snack.

해설

1 ④

④ 동사 – 형용사 / 나머지는 명사 – 형용사

2 ②

woman – women (복수형)

3 ②

active – more active – the most active

4 ①

how many + 셀 수 있는 명사, how much + 셀 수 없는 명사

5 ①

① 동사(~을 좋아하다) / 나머지는 전치사(~처럼)

6 ③

③ boring(형용사)을 꾸며 주는 부사(꽤, 매우) / 나머지는 형용사(귀여운)

7 ②, ⑤

a lot of와 lots of는 수량 형용사로 셀 수 있는 명사와 셀 수 없는 명사 모두 수식 가능

8 ⑤

through ~을 통하여

9 ④, ⑤

④ 빵이 테이블 아래에 있으므로 under the table.

⑤ 우유가 치즈 옆에 있으므로 next to the cheese

10 ②

보기와 ②의 hard: 딱딱한

11 ③

some은 긍정의 평서문에, any는 부정문에 쓰임

12 ②

Steak A는 Steak C보다 더 싸므로 more expensive → less expensive 또는 cheaper

13 ②

빈도부사의 위치는 일반동사 앞, be동사, 조동사 뒤, go often → often go

14 ②

조동사 can이 있는 문장에 대한 동의, So am I. → So can I.

15 ③

①, ②, ⑤는 주어가 복수, meets → meet, closes → close, washes → wash, ④ 주어가 단수, boil → boils

16 ③

③ more cool → cooler (more는 2음절 이상 비교급)

17 ②

ⓐ merry → merrily / ⓒ health → healthy /

ⓓ oxen → ox / ⑨ act different → act differently

18 ④

① greatly → great / ② herself → myself /

③ That → Those / ⑤ book → books

19 ④

is good at(~을 잘하다) → is good for(~에 좋다)

20 ⑤

will fun → will be fun (조동사 뒤에는 동사원형)

통합유형 **5-2**　　pp.126-130

1 ⑤	2 ③	3 ⑤	4 ④	5 ④
6 ②	7 ②	8 ⑤	9 ④	10 ③
11 ③	12 ④	13 ③	14 ③	15 ④
16 ⑤	17 ②	18 ③	19 ③	20 ④

서술형

1 ⓐ exited　　ⓑ like

2 A town is larger than a village but smaller than a city.

3 It is next to my house that a movie star lives.

4 But Minju is not taller than Jihun.

5 Winter is the coldest season of the year.

6 Jane is younger than Sujin.

7 I don't like sports as much as Tom.

8 The more I think about the puzzle, the more confused I get.

9 Hard work is the most important of all.

10 So am I.

해설

1 ⑤

life → lives (-f(e)로 끝나는 명사 → -ves(복수형))

2 ③

display – display

3 ⑤

free 무료의, 무료로 ① ~이 없는 / ② 자유로이 / ③, ④
한가한

4 ④

④ about 약~ / 나머지는 ~에 관하여

5 ④

비교급 강조 부사: even, still, far, much, a lot
*very: 원급 수식

6 ②

less(덜) → more(더)

7 ②

so: 그래서 / so ~ that 주어 can't... 너무 ~해서 ...할
수 없다

8 ⑤

일반동사의 과거형이 쓰인 문장에 대한 답이므로 앞 문장
과 같이 조동사 did 사용

9 ④

as + 형용사, 부사의 원급 + as, as often as
possible 가능한 한 자주

10 ③

비교급 + than 구문, floats와 sinks라는 동사의 의미
로 봐서 lighter – denser

11 ③

ⓐ make A out of B: A를 B로 만들다 / ⓑ, ⓒ
change/turn A into B: A를 B로 바꾸다

12 ④

ⓐ look at ~을 보다 / ⓑ walk with ~와 함께 걷다
ⓒ say hello to ~에게 인사하다

13 ③

a cat and a dog이 복수이므로 there is → there
are

14 ③

three-meters-long이 형용사로 쓰여 뒤에 있는
rope를 꾸며 주므로 meters의 s를 생략

15 ④

expensiver → more expensive

16 ⑤

① leafs → leaves / ② potatos → potatoes /
③ sheeps → sheep / ④ man → men

17 ②

① go → goes / ③ cooks → cook / ④ likes →
like / ⑤ visit → visits

18 ③

① waters → water / ② cups → cup / ④ five
pieces of banana → five bananas / ⑤ slice
of pizzas → slices of pizza

19 ③

① middle school students → a middle
school student / ② in → on / ④ in the 19th
→ on the 19th / ⑤ events → event

20 ④

① wrinkle → wrinkly / ② I always have
thought → I have always thought / ③
Beside → Besides / ⑤ you should proud of
it → you should be proud of it

통합유형 **5-3**　　　pp.131-135

1 ①	2 ⑤	3 ③	4 ②	5 ③
6 ③	7 ③	8 ②	9 ②	10 ①
11 ①, ⑤	12 ②	13 ①	14 ④	15 ③
16 ②	17 ④	18 ①, ⑤	19 ③, ⑤	20 ①

서술형

1 Mrs. Kim went to X bed at ten. A strange
noise woke her up at X dawn. She went to

231

the living room. Suddenly a young man and a dog ran out of the kitchen. The dog was very big.

2 He is a good singer.

3 Thomas has three times as many books as Jane.

4 You are three years younger than I.

5 Good attitude is the most important thing in life.

6 She should be as old as I.

7 I guess that the role of paper money will get smaller and smaller.

8 Because he doesn't like reading books, he seldom(=hardly) goes to the library.

9 Under the desk are two cats.

10 The more harm we do to the Earth, the worse our lives get.

해설

1 ①
① 동사 – 명사 / 나머지는 명사 – 동사

2 ⑤
⑤ the UK 영국, England 영국의 잉글랜드 지방 / 나머지는 나라 – 언어

3 ③
on + 요일, at + 시간, in + 계절

4 ②
some은 긍정의 평서문, any는 부정문에서

5 ③
of ~으로 된, learn of ~에 대해 배우다, arrive at ~에 도착하다, jump up ~를 펄쩍 뛰어 오르다

6 ③
so(그래서) + 결과, from(~로부터) + 출처, to ~ ~에게

7 ③
too: 긍정문 ~도 또한, either: 부정문 ~도 또한

8 ②
② 복수명사가 주어 자리에 있으므로 there are, 나머지는 there is

9 ②
비교급 + than

10 ①
more and more 점점 더 많은

11 ①, ⑤
a lot of(많은) + 셀 수 있는/없는 명사 모두 수식, a little(조금의, 약간의) + 셀 수 없는 명사 수식 *의미상 긍정의 의미가 와야 하므로 little(거의 없는)은 정답이 될 수 없음

12 ②
부정 주어 + 비교구문, 비교급 + than any other + 단수명사: 모두 최상급의 의미

13 ①
② would he → he would / ③ strong somebody → somebody strong / ④ wrong anything → anything wrong / ⑤ wonderful something → something wonderful

14 ④
① so do I → so can I / ② so does my sister → so is my sister / ③ so do Robert → so does Robert / ⑤ so does Anne → so would Anne

15 ③
① to home → home / ② carefuler → more careful / ④ you → yours / ⑤ during → for

16 ②
① prettyer → prettier / ③ expensive → more expensive / ④ thing → things / ⑤ most → the most

17 ④

① spoon → spoons / ② are → is / ③ see → seeing / ⑤ sandwiches → sandwich

18 ①, ⑤

① Do often you go → Do you often go / ⑤ every countries → every country

19 ③, ⑤

③ a little → a few / ⑤ a few → a little, a little + 셀 수 없는 명사 (a few + 셀 수 있는 명사)

20 ①

ⓒ farther → further / ⓓ a happier → the happiest / ⓔ the more → the most

통합실전 문제 1~10

통합실전 **1** *pp.138-142*

1 ①, ⑤	**2** ②	**3** ⑤	**4** ④	**5** ①
6 ①	**7** ⑤	**8** ③	**9** ⑤	**10** ③
11 ②	**12** ③	**13** ④	**14** ③	**15** ④
16 ①	**17** ②, ④	**18** ①, ③	**19** ③	**20** ②

서술형

1 Did he read an interesting book yesterday?

2 No, it isn't.

3 You will go back to LA to study, won't you?

4 I am hoping to travel to Europe this summer.

5 I am always given a lot of money by Mom.

6 ①- The boy who likes Susie is wearing red pants.

- The boy who is wearing red pants likes Susie.

② - I visited a big shopping mall which opened on May 16th.

- The shopping mall which I visited opened on May 16th.

7 He has lived in America for four years.

8 seeing → to see

9 Watch A is 15 dollars cheaper than watch B.

10 I go jogging every day to be healthy.

해설

1 ①, ⑤

① 명사 – 형용사 / ②, ③, ④ 형용사 – 부사 / ⑤ 명사 – 부사

2 ②

① 둘레의 – 약 / ② 던지다 / ③ 층 – 바닥 / ④ 고기 – 고기 잡는 것 / ⑤ 차가운 – 감기

3 ⑤

목적어로 쓰인 접속사 that

4 ④

동사 앞 also: 또한 (too는 문장 끝에 위치)

5 ①

시간을 나타내는 비인칭주어 / 나머지는 지시대명사

6 ①

주어 backpack, 능동 의미의 boring

7 ⑤

be in+장소 ~에 있다, be late for ~에 지각하다, next to ~ 옆에

8 ③

try to + 동사원형: 애쓰다, without ~ing: ~없이(전치사 뒤 동명사), decide to + 동사원형: ~하기로 결심하다

9 ⑤

보기와 ④ 주어로 쓰인 동명사 / ① 보어로 쓰인 동명사 / ②, ③ 목적어로 쓰인 동명사 ⑤ baby를 수식하는 현재분사

10 ③

　　③ 의문사 언제 / 나머지는 접속사 '~할 때'

11 ②

　　① meets → meet / ③ cost → costed me / ④
boil → boils / ⑤ wash → washes

12 ③

　　① goes → go / ② has → have / ④ has →
have / ⑤ doesn't → don't

13 ④

　　Mom bought a toy for me. (Mom bought
me a toy.)

14 ③

　　① doesn't → don't / ② too → either / ④ 조동사
는 연이어 못 씀 / ⑤ Your → You

15 ④

　　① is't → isn't / ② I'am → I'm / ③ studying →
study / ⑤ This's → This is

16 ①

　　② doesn't → isn't / ③ is → are / ④ isn't →
doesn't / ⑤ going → go

17 ②, ④

　　① doesn't → don't / ③ don't → doesn't / ⑤
Does → Did

18 ①, ③

　　① are → is / ③ come → comes 선생이자 의사
동일인

19 ③

　　play → plays

20 ②

　　ⓐ has → have / ⓑ have answered → have
been answered / ⓓ will → would / ⓔ is →
are

통합실전　**2**　——————　pp.143-147

1 ④	**2** ②	**3** ④	**4** ⑤	**5** ①, ③
6 ④	**7** ④	**8** ④	**9** ①	**10** ③
11 ④	**12** ③	**13** ②, ⑤	**14** ⑤	**15** ③
16 ③	**17** ①	**18** ②	**19** ③	**20** ①

📋 **서 술 형**

1 She doesn't play the piano every day.

2 They are playing soccer.

3 He decided to take a taxi <u>to arrive on time</u>.

4 Tom has a big house which is too big for him
to live alone.

5 This poem <u>was written by him</u>.

6 Don't speak during class.

7 You should return the books within one
week.

8 What an interesting movie it is!

9 I am good at washing the dishes.

10 Because <u>she has been sick for three days</u>.

해설

1 ④

　　stopping 단모음 + 단자음 = 단자음 하나 더 쓰고 ~ing

2 ②

　　①, ③, ④, ⑤ 형용사 : 명사 / ② 동사 : 형용사

3 ④

　　Yes, he does.

4 ⑤

　　①~④ 목적어로 쓰이는 접속사 / ⑤ 지시대명사

5 ①, ③

　　사역동사 + 목적어 + 동사원형

6 ④

　　with, for a change 기분전환으로, on, like

7 ④

  ①, ②, ③, ⑤ be / ④ talk about ~에 대해 이야기하다

8 ④

  보기: 보어로 쓰인 명사적 용법 / ④ 목적보어로 쓰인 명사적 용법 / ①, ③, ⑤ 형용사적 용법 / ② 부사적 용법의 원인

9 ①

  보기: 경험 / ②, ③ 계속 / ④ 결과 / ⑤ 완료

10 ③

  He is not as smart as I am.

11 ④

  ① because of → because / ② Is → Are / ③ amn't → am not / ⑤ wrong something → something wrong

12 ③

  ① doesn't → isn't / ② fashionably → fashionable / ④ or → and / ⑤ going → go

13 ②, ⑤

  ② live usually → usually live / ⑤ will get → get

14 ⑤

  ① not 삭제 / ② doesn't 삭제 / ③ speaking → speak / ④ cooks → cook

15 ③

  friend → friends

16 ③

  ⓐ is → are / ⓑ speak → speaking / ⓒ there 삭제 / ⓓ and → or / ⓖ cloudy → cloud

17 ①

  ⓑ to 삭제 / ⓒ are → do / ⓕ play → plays / ⓖ Does → Do

18 ②

  ⓐ Doesn't → Don't / ⓓ became → to become 또는 becoming / ⓔ Does → Do

19 ②

  you're not → I'm not

20 ③

  ⓐ badly → bad / ⓑ eat → to eat / ⓓ doesn't → don't / ⓔ is → are

통합실전 ③   pp.148-152

1 ①	2 ④	3 ②	4 ②	5 ②
6 ③, ⑤	7 ⑤	8 ③	9 ④	10 ①
11 ⑤	12 ③	13 ④	14 ②	15 ③, ④
16 ①, ③	17 ④	18 ①	19 ④	20 ③

서술형

1 Does he take a shower after playing soccer?

2 While hamburger came into Korea with western culture, Bulgogi is spreading to other countries with our culture.

3 Henry is the tallest of the three students.

4 How well she speaks English!

5 The food which(=that) my family loved was very delicious.

6 The sound made me surprised.

7 ① ⓐ

  ② The bat is longer than the umbrella.

8 The machine will be fixed by me tomorrow.

9 Tom has to do the dishes.

10 Tom doesn't have to mop the floor.

해설

1 ①

  ① 유사 관계 / 나머지 상위 개념 : 하위 개념

2 ④

  ①, ②, ③, ⑤ are / ④ Do

235

3 ②

전치사 뒤에는 동명사가 옴

4 ②

부가의문문, 3인칭 주어, 일반동사 현재 긍정이므로
doesn't he

5 ②

보기: 바로, 부사 / ①, ⑤ 올바른 / ③, ④ 오른쪽의

6 ③, ⑤

지각동사의 목적보어는 동사원형 또는 현재분사

7 ⑤

①, ④ 목적격 관계대명사 생략 가능 / ②, ③ 목적어로 쓰인 접속사 생략 가능 / ⑤는 지시형용사 생략 불가

8 ③

since ~ 이후로, take a picture of ~의 사진을 찍다

9 ④

can go ~ and buy, enjoy listening ~ and
reading

10 ①

보기: 부사적 용법의 원인 / ① 명사적 용법의 목적어 /
②~③ 부사적 용법의 목적 / ④ 부사적 용법의 원인 / ⑤
부사적 용법의 반대 결과

11 ⑤

① doesn't → don't / ② play soccer (the 삭
제) / ③ are → were / ④ She's → She was,
because of → because

12 ③

① shocking → shocked / ② looked → looking
/ ④ has → had / ⑤ how → what ~ like (전치사
와 함께 쓸 수 있는 것은 의문대명사 what)

13 ④

① have → having / ② doing → do / ③ finding
→ find / ⑤ meet → meeting

14 ②

① Does → Do, is washing → wash / ③

meeting → meet / ④ bikes → bike / ⑤ am →
are

15 ③, ④

③ school이 주어이므로 is / ④ must solve →
must be solved

16 ①, ③

② is → are / ④ bored → boring / ⑤ has → have

17 ④

① has → have / ② Does → Do / ③ has not →
doesn't have / ⑤ listens → listen

18 ①

play → plays / play not → doesn't play / and
→ or / reads → read / shopping → to shop /
am → are

19 ④

lately → late

20 ③

ⓐ exciting → excited / ⓑ seeing → see / ⓓ
enter → entered / ⓔ were → was

통합실전 ④ pp.153-157

1 ②	2 ③	3 ③	4 ②	5 ①
6 ⑤	7 ③	8 ①	9 ④	10 ③
11 ②	12 ②, ⑤	13 ③, ⑤	14 ②, ⑤	15 ④
16 ③	17 ①	18 ④	19 ②, ③	20 ①

📋 **서 술 형**

1 ① He is studying in the library.

② They are taking an English lesson.

③ I am having dinner.

2 Are there many interesting shows on TV?

3 This is a book which(=that) tells us many
interesting stories.

4 Lee Juil, a famous comedian, showed a lot of interesting actions to audience.

5 Why don't you stop computer games?

6 What were they doing?

7 Many great plays <u>were</u> <u>written</u> <u>by</u> William Shakespeare.

8 Her <u>eyes</u> <u>are</u> as bright as a star.

9 ① What <u>an expensive car it is</u>!
  ② How <u>expensive the car is</u>!

10 ① It <u>tastes</u> sour and sweet.
  ② It <u>felt</u> smooth.

해설

1 ②
  ② 요리하다 – 요리기구 / 나머지는 동사 – (사람) 명사, 직업

2 ③
  of ~ 중에서 / to the park 공원으로 / with my boy friend 남자친구와 함께 / after school 방과 후에

3 ③
  ⓐ, ⓓ, ⓔ Does / ⓑ, ⓒ Do

4 ②
  분사구문의 현재분사: 그를 알게 되었을 때

5 ④
  solved를 수식하는 부사 / are(있다)를 수식하는 부사 / think를 수식하는 부사 hard 열심히

6 ⑤
  be동사 쓰인 문장의 부정명령은 Don't be

7 ③
  in front of the door → on the rug (카페트 위에)

8 ①
  ① like 전치사 / ② 영어, 영국인 / ③ 왼쪽, leave 남기다의 과거형 / ④ ~인지 아닌지, 만약 ~한다면 / ⑤ 접속사, 지시형용사

9 ④

① 목적어 / ② 목적보어 / ③ 목적어 / ⑤ 부사적 용법의 목적 / ④ 주어

10 ③
  키가 큰 순서 Jack ⓑ 〉 Tom ⓒ 〉 Mike ⓐ

11 ②
  ① Did → Was / ③ at → by / ④ are → is / ⑤ take → takes

12 ②, ⑤
  ① sleep → asleep / ③ legs → leg / ④ 조동사 2개 연이어 쓸 수 없음

13 ③, ⑤
  ① don't → aren't / ② doesn't → don't / ④ is → am

14 ②, ⑤
  ① goes → go / ③ do → are / ④ likes → like

15 ④
  has → have

16 ③
  is → are

17 ①
  ⓓ good → a good / ⓔ Is → Are

18 ④
  ① is / ② is / ③ is / ⑤ are

19 ②, ③
  ⓑ seen → saw / ⓒ run → ran

20 ①
  are you → aren't you

통합실전 **5** ─────────── pp.158-162

1 ③	2 ③	3 ②, ④	4 ⑤	5 ⑤
6 ⑤	7 ④	8 ③	9 ④	10 ④
11 ④	12 ③	13 ①	14 ⑤	15 ③
16 ④	17 ②	18 ③	19 ①, ④	20 ②

서 술 형

1 She looked for her ring until she found it.

2 ① Have you ever <u>eaten</u> Indian food?

② He gave some money to the person <u>sitting</u> on the street.

3 He threw the ball to the girl <u>wearing</u> a red cap.

4 ① I was also afraid of being laughed at.

② If I have a garden, I will make it beautiful.

5 Kevin is <u>the same age as(=as old as)</u> Anna.

6 ① His dad bought a new bike for him.

② His grandma gave pocket money to him.

7 Some people say that the earth <u>is being damaged</u> by human activity.

8 I lost the umbrella which(=that) my mother gave to me.

9 Everything <u>sounds like a lie</u>.

10 Her hands <u>felt warm</u>.

해설

1 ③

③ 명사 – 형용사 / 나머지는 동사 – 명사

2 ③

③ 가주어 / 나머지는 요일, 날씨, 명암의 비인칭주어

3 ②, ④

보기, ②, ④ 형용사적 용법 / ① 명사적 용법 목적어 / ③ 부사적 용법 목적 / ⑤ have to 동사원형(~해야 한다)

4 ⑤

⑤ 허가 / ①~④ 추측(~일지도 모른다)

5 ⑤

보기: 보어로 쓰인 동명사 / ① 목적어 / ②, ④ 전치사의 목적어 / ③ 주어로 쓰인 동명사 / ⑤ 진행형으로 쓰인 현재분사

6 ⑤

be covered with ~로 덮여 있다 / 나머지는 by

7 ④

ⓐ 수동의 의미 surprised / ⓑ 주어가 places이므로 are / ⓒ enjoy가 동명사를 목적어로 하기 때문에 gambling

8 ③

4형식을 3형식으로 쓸 때 write는 to, ask는 of, make는 for를 쓴다.

9 ④

무엇 what / 어떤 (상태) how

10 ④

beautiful – more beautiful – the most beautiful

11 ④

① a와 소유격은 동시에 쓸 수 없음, a 삭제 / ② year → years / ③ glass → glasses(안경) / ⑤ 빈도부사 often의 위치는 일반동사 앞 drink often → often drink

12 ③

① wasn't it → aren't you / ② didn't → doesn't / ④ do you → don't you / ⑤ isn't → doesn't

13 ①

to carry → carry (make는 사역동사)

14 ⑤

① beautifully → beautiful / ② palely → pale / ③, ④ look + 형용사, look like + 명사: ~처럼 보이다

15 ③

Get → Getting (동명사 주어)

16 ④

① to lock 또는 locking / ② make → making / ③ going shopping → go shopping / ⑤ I'm → I was (시제 일치) turn off the water 수도를 잠그다

17 ②

① friend → friends / ③ you → your / ④ Are → Is / ⑤ are → is

18 ③

① something healthy: ~thing는 후치 수식 / ②
was → were / ④ Were → Was / ⑤ go → went

19 ①, ④

hate, start는 부정사, 동명사 모두 가능 / ② to 삭제 /
③ to turn → turning / ⑤ passing → to pass

20 ②

to visit → visiting

통합실전 **6** pp.163-167

1 ④	**2** ②	**3** ①	**4** ③	**5** ⑤
6 ⑤	**7** ②	**8** ②	**9** ①	**10** ④
11 ⑤	**12** ②	**13** ②	**14** ②	**15** ③
16 ①	**17** ③	**18** ②	**19** ③	**20** ⑤

서술형

1 The most surprising thing about the writer is
his age.

2 This creative food with apples was made by
my mother.

3 ① Wash your hands before lunch.
② Be quiet in class.

4 The concert made them excited.

5 Today's lunch is more delicious than
yesterday's lunch.

6 Have you ever read the book?

7 She does housework because my mother
makes her do that.

8 It took about 5 hours for me to read this
book.

9 ① The Central Park in New York is one of the
largest parks in U.S.

② I have been tired since I didn't slept well
last night.

10 ⓐ bought   ⓑ didn't
ⓒ gave   ⓓ used
ⓔ took

해설

1 ④

반의어

2 ②

Do I ~? 의문문이므로 you do로 대답

3 ①

내용상 의무의 조동사 필요

4 ③

There are + 복수 명사

5 ⑤

선행사에 the last가 있으면 관계대명사는 that / 소유격
관계대명사는 항상 뒤에 명사가 옴

6 ⑤

현재완료의 완료 용법 ① 경험 / ②, ④ 계속 / ③ 결과

7 ②

② 불필요함을 의미 / 나머지는 금지

8 ②

ⓐ 시간 접속사, ⓑ 의문사 / 나머지는 시간 접속사로만 쓰
임

9 ①

every는 뒤에 단수명사가 옴 / not은 be동사 뒤에 /
why don't you + 동사원형~? ~하는 게 어때?

10 ④

감탄문 어순: what + (a/an) + 형용사 + 명사 + 주어
+ 동사

11 ⑤

나열의 and가 내용상 적합

12 ②

접속사 if/whether가 있어야 자연스러움

13 ②

① This's → This is / ③ is't → isn't / ④ small → short / ⑤ isn't → aren't

14 ②

3인칭 단수 주어이므로 go → goes

15 ③

3인칭 단수 주어이므로 play → plays

16 ①

② going → go / ③ doesn't → isn't / ④ is → are / ⑤ isn't → doesn't

17 ③

① makes → make / ② don't → doesn't / ④ Do → Does / ⑤ cans → can

18 ②

has → have

19 ③

that directly takes me there from my house

20 ⑤

feels → feels like

통합실전 ⑦ ————— pp.168-172

1 ⑤	2 ④	3 ③	4 ②	5 ③
6 ②	7 ③	8 ④	9 ⑤	10 ④
11 ④	12 ④	13 ⑤	14 ③	15 ②
16 ④	17 ③	18 ①	19 ②	20 ③, ④

서술형

1 We want you <u>not to eat or drink anything</u> inside.

2 They go to an orphanage every Sunday.

3 I will take a swimming lesson next year.

4 The cheetah runs faster than the horse.

5 I like these shoes which(=that) my wife bought for me yesterday.

6 Make <u>sure</u> <u>you</u> <u>don't</u> <u>carry</u> heavy things.

7 He <u>has been solving the problems for two hours.</u>

8 My dream is traveling around the world.

9 ① He went to the bookstore to buy some school textbooks.

② If you don't practice hard, you will fail in the finals.

10 ① ⓓ It was difficult for her to learn to make those dishes.

② ⓔ Jane tells us about her first try at cooking Korean food.

해설

1 ⑤

강한 금지를 나타내는 must not ~하지 말아야 한다

2 ④

손은 두 개이므로 one ~(한 손은) the other ~(다른 한 손은)

3 ③

③ 접속사 / 나머지는 의문사

4 ②

② 명사절 접속사 / 나머지는 조건절 접속사

5 ③

주어가 여성, herself ① themselves / ② yourself / ④ herself / ⑤ ourselves

6 ②

② 명사적 용법의 보어 / 나머지는 명사적 용법의 목적어

7 ③

가주어–진주어 구문 (it ~ to부정사)

8 ④

금지 표현, should not + 동사원형

9 ⑤

　⑤ 3형식 / 나머지는 5형식

10 ④

　확정적 과거이므로 과거시제 / for + 숫자 기간 /
　before가 쓰인 현재완료 표현

11 ④

　④ 주격 관계대명사 / 나머지는 목적격 관계대명사

12 ④

　목적격 관계대명사는 생략 가능

13 ⑤

　①, ③, ④ 간접의문문의 어순: 의문문 + 주어 + 동사 /
　② quiet → quietly

14 ③

　run → runnig (능동의 현재분사, 후치 수식)

15 ②

　① cutted → cut ③ to do → do ④ copied →
　copy ⑤ ran → run

16 ④

　look at은 지각동사이므로 to smile → smile/
　smiling

17 ③

　ⓐ go → goes / ⓑ weekends → weekend /
　ⓕ works → work

18 ①

　ⓒ friend → friends / ⓓ do → does / ⓔ goes
　→ go

19 ②

　ⓐ to fix → be fixed / ⓑ greatly → great / ⓓ
　for → since

20 ③, ④

　ⓒ is → are / ⓓ for → of

통합실전 **8**　　　pp.173-177

1 ④	**2** ⑤	**3** ④	**4** ①	**5** ①
6 ③	**7** ⑤	**8** ①	**9** ③	**10** ⑤
11 ①	**12** ②	**13** ⑤	**14** ④	**15** ⑤
16 ③	**17** ④	**18** ④	**19** ③	**20** ④

서술형

1 He <u>has been baking</u> some cookies in the kitchen.

2 ⓐ <u>younger</u>

　ⓑ <u>older</u>

3 If it is fine tomorrow, I will take a walk on the park.

4 We have been together for a year.

5 Would you mind <u>my</u> <u>taking</u> pictures in this natural science museum?

6 She wanted a doll <u>which can dance</u>.

7 I have a brother <u>who became a doctor</u>.

8 ① I go to a park <u>to ride a bike</u>.

　② I go to a shopping mall <u>to buy sneakers</u>.

　③ I go to the bank <u>to open a bank account</u>.

　④ I go to a gym <u>to exercise</u>.

9 Once she decides to buy something, she never gives up.

10 A: How <u>was the Bulgogi cooked by my mother</u>?

　B: It was <u>the best food (that) I've ever had</u>.

해설

1 ④

　④ 놓치다 / ① 좋아하다 – ~처럼 / ② 만들어 주다 – 벌
　다 / ③ 물을 주다 – 물 / ⑤ 도움 – 손

2 ⑤

나머지는 and와 or를 서로 바꾸어야 함

3 ④

사역동사의 목적어와 목적보어가 수동관계이면 목적보어

자리에 과거분사 사용

4 ①

주어진 문장은 부사적 용법의 목적(~하기 위해)

5 ①

ⓐ ~의 of / ⓑ ~에게 to / ⓒ ~ 때문에

6 ③

she의 소유격 her – 목적격 her – they의 목적격

them

7 ⑤

허가의 may / 나머지는 추측

8 ①

① 지시대명사 / 나머지는 가주어

9 ③

They를 받으므로 itself → themselves

10 ⑤

명사절을 이끄는 접속사 that ①, ③ 지시형용사 ②, ④

지시부사

11 ①

부정명령문은 Don't/Never + 동사원형

12 ②

① far → long / ③ will late → will be late / ④

is → are / ⑤ don't → doesn't

13 ⑤

① many → much / ② goes often → often

goes / ③ the soccer → soccer / ④ Sundays

→ Sunday

14 ④

① goes → go / ② not can → cannot / ③ does

→ do / ⑤ will hang out not → will not hang

out

15 ⑤

weekends → weekend / thing → things /

watch → watched / ride → rode

16 ③

ⓐ go often → often go / ⓑ sets → set /

ⓓ song → songs / ⓔ fireflys → fireflies

17 ④

ⓐ feeding → feeds / ⓒ to home → home /

ⓕ men → man, uncles → uncle

18 ④

ⓐ do → doing / ⓑ love → loves / ⓕ stoped

→ stopped

19 ③

① writes → wrote / ③ thirsty so that → so

thirsty that / ⑥ so loudly that → loudly so

that

20 ④

4형식 간접목적어 앞에는 전치사를 붙이지 않음

통합실전 **9** pp.178-182

1 ①	2 ③, ④	3 ①	4 ⑤	5 ③
6 ④	7 ②	8 ①	9 ①	10 ③
11 ②	12 ②	13 ④	14 ③	15 ②
16 ①, ②, ④	17 ③	18 ⑤	19 ①	20 ④

서술형

1 My father hurried in the morning <u>not to be</u> <u>late</u> for work.

2 Aren't you upset, are you?

3 She has been taking a swimming lesson for a year.

4 Family is more important than work.

5 You need a <u>swimsuit to wear in summer vacation.</u>

6 ① will keep → keep

② to use → using

7 The shopping mall which(=that) is near my house is huge.

8 The role of the robot <u>will get bigger and bigger.</u>

9 ① are melting → is melting

② has rise → has risen

③ because → because of

10 ① I was given some cookies by her.

② A new bicycle was bought for my brother by Father.

해설

1 ①

① 상태 변화 동사 / 나머지는 차례, 돌다, ~이 되다

2 ③, ④

감탄문 어순: What + a(n) + 형용사 + 명사 + 주어 + 동사(복수명사일 때 a(n) 못 씀) ~!, How + 형용사 + 주어 + 동사 ~!

3 ①

가정법 과거 (if + 주어 + 과거형 동사, 주어 + would / should / could / might + 동사원형)

4 ⑤

ⓐ ~하는 것 (그녀가 말하고 있는 것) / ⓑ 이유 that's why ~: ~하는 이유이다

5 ③

so ~ that … can't 문장은 too ~ to부정사 구문으로 전환

6 ④

주격 관계대명사 / 나머지는 의문사

7 ②

keep ~ing 계속 ~하다

8 ①

must not 금지, don't have to 불필요

9 ①

사물 주어 + ~ing (능동), 사람 주어 + ~ed (수동)

10 ③

forget + to부정사: ~할 것을 잊다, 사람 주어 + ~ed, 현재완료에는 before (ago는 과거형에 쓰임)

11 ②

선행사가 사물이므로 which

12 ②

① ask → asks / ③ am → will be / ④ won't like → likes / ⑤ will go → goes

13 ④

주어가 복수이므로 goes → go

14 ③

시제 일치, get → could get

15 ②

my brother를 받는 대명사 소유격이므로 Its → His

16 ①, ②, ④

① practice → practicing / ② Will you to → Will you go to / ④ visits → visit

17 ③

friend → friends

18 ⑤

앞의 문장이 긍정문이므로 either → too

19 ①

② a → an, has → have / ③ teach → teaches / ④ have → has / ⑤ sings → sing

20 ④

ⓐ make는 간접목적어를 주어로 쓸 수 없음 / ⓑ sent → was sent / ⓒ to → for

통합실전 **10** — pp.183-187

1 ④	**2** ①	**3** ⑤	**4** ③, ⑤	**5** ①
6 ③	**7** ③, ⑤	**8** ⑤	**9** ②, ④	**10** ⑤
11 ②, ③	**12** ⑤	**13** ①	**14** ④	**15** ⑤
16 ①, ③, ⑤	**17** ②	**18** ④	**19** ⑤	**20** ③

서술형

1 Taking a warm bath <u>made me feel relaxed.</u>

2 ① Run   ② and

3 How <u>kind</u> <u>the</u> <u>stranger</u> <u>is</u>!

4 Our club members who(=that) talked well on the topic got the first prize in a debate competition.

5 ① His mom <u>told him the story.</u>

  ② The birds <u>are taken care of</u> by Susie.

6 Jun, my best friend, loves playing computer games very much.

7 ① isn't it → aren't you

  ② doesn't he → didn't she

  ③ will you → shall we

8 ⓒ My baby made this toy broken.

  ⓔ I got the man to carry my backpack.

9 Susie is <u>younger than</u> Tom.

10 ① Tom is shorter than Susie.

   ② Tom is heavier than Susie.

해설

1 ④

동사 뒷부분이 완전한 문장이므로 접속사 that

2 ①

① 동명사 / 나머지는 현재분사

3 ⑤

보기: 현재완료 경험 ①, ② 결과 / ③, ④ 계속

4 ③, ⑤

불필요 표현: don't have to ~, need not ~, don't need to ~

5 ①

② sung → sing / ③ to run → run / ④ have burn → burn / ⑤ being smile → smile

6 ③

It ~ to+동사원형

7 ③, ⑤

보기: as 원인 접속사 ①, ② 전치사 / ④ ~할 때, ~하면서

8 ⑤

보기: 부사적 용법 중 형용사 수식, ~하기에

9 ②, ④

동사 want가 나오므로 빈칸에는 동사원형만 들어갈 수 있음

10 ⑤

ⓐ 주절이 단순과거, 시제 일치 / ⓑ 사람 주어 + ~ed (수동) / ⓒ Since ~, 현재완료 구문

11 ②, ③

② to → for / ③ for → of

12 ⑤

① clean → to clean / ② solving → to solve / ③ return → to return / ④ stopping → to stop

13 ①

② make → makes / ③ exciting → excited / ④ make → makes, carefully → careful / ⑤ many → much, make → makes

14 ④

go → to go

15 ⑤

① years → year / ② took → was taken / ③ very → much(=still, far, even, a lot) / ④

who → that

16 ①, ③, ⑤

② doesn't → don't / ④ will be → is

17 ②

wake up me → wakes me up 시간, 조건 부사절
에서는 현재가 미래를 대신

18 ④

선행사 carrots가 복수형이므로 was → were

19 ⑤

do → am talented ~에 재능이 있는

20 ③

시제 일치, ⓐ gather → gathered / ⓑ have →
had

최신 신경향 기출 서술형 100

pp.190-204

Chapter 01

1 Does G. Dragon sing very well?

2 My mother doesn't teach English.

3 ① She name is Happy. → Her name is Happy.

② We is good friends. → We are good friends.

4 What a beautiful picture it is!

5 Can I borrow your bag just for today?

6 Why don't you talk to your friends in English?

7 Listen to your friends, and you will make
friends.

8 Don't play soccer(=with a ball) in your
classroom.

9 A fish doesn't swim in the ground. /
It swims in the sea.

10 ① get → getting   ② leaf → leaves

11 ① student → students   ② cry → cries

12 ① ⓐ Does → Do   ② ⓔ Are → Do

13 ① ⓑ her eyes → his eyes

② ⓓ play → to play(=playing)

③ ⓔ gets up → get up

14 ① Kelly shows Thomas ⓐ her picture.

② Ms. Lee reads ⓑ her students a book.
She thinks that ⓒ her students like it.

15 ① They are from Korea.

② They are not from Korea.

③ Are they from Korea?

Chapter 02

16 She is riding a bike.

17 She is going to sing her favorite songs.

18 I'm going to see lots of interesting things
there.

19 Gongmin has been the captain of our
baseball team since January.

20 English is taught to us by him.
We are taught English by him.

21 An interesting story was told (to) us by him.

22 She has to be as old as I.

23 ① well → good

② deliciously → delicious

③ happily → happy

24 ① may hit → may be hit

② safely → safe

25 give → was given

26 Have you been to the new art museum?

27 Ben is sleeping on the sofa.
Kate is eating an apple.

28 ① looked for → looked like

② was listening → were listening

29 Tom has been studying at H Middle School

since he was 14.

30 ① will become → become

  ② happily → happy

31 I have never seen her <u>since we graduated</u> <u>from elementary school</u>.

32 ① found → find

  ② stop → stopped

  ③ clearly → clear

Chapter 03

33 listening

34 Yong thinks that <u>reading</u> <u>books</u> is fun.

35 Does <u>he have a pen to write with</u>?

36 Never give up <u>without trying</u>.

37 My father <u>made</u> me fix <u>his computer</u>.

38 Do you know <u>how to use</u> these chopsticks?

39 Bonnie wants Jake not <u>to be late for her</u> <u>birthday party</u>.

 Narah wants Henry <u>not to eat too much</u> <u>chocolate</u>.

40 It may not be easy <u>for him to write a book</u> <u>in English</u>.

41 Let's <u>look for a chair to sit on</u>.

42 We <u>should not spend our time on playing</u> <u>games on the smartphone</u> at school.

43 ① Jane is good at <u>singing</u> as well as <u>dancing</u>.

  ② Tom enjoys not only <u>cycling</u> but also <u>car</u> <u>racing</u>.

44 I will have my brother <u>repair</u> <u>my</u> <u>bicycle</u>.

45 She is too young to drive a car.

46 You <u>should promise not to cheat again</u>.

47 The students <u>should not mind studying</u> <u>English</u>.

48 ① My dream <u>is to meet a famous</u> <u>Hollywood star</u>.

  ② Our plan <u>is to go fishing tomorrow</u>.

49 Mother <u>had Father repair the washing</u> <u>machine</u>.

50 I stopped talking on the phone <u>so that</u> <u>people in the library could study</u>.

51 ① cleaning → clean

  ② by → with

52 ① overcoming → to overcome /

   keep → keeping

  ② master → mastering

53 ③ Juyoung's family goes hiking once a month.

  ④ There is one more event in March.

54 ① ⓒ

  ② plays → play(=playing)

  ③ 지각동사 목적격 보어로는 동사원형이나 진행형이 온다.

55 ① ⓐ to learn → learning

  ② ⓓ to read → reading

56 ① broke → broken

  ② fixed → fix

  ③ painting → painted

Chapter 04

57 The door opened <u>of itself</u>.

58 ① Though he is poor, he helps other people.

  ② If you are not ready, you don't have to go tomorrow.

 (*Though the radio is very old, it works well.

 *Because it is sunny, many people are playing in the park.)

59 James as well as Alice comes from America.

60 Some of my friends live in Sidney.

61 ① She was both thirsty and hungry.

 ② She can eat either a pizza or a cake.

62 If she doesn't come to the party tomorrow, I will be sad.

63 The teacher who(=that) all the students like is very famous.

64 The cats which(=that) I raised in my backyard are now four years old.

65 Choose any place that you want and plant any vegetables that you like.

66 The man who(=that) lives next door is friendly.

67 Juliet is the girl who(=that) fell in love with Romeo.

68 There is something important in his plan.

69 This princess doll will be given to my girlfriend.

70 This is the gym which(=that) I often exercise at.

 (*This is the gym at which I often exercise.)

71 I was so curious that I decided to read the text messages.

Chapter 05

72 water

73 ① A table is in front of the sofa.

 ② Two dogs are on the sofa.

74 In Gosung, Tom's family grows vegetables like onions and tomatoes.

75 When you catch a cold, drink lots of water.

76 ⓔ from → in

77 In front of the chair is the dog.

78 This experiment is not as easy as the last one.

79 Mom told me to come back home as soon as possible.

80 ① deliciously → delicious

 ② to → in

81 So do I.

82 There were few people shocked at the news.

83 ① an advice → a piece of advice

 ② spend → spending

84 Behind the city hall is the hotel which you will stay at.

통합문제

85 I went to the library to find a book about traveling.

86 ① Mr. Watson has taught us English since last year.

 ② Taking a walk is a good exercise.

87 ① running　　② to sleep/sleeping

 ③ passed　　④ sleeping

88 The man wearing a red hat is my brother.

89 ① and → or

 ② eating → to eat

 ③ because of → because

90 ① ⓐ bear → was born

 ② ⓑ bad → badly

 ③ ⓔ ride → riding

91 I had better not eat more food.

92 ① spent → spend

 ② cook → cooking

93 Your parents will let you do the things

which you really want to do.

94 ① making → to make

② some flower → some flowers

③ sadly → sad

95 ① That student must be Kelly.

② David is taking a walk with the student.

③ That student whom(=that) David is

taking a walk with must be Kelly.

96 ① students → student

② names → name

③ good something → something good

97 ① has → have

② loves → love

98 ① made → were made

② different → differently

③ because of → because

99 Inline skaters put on special inline skates

made for doing difficult tricks.

100 ① So does her sister.

② Neither did I.